Unveiling Your Sacred Truth

The innermost essence of all of the Buddha's teachings,
together with a supplementary explanation of the methods for entering
into the profound path of the Kalachakra Six Vajra Yogas.

བདེ་གཤེགས་སྙིང་པོའི་འཇུག་རིམ་རྗེ་གས་ལྷུན་གསར་པའི་ཁྱད་ཆོར་

༄༅།།རབ་ལམ་རྗེ་འི་རྣལ་འབྱོར་དྲུག་ལ་འཇུག་ཚུལ་འགྲོས་དོན་དང་བཅས་པ་ཀུན་འདུས་རྒྱལ་བསྟན་ཡང་སྙིང་།།

— BOOK THREE —

The Enlightened Reality

by Shar Khentrul Jamphel Lodrö

ཤར་མཁན་སྤྲུལ་རིན་པོ་ཆེ་འཇམ་དཔལ་བློ་གྲོས

Dzokden

Author: Shar Khentrul Jamphel Lodrö

First Edition

ISBN (Paperback): 978-1-958229-61-3
ISBN (ePub): 978-1-958229-62-0

Published by:
Dzokden

This work was produced by Dzokden, a non-profit institution operated entirely by volunteers. This organization is dedicated to propagating a non-sectarian view of all the world's spiritual traditions and to teaching Buddhism in a way that is both completely authentic and at the same time practical and accessible to Western culture. It is especially dedicated to spreading the Jonang tradition, a rare gem from a remote part of Tibet that preserves the precious teachings of the Kalachakra.

For more information about scheduled activities or available materials, or if you would like to make a donation, please contact:

Dzokden
3436 Divisadero Street
San Francisco, CA 94123
USA
www.dzokden.org
office@dzokden.org

Contents

ༀ༔ །ཤ་རྃ་རྃ་སྭ་སྣང་རྗེ་བཙུན་ཆེན་པོ་ཀུན་...

至尊藏哇赤列南杰觉囊派第四十七任法王填塘藏哇大藏寺金刚寺主

HIS HOLINESS TSANGWA TRINLÉ NAMGYAL

The 47th Vajra Throne Holder of the Great Eastern Monastery of Dzamthang Tsangwa and Lord of the Jonang Dharma.

[Tibetan text — five paragraphs of dbu-can script]

[seal]

[Three lines of Tibetan colophon text]

གཙང་བ་སྤྲུལ་འཛིན་བཞུགས་...

无上怙主殊胜化身吉美多杰尊胜第八任藏哇活佛

The 8th Tsangwa Geitrul, Supreme Incarnation of All the Victorious Ones, Jigmé Dorjé

Preface by
His Holiness Jigmé Dorje

Shar Khentrul Jamphel Lodrö has attained great faith in the teachings of Tibetan Buddhism through his intensive study of the five traditions of Nyingma, Sakya, Kagyu, Jonang and Geluk. On the basis of these teachings, he has written many great books on subjects such as the history of the Dharma and non-sectarian philosophical views. Through this work he has brought great benefit to the doctrine.

While having studied under many great masters from each of the traditions, his root master was the truly learned and accomplished master Jetsun Lama Lobsang Trinlé, also known as Lama Trinlé Tsang. From him, he spent a long time learning the complete teachings of Sutra and Tantra, specifically, the six branch practices of the Kalachakra Completion Stage. In recognition of his great effort to achieve mastery of all traditions, Jamphel Lodrö was awarded the title of Rimé Master by his root teacher. In particular, he was given the highly blessed Khenpo-hat which had been worn by Lama Lobsang Trinlé throughout that master's life. This hat carries with it profound blessings and is a sign that Jamphel Lodrö will bring great welfare to beings in the future.

As a child, Jamphel Lodrö was recognised as the immediate reincarnation of the Golok lama Getse Khentrul; however, this truth was kept secret in order to expel obstacles to his life. Many years later, with permission from his root master and after all obstacles had been dispelled, the seal was lifted and he was publicly recognised as the second incarnation of the Washul Lhazu Lama—Ngawang Chözin Gyatso.

Presently, he has been giving extensive teachings on the sutras of definitive meaning and the profound philosophical views of Zhentong Madhyamaka, as well as the preliminary practices which form the foundation for the practice of Kalachakra. He has made great effort to make these teachings available in the Tibetan and English languages, with the aim to eventually translate them into many other languages in

The Great Monastery of Dzamthang Tsangwa

the future. Due to his determination to make the Zhentong philosophy accessible, many people all over this world have received great benefit and for that I am very grateful. I rejoice and thank him on behalf of all Jonang practitioners, and fully support him in his many activities.

I would particularly like to express my highest regard for his courage to take responsibility for the most rare and profound teachings of the Kalachakra as an authentic holder of the lineage, as well as for his emphasis for all traditions to come together in the name of global peace and harmony. From the bottom of my heart, I rejoice in these great deeds for they are truly the causes for a golden age to arise.

To all those who are currently supporting Khentrul Rinpoché to achieve these activities, I would like to express my heartfelt thanks to you and rejoice in the vast merit that you are creating. It is most rare to have the opportunity to encounter these teachings which can bring so much peace and harmony to this world. I make prayers and aspirations that in the future, we will all gather together in the sublime northern realm of Shambhala.

Written at the Dharma palace of the Great Eastern Monastery of Dzamthang Tsangwa by the 47th Vajra Throne Holder Tsangwa Geitrul, Supreme Incarnation Jigme Dorje on the sixth month of the fire monkey year during the 17th rabjung (August, 2016).

Shar Khentrul Jamphel Lodrö Rinpoché

Acknowledgments

Throughout its long history, the teachings of Kalachakra have gradually emerged over the centuries at critical moments in the development of our world. In the land of Shambhala, it passed from the royal courts of Kalapa to the outer regions. It then made its way from Shambhala to India where it eventually passed to the snow capped mountains of Tibet. Now, over the course of the last one hundred or so years, a new transmission has slowly been occurring. From the ancient wisdom of the Tibetan masters, Kalachakra has found its way into the rest of the world.

The *Sacred Truth Series*, of which this book is the last instalment, represents a major step forward in this evolutionary process. Where previously there were only pockets of information and general presentations, we can now access a complete path structure that shows us how the wisdom of Kalachakra can be used to develop all the foundational realisations, leading to the enlightened result of Buddhahood. From within this unified context, we can gain profound insight into the complete range of the Buddha's teachings, to penetrate deeply into their most definitive of meanings.

It is, therefore, on behalf of all Khentrul Rinpoché's students that I would like to express our eternal gratitude for the immeasurable kindness that Rinpoché has shown in making these teachings available to us in a way that is truly profound and yet amazingly accessible. It has taken many years for the conditions to come together for these materials to take shape and this is entirely due to Rinpoché's unwavering devotion to the teachings and his undefeatable strength of will. He is truly an inspiration to us all.

To all those who have been fortunate enough to support Rinpoché in this project, I would like to express my sincerest appreciation. Each of your contributions has made it possible for this wish-fulfilling jewel to manifest. I would particularly like to thank Vanessa, Holly, and Dorothy for working so hard to polish the chapters and provide invaluable feedback. This is truly a team effort and without you, I know this could not have been achieved. I would also like to recognise the silent support of Julie O'Donnell and Jackie Bao, who made sure that things like food and shelter were never an obstacle.

As a textbook for practice, the writing style of this book focuses on providing an essential synthesis of many different materials that are currently available. This would not have been possible without the many hours of discussion with Rinpoché, as well as the continued support offered by Edward Henning and David Reigle. I have learned so much from each of you and for that I am very grateful.

Finally, while I have done my best to communicate the teachings of the Kalachakra lineage as clearly and authentically as possible, due to my own limitations I am well aware that I may have inadvertently introduced mistakes. Therefore, with the aim of refining our presentation of the path in English, we welcome any feedback or corrections you may have to offer. This is definitely a work in progress and we expect it will continue to evolve over time.

I dedicate any merit that has been generated through the writing and production of this text to the flourishing of the profound Jonang Dharma—the gateway to the complete teachings of Kalachakra.

May this text become a cause for all sentient beings on this planet to achieve the sublime realm of Shambhala and to subsequently actualise their greatest potential of a fully enlightened Buddha.

May the perfection of peace and harmony that is the union of immutable great bliss and empty-form arise where it has not yet arisen, and may that which has already arisen, not diminish but increase more and more.

May we each complete the profound path of the Six Vajra Yoga and so attain the ultimate state of the Primordial Buddha for the sake of all sentient beings.

Joe Flumerfelt
Belgrave, Australia
October 2016

Introduction

Unveiling Your Sacred Truth was written to expound the spiritual path as taught by Buddha Shakyamuni. Throughout this text I have attempted to present the core tenets of Buddhism in an approachable way without losing the essence of the Buddha's ancient wisdom. It is my hope that Unveiling Your Sacred Truth will enable you to live purposefully and compassionately.

When you pick-up a Dharma book such as this one, you are not simply reading the words of the author. Through *Unveiling Your Sacred Truth* you connect with the unparalleled wisdom of the Buddha and come to know the great practitioners of the past and present who realised Buddha-Dharma for themselves. This Buddhist ancestry, known as a lineage, is critical for spiritual development as it is their stories, commentaries and realisations that we rely upon for guidance and inspiration.

The Buddha's teachings were taught for an extensive variety of people, each experiencing dissatisfaction and suffering in different ways. As a result, there are different levels of benefit from studying these teachings that we can all aspire to achieve. On the most basic level, we can each find practical tools to help us lessen our day-to-day stresses and to live a more meaningful life. On a deeper level, we can realise our incredible potential and cultivate the causes for long lasting, genuine happiness, both for ourselves and others.

Of all the Buddha's teachings, the system that I personally feel most connected with is that of the Kalachakra Tantra. In my opinion it is the most skilful system for realising this extraordinary potential and for actualising enlightenment within a single lifetime. While most people relate these teachings to advanced esoteric practices, the Kalachakra Path is in fact a complete system which is suitable for practitioners at all stages of their spiritual development.

OVERVIEW OF THE KALACHAKRA PATH

Kalachakra literally means *wheel* (chakra) of *time* (kala). It is the name given to a system of practices that originated with the Buddha Shakyamuni and has been passed down through the ages in an unbroken lineage to this day. The Kalachakra system is focused on helping people make sense of their experiences in a way that allows them to cultivate greater peace and harmony in their personal lives and their relationships with others.

The Kalachakra is unique in that it provides teachings on a comprehensive scope of topics that support a variety of practitioners at different stages of spiritual development. Within one unified framework, we find a wealth of profound wisdom that is both immediately relevant and direct in its approach.

The main subject matter of *Unveiling Your Sacred Truth* is the presentation of the complete Kalachakra Path. The path is progressive in nature, providing clear step-by-step instructions for guiding you through the many layers of your lived experience. I have broken this path up into three separate books, where each book examines one specific layer of reality, moving in a linear fashion from gross to subtle. As such, it is recommended that the material be studied in sequence so that the necessary foundations can be developed for each subsequent practice.

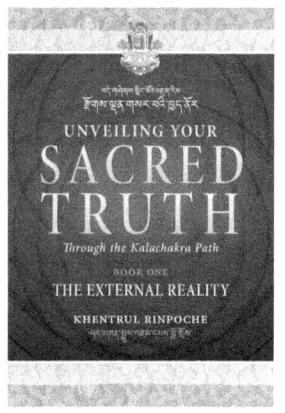

Book One:
The External Reality

We begin our journey by first studying the characteristics of our immediate experience. Specifically, we are looking at the ordinary world that we encounter each and every day, with the aim of developing the wisdom that will allow us to live more meaningful and balanced lives. At this stage, emphasis is on pragmatic strategies, firmly rooted in an experiential approach to understanding reality.

This book introduces many potentially new ideas that will challenge us to think more broadly about the nature of our shared universe. These ideas form the basis for understanding a Buddhist worldview which in turn is the foundation for a profound system of contemplative practice.

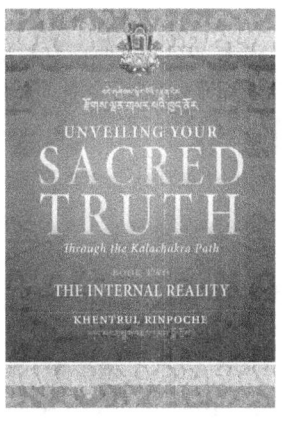

Book Two:
The Internal Reality

By focusing outward, we can develop strategies for coping with whatever comes up in our lives; finding ways to apply our wisdom in order to act constructively in the face of adversity, but no matter how effective our strategies may be, they are unable to generate the long lasting transformation that is capable of breaking the cycle of our suffering and opening the door to genuine happiness. For this, we must turn inward. We must look directly at our own mind and experience its underlying nature.

In the second book, we explore the experiential world of appearances and how those appearances actually exist. While we continue to work with concepts on a theoretical level, we increasingly shift our emphasis towards direct experience. It is not enough to simply understand what is occurring, we must develop first-hand awareness of what these concepts are describing. It is when we convert understanding into experience that we truly integrate these ideas into our way of being. This process of transformation is facilitated through what is known as the *Kalachakra Preliminary Practices*.

Book Three:
The Enlightened Reality

By working with our internal reality we slowly refine our capacity to distinguish between the impure appearances of the external reality and the pure appearances of the enlightened reality. Like a radiant sun hidden behind a wall of clouds, our true nature has been hidden from us by layers of obscuring delusions. Initially all we had to work with were the deluded perceptions of our ignorance, but as we progress, the light of wisdom has begun to manifest. Although there are still many clouds veiling the sun, we can now at least see the glow of its rays emanating from behind the clouds. With continued determination and the right methods, we can soon experience the warmth of its light directly.

In this third book, we turn our focus towards achieving a direct realisation of Buddha-nature—the sublime emptiness endowed with all aspects. With this highest of realisations we follow in the footsteps of the great Bodhisattva Kings to rapidly purify our minds of all remaining obscurations. To achieve this, we need to rely on the profound methods of Buddhist Tantra.

Traditionally, many of the teachings found in this book were reserved for those who had received empowerment into Highest Yoga Tantra. This restriction was originally meant to ensure that students only engaged with the practices of Tantra under the guidance of a qualified vajra master. While this still remains the best way forward, due to the relative ease with which the general public can now access esoteric teachings, it has become increasingly important for students to develop clarity regarding how these higher paths are practiced.

For this reason, I have chosen to take a mixed approach to the material presented in the coming chapters. In order to provide a clear understanding of the way the path unfolds, I have included an essential presentation of the theoretical foundations and structures that form the practice of Kalachakra Tantra. The only teachings absent are the specific pith instructions for engaging in the Kalachakra Completion Stage. These precious teachings are only bestowed on those who have received the necessary empowerment and who are devoted to both the Guru and the Kalachakra Path. It is my hope that the information you find here will inspire you to seek a qualified master and to dedicate yourself to practicing this path.

This book is divided into three main parts: (1) establishing a close bond with the Guru; (2) generating the enlightened mandala and (2) actualising the state of Kalachakra. Each part represents a key phase in how we relate to our most sacred truth and how to make that truth manifest in our experience.

Establishing a Close Bond with the Guru

Our exploration of Kalachakra Tantra begins with a discussion of the *unique aspects of the Vajrayana* and how its resultant approach can be used to achieve realisations in a very short period of time. This provides us with a general context for following the remaining teachings in this book, as well as reminding us of their incredible profundity. By developing appreciation for the precious qualities of this path, we strengthen our faith and determination to put these teachings into practice.

On this basis, we then turn our attention to the very root of all tantric practice—the Guru. This often misunderstood subject demonstrates how the practice of *devotion towards the Vajra Master* is an extremely skilful method for cultivating vast quantities of merit and developing a pure perception of reality. It is this pure perception that is expanded and refined by the subsequent practices. To provide a general structure for our discussion, we rely on the classic text *Fifty Verses of Guru Devotion* by Ashvaghosha. By familiarising ourselves with the advice it contains, we establish a meaningful relationship with our Vajra Master that can carry us through to enlightenment.

While devotion toward an external Guru provides a good starting point, it is still provisional in nature. Ultimately we need to transcend the notion of the Guru as an external entity and connect with the Guru as an expression of our own inner nature. Through the practice of *Guru Yoga* we learn to open our hearts to the guiding influence of our most sacred truth and to use that influence as a gateway for achieving realisations.

Generating the Enlightened Mandala

The first phase of formal tantric practice is the *generation stage*. It is primarily concerned with expanding the pure perception generated with Guru Yoga to incorporate all aspects of our experience. This process is established when we are introduced to the enlightened mandala in the empowerment ceremony known as the *Seven Empowerments of a Growing Child*. Through this ceremony, we enter into a vajra relationship with the vajra master who bestows the empowerments. This involves taking a series of *tantric vows and commitments* designed to cultivate pure perception and provide us with an ethical framework for tantric practice.

Once we have received empowerment, we are now ready to begin our study and practice of the Kalachakra generation stage. With more than

636 deities, the *Enlightened Mandala of Kalachakra* is one of the largest and most expansive mandalas of all Buddhist systems and therefore requires considerable effort to fully understand. By focusing on the essential nature of its different features we can create a meaningful working model that can then be developed and expanded over time.

The main method for familiarising ourselves with the enlightened qualities of the mandala is through the profound practice of *Deity Yoga*. In this training we dissolve our ordinary conception of self and visualise ourselves arising in the enlightened aspect of Kalachakra and Vishvamata. In this way we stop identifying with ordinary appearances and instead cultivate a divine pride that recognises the ways our enlightened nature manifests.

Actualising the State of Kalachakra

Through the various practices of the generation stage we are able to purify our mind and achieve significantly more subtle states of awareness. Such a mind is considered ripe for experiencing its own ultimate nature through the *Four Higher Empowerments*. During this empowerment ceremony, we receive unique pointing-out instructions for experiencing Buddha-nature in accordance with the Kalachakra view. It is the experience of this view that marks our transition into the *Completion Stage*.

While the generation stage emphasised building a symbolic representation of our enlightened reality, the completion stage recognises that we must ultimately transcend these concepts to directly experience that reality. For this reason, the completion stage focuses on non-conceptual methods to manipulate the state of our mind in order to achieve non-dual awareness.

The basis for these methods is a detailed understanding of the *subtle energetic system* present in all human beings. By recognising the correlations between the movement of energy within this system and the corresponding states of mind they produce, it is possible to work indirectly with the mind without resorting to dualistic concepts. Through powerful techniques such as the *Three Isolations*, we can completely dissolve the conceptual mind and thereby create the conditions for the sublime emptiness of suchness to arise.

As we reach this point, the common and uncommon preliminaries have been completed and we are ready to enter the main practice of the *Six Vajra Yogas*. These advanced practices require us to work very closely with a qualified master to ensure they are performed safely and correctly. Traditionally, the pith instructions are only granted once the Vajra Master has determined a student is ready. Until then, studying and familiarising ourselves with the structure of these practices is an excellent way of strengthening our aspiration to practice and creating the causes to receive the instructions.

With the completion of the teachings on the Six Vajra Yogas, we have all that we need to achieve enlightenment within a single lifetime. All that remains is the actualisation of these teachings. To this end, we will conclude with a discussion of how the extraordinarily skilful methods contained within the transitional periods of the *Six Bardos* can be used to maximise the opportunities afforded us through the cycle of life and death. By bringing wisdom into this process, we can ensure we do not waste a single moment of this precious human life, but instead use it in a meaningful way to bring incredible benefit to sentient beings.

GETTING THE MOST OUT OF THIS BOOK

As you read through the material, it can be helpful to keep a few key points in mind. The following is some general advice that applies to any form of Dharma study, whether reading a book or listening to a teaching.

The Right Attitude for Studying Dharma

When we encounter the Buddhist teachings, it is important to generate an attitude of great enthusiasm. If we can recognise that through these teachings we are being introduced to ideas that can ultimately lead us to greater peace and happiness, this should be a relatively easy task. That being said, cultivating a bright and alert mind is a skill that takes time to develop and prolonged effort is needed to overcome the different obstacles that may arise. One teaching that highlights these difficulties is known as the *Three Defects of a Pot*:

    1.   We should not be like an **upside-down pot** on which liquid is

being poured, being distracted or so closed minded that the teachings cannot penetrate. Listen with an open mind, a ready mind.

2. Nor should we be like a **pot with a hole in it**. No matter how much liquid is poured in, it drips away and we retain nothing of what is learnt.

3. Finally, do not be a **pot containing poison**. Avoid falling prey to preconceptions and fixed ideas. This will cause you to misconstrue what you hear and manipulate Dharma into something it is not, like nectar poured into poison.

As you read through each chapter, try to maintain an open, receptive attitude that is fully engaged in the material and free from any preconceptions or judgemental attitudes. Every now and again check to see the quality of attention you are bringing to your reading. Remind yourself of this simple teaching whenever you need the inspiration to improve your method of study.

Stopping to Reflect

It is important that we don't allow ourselves to become overwhelmed by the complexity of the Kalachakra System. Breaking up your reading with short periods of personal reflection can provide you with valuable insights into how the material relates to your personal experience.

I would suggest that you develop a methodical and gradual approach to this material. First select a passage of the text, read through the material a few times and make sure you are really understanding what is being said, then put the book down and consider how these teachings relate to your life. Think of examples from your own experience that illustrate the various principles.

Another good habit to develop is to write down questions that arise while reading. Keep a notepad nearby and when a question comes up, simply jot it down. When you are finished reading a section, look back at your questions and see if they have been answered. If the questions persist, consider discussing the topic with a teacher or another Dharma friend when the opportunity arises.

Taking Joy in the Journey

Finally, no matter what your motivation, I am confident that if you can maintain an open heart and an open mind, the timeless wisdom of the Buddha-Dharma has the capacity to bring you benefit.

Remember that this is a journey of discovery—a process of transformation. It will take time for the concepts and practices to develop in your mind and therefore it is important to be patient with yourself. Work through the ideas at your own pace, taking as much time as you need. After reading through a few chapters, go through them again and see if your understanding has shifted. Often you may find that later teachings shed new light on earlier ones, peeling back layers and uncovering a deeper meaning.

Above all, cultivate a sense of joy in having this precious opportunity. It shouldn't be dry or tedious. Instead think of it like an adventure and revel in the challenges that it presents. In Buddhism we talk about planting the seeds for future realisation. This simply means that any confusion we face here and now is the basis for future understanding to arise.

"In the beginner's mind there are many possibilities,
but in the expert's mind there are few"
— Shunryu Suzuki —

PART ONE

Establishing a Close Bond with the Guru

CHAPTER ONE

The Resultant Path of Kalachakra Tantra

Since beginningless time, we have cycled continuously in samsaric existence. Dominated by our afflictions, we engage in countless actions that condition our experience and drive us into unsatisfying situations. It is a pattern we have repeated over and over again and will potentially continue to do so for an eternity.

It is therefore extraordinary that at this particular moment in time, we have attained a precious human rebirth filled with amazing possibilities. It is as if we have been granted a wish-fulfilling jewel that holds the promise of everything our hearts have ever desired. Right now we have the incredible opportunity to break the cycle we have been chained to and achieve not only liberation from suffering, but also the complete enlightenment of Buddhahood.

What makes this life so extraordinary is that we have been born in a world where a Buddha has manifested to teach the Dharma, and these teachings remain today, accessible to us through the great compassion of authentic lineage masters. What is even more astounding is that the Buddha did not teach only one path to achieve enlightenment. Recognising the different capacities of sentient beings, he taught methods which embraced their varying needs. For this reason, the Buddha turned the wheel of both Sutra and Tantra.

Known as the *causal vehicle*, the Sutrayana emphasises creating the causes for Buddhahood by working with karma to plant seeds that when nurtured, give rise to desired results in the future. It is essentially a process of change we try to control in a very specific way. This is illustrated in the step-by-step approach it takes to the afflictions, where we work with our conventional reality by applying antidotes and minimising the effects of destructive patterns. Our aim is focused on the removal of obscurations, and not on the result the practice will produce. In this way, the Sutrayana is more concerned with the process of uncovering rather than what is being uncovered.

The approach taken in the Tantrayana is quite different. Regardless of our apparent limitations and the situations we undergo, we remind ourselves of the underlying purity of our nature. As we realise that everything we experience is ultimately rooted in the enlightened qualities of our own Buddha-nature, there is nothing that needs to be created. We need only transform our perception of reality where negative emotions are not seen as obstacles, but as supports for achieving realisation. This approach is known as the *resultant vehicle* because the focus here is on recognising how the resultant state of enlightenment manifests in our life right now.

As the Kalachakra Path is based on the teachings of the Kalachakra Tantra, it technically belongs to the Tantrayana. The teachings of the Sutras, however, are used as the foundation to ripen our mind, enabling us to effectively use the profound methods presented in the Tantras. In this way, the Kalachakra Path incorporates both Sutra and Tantra.

In this chapter we will explore some of the key features of Buddhist Tantra in an effort to understand how the Kalachakra approaches practice and how this approach can ultimately lead us to achieve enlightenment within a single lifetime. By developing faith in these characteristics, we develop the courage to put these teachings into practice and receive the many benefits they produce.

THE MANY NAMES OF TANTRA

A common characteristic in Tantra is the use of synonyms when referring to specific concepts. This practice mirrors our experience of reality, as while everything has the same fully-established nature, that nature functions as the basis for an infinite variety of manifestations. Similarly, multiple labels serve to highlight different aspects of a given meaning. By learning to recognise these nuances, we can gain a deeper and more robust understanding.

The word *tantra* literally translates as a "continuum". It refers to the continuity of our Buddha-nature that is never broken, regardless of how distorted our perception of reality may be. *Tantrayana* is the path which emphasises revealing this sublime continuum.

Another name used interchangeably with tantra is *mantra*. Literally translated as "protecting the mind", the *Mantrayana* is the path that protects the mind from the ordinary appearances generated by delusion. Acting as a constant reminder of the underlying purity of our experience, it prevents us from slipping back into deluded states of mind.

The word mantra is also used in reference to the practice of reciting mantras as a way of familiarising the mind with its enlightened qualities, while also purifying the winds of our subtle energetic body. As we will see in the coming sections, reciting mantras is not the only form of protection offered by the Mantrayana. There are also many powerful visualisation practices and yogic techniques that serve to clear our ordinary perception, allowing us to experience reality as it is. This wealth of methods is what ultimately provides our mind with the greatest protection.

Throughout this series of books, the term *vajra* has often been used when speaking about the ultimate truth. This very important word can be loosely translated as "indestructible" or "inseparable" and has the connotation of being unbreakable like a diamond. The *Vajrayana* is therefore an indestructible path as nothing can destroy our sacred truth which is the ultimate, fully-established nature of reality, unborn and unceasing. No matter how many clouds gather in the sky, they can never harm the sun. Similarly, the adventitious defilements of conventional reality can never damage the ultimate truth of our Buddha-nature.

Whatever term we choose to refer to the teachings of Tantra, every word, every line of text, every idea brings us back to the source, back to our sacred truth. Whether directly or indirectly, everything points to our ultimate nature. Through establishing our awareness of this truth, we become a *Vidyadhara* or "awareness holder". Since the result of practicing the Vajrayana is to achieve the state of a Vidyadhara, it is also known as the *Path of the Vidyadharas*.

Finally, when compared with the Sutrayana, the direct approach of Tantra is able to produce results in a more efficient manner. Due to its profound methods, a practitioner of Tantra can habituate their mind to Buddha-nature in a fraction of the time. What would usually take three countless aeons through the practice of Sutra can be achieved with Tantra like a flash of lightning, bringing instantaneous realisation. For this reason, it is often referred to as the *Lightning Vehicle* or the *Quick Path*.

DISTINCTIONS BETWEEN SUTRA AND TANTRA

As we transition into the unique practices of the Kalachakra Path, it is important to cultivate a clear understanding of the ways the practice of Tantra differs from that of Sutra. Recognising the superiority of Tantra is fundamental to cultivating faith in the Kalachakra Path.

Common Features

Before we examine their differences, we should first consider the ways in which Sutra and Tantra are similar. This can help us avoid giving rise to misconceptions or wrong views that could eventually lead us to abandon the teachings of the Sutrayana. There are three main features common across Sutra and Tantra: (1) intention, (2) view and (3) attainments.

Intention

As both the Sutrayana and the Tantrayana are included within the Mahayana, they share the same motivation—the altruistic intention of *Bodhicitta*. Only with this supreme intention can the profound methods of Tantra produce the result of full enlightenment.

The only difference between the Bodhicitta of Sutra and the Bodhicitta of Tantra is their intensity. Whereas a Bodhisattva is usually willing to spend three countless aeons training in the *Six Perfections* and the *Four Ways of Gathering a Following*, a Tantric practitioner finds this period of time to be unacceptable. Overcome by the strength of their compassion, they seek the most skilful methods to accomplish their aim as quickly as possible. From their side, in terms of their own benefit, the time it takes is irrelevant, but from the perspective of the suffering sentient beings, they do not wish to waste a single moment.

This is why establishing the motivation of a Bodhisattva was explored so extensively in Book Two of this series. In many ways, Tantra is like rocket fuel that when used correctly, can provide the power to go higher than we've ever gone before. However if it is misused, it can also be incredibly destructive. Bodhicitta is our safeguard that ensures such power is aimed in the right direction.

View

Both Sutra and Tantra share the ultimate view of reality as being a sublime emptiness endowed with all enlightened qualities. This is the view presented in the definitive teachings of the Third Turning of the Wheel of Dharma. The only difference between the two views is that Tantra provides more details regarding the characteristics of ultimate truth and is therefore able to generate a more subtle experience of its nature, but the essential meaning is virtually identical.

We should however be aware that while Sutra and Tantra share the same view of ultimate reality, this does not mean that the suchness described in Tantra is the same as the emptiness of self as presented in the Second Turning. The emptiness of self describes the dependent nature of dualistic appearances, whereas suchness describes the fully-established nature of non-dual awareness. It is this resultant state of suchness that is used as the basis for Tantra. Failing to correctly understand this difference will unfortunately limit an individual's practice of Tantra to conventional reality, preventing them from penetrating to the definitive meaning.

Attainments

When considering the Path of a Bodhisattva, Sutra and Tantra both lead to the same result of full enlightenment. Although the methods they use to achieve this result are different, the actual attainments are not. For instance, the realisation of emptiness in the Sutras is the same realisation as that achieved in the Tantras.

Both approaches converge on the realisation of suchness, which ultimately clears the cognitive obscurations, giving rise to the enlightened mind of a Buddha. This is important to keep in mind to avoid any sense of inflated pride related to practicing a Tantric path. While the skilful means of Tantra may be superior for some practitioners, we should never denigrate or belittle the practices of those dedicated to the Sutra approach.

Uncommon Features of Tantra

Having established a common basis between Sutra and Tantra, we now turn our attention to the specific benefits of practicing the Vajrayana. Five features make Tantra superior to other forms of practice: (1) it is suited for those with sharp faculties; (2) it is vast in nature; (3) it has an abundance of methods; (4) the clarity of its view and (5) the lack of hardship in its practice.

Suited for Those with Sharp Faculties

When the Buddha arose from his meditation under the Bodhi tree, he did not immediately share his discoveries, but remained silent for many weeks, abiding in the incredible profundity of his realisation. The Buddha knew that the ultimate nature of reality was simply too subtle to be comprehended by those whose minds were not yet ready. He therefore chose to teach different provisional steps that would allow his students to mature to a point where they would be able to comprehend the sublime definitive meaning.

Based on their level of spiritual development, students can be divided into groups, identifying them as beings with lesser, middling or greater faculties. These labels do not imply a value judgement regarding the intelligence of a practitioner, but rather suggests that due to their present perspective, they are capable of engaging with certain levels of practice. For instance, as a student in high school would have difficulty working with material meant for a university student, they would gain more benefit from studying at their level of comprehension.

Tantra is designed for students with "sharp" faculties as it requires a keen sense of discernment that is capable of working with reality in a very direct way. A practitioner of Tantra brings everything into the path, including experiences normally considered negative or non-virtuous. This directness is what gives Tantra its incredible speed and makes it such an efficient system of practice. For those who are ripe, this path is extremely powerful, however for anyone not ready, it can be quite challenging.

For this reason, the Buddha taught the Sutras as a skilful way of preparing students. As the directness of Tantra can be difficult for some practitioners, focusing on using the Sutras to accumulate more merit and wisdom can be a more beneficial approach. Generating merit gives the mind the strength needed to face reality head on, while the wisdom provides the context for integrating different types of experiences. In this way, by working with the Sutras there is no one who cannot develop the sharpness of mind that Tantra requires.

Vast in Nature

The Sutrayana approach makes heavy use of distinguishing between what should be abandoned and what should be adopted. This form of selective bias is used to train in virtue where provisionally we concentrate on the "good" while turning away from the "bad".

Tantra recognises that these distinctions of good and bad are ultimately unnecessary as all phenomena are manifestations of the innate purity of ultimate truth. All phenomena, regardless of our relationship to them, are a valid source for establishing a direct experience of reality. By dissolving all forms of artificial bias, Tantra achieves a quality of vastness not present in the Sutras. Specifically, there are three types of vastness that are spoken of in the scriptures:

1. **Vastness of Focus:** The objects we use for practice are vast as there is no limitation to what can be brought into the path. Everything can be included, without exceptions.

2. **Vastness of Support:** The blessings we receive by practicing Tantra are vast, because we are never for a single moment separated from the influence of our enlightened nature. As long as we uphold our vows and commitments, we will produce vast stores of merit.

3. **Vastness of Conduct:** The activities we engage in are vast because Tantric practice is modelled after the conduct of the Buddhas and Bodhisattvas. Instead of behaving in accordance with an ordinary view, we try to emulate the way highly realised beings engage with the world.

This aspect of vastness gives Tantra its incredible power. It reminds us that all imputations are insubstantial, lack any real essence and so are inherently empty by nature. When we recognise that these illusory appearances have never existed at all, we are able to see that the ultimate truth is actually a sublime emptiness that is empty of these projections. Such a realisation is the difference between experiencing reality from the perspective of delusion or from the perspective of enlightened wisdom.

Abundance of Methods

As the focus of Tantra encompasses the entirety of reality, it is only fitting that it also contains an abundance of methods for working with that reality. The great wealth of rituals and meditative practices presented in the Tantras are divided into a number of *classes* based on the spiritual development of the practitioner. Through the lower classes, we purify our mind so we can eventually practice the higher classes specifically designed to suit our individual karmic propensities.

This movement from general to specific is one of the reasons there are so many systems of practice. As we each have unique karmic propensities, our subtle bodies have developed in a way that reflects this diversity. Consequently, some yogic techniques are more effective for specific types of minds and therefore knowing which system and practices are most suitable for you will require working with a qualified vajra master.

In addition to the sheer quantity of practices, Buddhist Tantra is also unique in the way it skilfully combines both method and wisdom into a single process. When practicing in accordance with the Sutras, method and wisdom are cultivated separately, leading to a process which alternates between working with conventional reality and ultimate reality. Because Tantra emphasises that all conventional phenomena manifest on the basis of ultimate truth, any practice which works with the conventional can cultivate merit while simultaneously generating greater awareness of Buddha-nature. This approach allows a Vajrayana practitioner to progress along the path at a much faster rate than someone following the Sutrayana.

Clarity of View

While both Sutra and Tantra are said to have the same view, this largely refers to how the view is experienced. When it comes to communicating the view however, there are a number of distinctions that can be made. The Tantras are said to have greater clarity than the Sutras, providing more detail regarding very subtle layers of experience. One example is the presentation of the subtle energetic system, found only within the teachings of Highest Yoga Tantra. The extraordinary detail allows practitioners to use a much broader range of phenomena as supports for their spiritual development.

The clarity of the Tantras is also evident in the way practices are presented. There is an enormous amount of detail regarding how specific rituals and meditations can be conducted and what results can then be expected. This clarity makes it possible to work with the complexities of reality in very precise ways.

Lack of Hardships

When comparing the subjective experience of practicing Sutra and Tantra, it is generally said that Tantra lacks the hardships that come from practicing the Sutra path for three countless aeons. Because it is possible to achieve enlightenment within a single lifetime, a practitioner of Tantra is able to avoid the hardship of experiencing the suffering of cyclic existence over many lifetimes.

As Tantra incorporates every aspect of reality into the path, there is also no need to emphasise the ascetic practices found in the Sutrayana. Rather than emphasising the restraint of conduct and limiting experience, a Vajrayana practitioner focuses on the blissful nature of their awareness as a powerful method for realising Buddha-nature. This skilful use of bliss removes any sense of hardship from the process, making it a joy to practice.

The point being made here is not that there are no challenges in practicing Tantra. For a mind that is not quite ripe, authentic tantric practice can be very confrontational. It is for this reason that we spend so much time preparing our mind with the preliminary practices so that we will have the strength to take full advantage of the skilful means that Tantra has to offer.

Uncommon Features of Kalachakra Tantra

Of all the tantric systems taught by the Buddha, the Kalachakra Tantra is considered the *King of Tantra* due to three unique and distinguishing qualities. The first is the *expansive scope* of the Kalachakra teachings. Within a single unified system, its vast range of topics provides an intricate understanding of how reality manifests to both sentient beings and the enlightened mind of a Buddha. Due to this expansiveness, the Kalachakra encompasses all other systems, giving context to their teachings and highlighting how everything fits together. This means that through the practice of Kalachakra, the essence of all systems is incorporated and through the practice of other systems, aspects of Kalachakra are emphasised.

The second quality is the Kalachakra's *clear presentation*. Although Tantra provides considerably more information than the Sutras, many of its systems are presented in cryptic and symbolic language, making them hard to interpret without the guidance of a qualified master. The Kalachakra, on the other hand, uses very direct language to describe extremely profound levels of experience. Whereas other systems become increasingly hidden as the approaches become more subtle, the Kalachakra provides details not found anywhere else. This clarity and directness makes it particularly well suited for times of degeneration when qualified masters are scarce and the possibility of confusion is high.

Finally, the unique practices of Kalachakra rely on the *profound methods* of empty-form and immutable bliss. Through working with empty-forms we cut through our dualistic obscurations and actualise an initial realisation of suchness. On this basis, we expand our realisation to integrate every aspect of our experience, from gross to very subtle levels, until we achieve the non-dual awareness of immutable bliss. The union of empty-form and immutable bliss is then used to burn up all karmic propensities and sever our connection to cyclic existence.

All systems of Highest Yoga Tantra can produce enlightenment within a single lifetime, however some are more direct than others. In the case of Kalachakra, it is one of the few systems capable of directly dissolving the aggregates and producing a *Great Transference Rainbow Body* without reliance on the death process. Such incredible efficiency and speed distinguish Kalachakra as being a particularly skilful means for the achievement of enlightenment in as short a time as possible.

THE ROLE OF SECRECY IN TANTRIC PRACTICE

When discussing the Vajrayana, the theme of *secrecy* is often encountered and as it tends to carry negative connotations in Western culture, it's worth discussing the role it plays in our practice.

The Vajrayana is sometimes called the *Path of Secret Mantra*, where the word "secret" refers to the subtle nature of the teachings. Gross phenomena are obvious and easily accessible to most people but as phenomena become more subtle, they become increasingly hidden from ordinary perception. This natural form of secrecy arises based on the perspective of the practitioner. As we train on the path, our mind becomes more subtle, thereby revealing aspects of our experience previously unavailable to us. Accordingly, the truth of the Vajrayana will not immediately be evident to everyone who encounters it and will instead remain a secret until their mind has properly ripened.

As a result of this natural secrecy, the intent of Tantric teachings can be easily misunderstood by those who are not ready to receive them. This can lead people to develop many misconceptions that distort the teachings, preventing them from producing the desired effects. When this occurs, the incredible power of Tantra is corrupted and can become the cause for suffering and delusion.

Recognising this potential for confusion, the Buddha used a number of checks and balances to safeguard the esoteric teachings. Unlike his Sutra teachings which were given to large public audiences, the Tantras were only bestowed to select groups of advanced practitioners. Before they could begin the practices, they were introduced to their ultimate nature through empowerments to ensure they developed the correct view.

Following in the footsteps of the Buddha, the esoteric teachings were passed from teacher to disciple in whispered lineages for many generations, before eventually being taught more openly. Historically speaking, secrecy has been strictest when the teachings are first introduced into a country or population. As more people develop the necessary foundations to understand the teachings, the secrecy tends to relax, allowing more people access to these teachings. This demonstrates that the level of secrecy is not fixed and changes over time, depending on the capacity of students.

In a world such as this one where high teachings have become readily available through the internet, many of the traditional checks and balances have broken down. The danger of developing wrong views is now much higher and for this reason, we need to consider which aspects of the teachings should remain secret and which should be made public.

My personal approach is to emphasise a discriminating wisdom that clearly identifies and differentiates the theoretical foundations used in Vajrayana practice. When we understand why we engage in a particular practice, we can be certain of the benefit it will bring to our mind. Failing to develop this wisdom will only cause us to become lost in empty rituals. Instead of connecting with the essence, we may focus too heavily on the symbolic manifestations, losing sight of the meaning they embody. I therefore encourage you to openly study the Vajrayana within the context of a path structure in order to be as prepared as possible.

When it comes to the actual practice of Tantra, I feel the traditional process is still the most effective. If a practice requires *empowerment*, that practice should not be recited until such a time as you can receive the necessary empowerments from a qualified vajra master. The opportunity to receive the *oral transmission* of the practice text and its *instructions* should then be sought out.

As the practices become more advanced, the pith instructions play an increasingly important role. Since most of these instructions are passed on as an oral tradition, the role of the vajra master becomes a vital part of your practice. This relationship will be discussed in greater detail in the coming chapters.

In order to maintain the strength of our practice, we should try to avoid speaking of the specifics needlessly. This is not because we are doing something shameful or regrettable, but because there is no benefit from such talk. By keeping our practice a private matter, not only do we protect the mind of those who might not understand, we also protect our own mind from developing spiritual pride.

THREE APPROACHES FOR REMOVING OBSCURATIONS

With a clear understanding of the unique features of the Vajrayana, we move on to discuss the different methodologies used in Buddhist practice. There are three distinct approaches: (1) abandonment, (2) transformation and (3) recognition. While the first is most closely related to the Sutrayana, the last two correspond to the approaches taken in the generation and completion stages of the Vajrayana. Understanding these approaches provides a context for the various practices presented later in this book.

Abandonment

The first approach involves the *abandonment* of afflicted states of mind such as the three poisons of ignorance, attachment and aversion. These afflictions are viewed as problems that need to be removed. By practicing the path in accordance with the Sutras, we learn the faults of these states of mind and develop the aspiration to let them go. This approach can be likened to a gardener finding a poisonous plant in their garden. Recognising the plant as dangerous, they take steps to uproot and destroy it.

The method used to remove afflictions is meditation on the antidotes which counteract the specific forms of ignorance that feed the affliction. For instance, we can meditate on the faults of attachment to counter the ignorance that thinks attachment is a good quality. We can then meditate on impermanence as an antidote to the ignorance which believes the object of attachment is a genuine source of happiness. The more familiar we become with the antidotes, the weaker the afflictions become until eventually they no longer have the power to impact the mind.

In this approach, the root of suffering is the ignorance which grasps onto reality as existing inherently in the way that it appears. The antidote towards this type of ignorance is to meditate on the dependent nature of phenomena and to realise the emptiness of self-entities. By completely habituating oneself to this realisation, all afflicted and cognitive obscurations are eventually abandoned, allowing the ultimate truth to manifest.

Transformation

As we move into the Vajrayana, the second approach is to focus on *transforming* ordinary appearances into pure perceptions. This is the method associated with the generation stage and is based on recognising that afflictions are merely distorted interpretations of reality. If we change our interpretation of them, they stop being afflictions and instead become supports for developing wisdom. This is similar to a skilled alchemist recognising that a poisonous plant can be transformed into medicine. Rather than destroying the plant, he is able to use it to bring benefit.

In practice, this method involves seeing all forms as enlightened deities, all sounds as enlightened mantras and all thought as manifestations of primordial wisdom. No matter what arises, we try to establish a pure view of the experience, recognising it as an aspect of our underlying Buddha-nature. The more we familiarise our minds with this enlightened level of reality, the less power our ordinary perception has to influence our experience.

As this approach involves replacing an impure view with a pure one, it can be considered conceptual in nature. As such, it provides a provisional method to purify the mind and bring us closer to our Buddha-nature. Ultimately, however, such an approach needs to be transcended in order to achieve a direct realisation of suchness.

Recognition

For the last approach, we rely on direct observation to *recognise* the ultimate nature of appearances. Instead of describing our experience with concepts, we focus on developing an awareness of the present moment that is free from grasping. Such an awareness allows us to see through conceptual imputations, revealing the underlying ways in which sublime emptiness manifests. As this approach transcends the concepts of pure and impure, it makes use of all forms of experience.

This would be like a person who is able to eat a poisonous plant without fear of harm. There is nothing that actually needs to be transformed, we simply observe reality as it is.

If we applied this method to a moment of anger, we would see it to be nothing more than an appearance within the mind, arising like a wave in the ocean to abide for a moment and then dissolving away. At no point is there anything that exists with any degree of substance or inherent qualities. By simply observing the appearance, we see that it liberates itself and is naturally pacified. This truth applies to all dualistic forms of consciousness.

The Kalachakra Path makes use of all three of the above approaches. Up to this point, we have mostly worked with the approach of abandonment in accordance with the Sutrayana. The next stage of our practice emphasises the approaches of transformation and recognition.

HOW ENLIGHTENMENT IS ACHIEVED IN THE KALACHAKRA TANTRA

Using the profound methods found in the Kalachakra Tantra our aim is to establish a pure view of the dependent nature of reality which is then used to directly experience the fully-established nature of absolute reality. To understand how enlightenment is achieved through this process, we once again analyse our ground, path and result, only this time from the perspective of the uncommon practices of the Kalachakra Path.

The Ground of Ordinary Appearances

The purpose of a spiritual path is to change the way we experience reality so we can transcend our limitations and actualise our potential. Its nature is transformation where we begin in one state and through our practice of the path, we produce another. Recognising this, the first step to effectively practice the path is to develop clarity regarding exactly what we intend to change.

In the context of Kalachakra, the ground to be purified is the conventional reality of the external and internal Kalachakras. These two levels of reality correspond to the objective and subjective appearances of a dualistic consciousness. If we think back to our understanding of the *Three Natures* (see Book Two), we recall that the dependent nature of reality arises on the basis of projecting imputed natures onto our experience of the fully-established nature of suchness. As long as these imputations remain, we will continue to experience reality from the perspective of a dualistic consciousness. However, if we stop projecting imputations, the dependent nature will dissolve and we will be left with an experience of reality as it is.

This presents us with a problem. The nature of the dualistic view is a dependent designation; as soon as the appearance of an object arises, there is also the appearance of a subject. Likewise, with the appearance of a subject, there is the appearance of an object. This means that in order to completely stop imputed natures, we need to stop all dualistic appearances without exception. If even one ordinary appearance remains, the dependent nature of reality will not dissolve.

For this reason the Kalachakra uses a four-fold model to understand the different types of appearances we need to purify to achieve our aim. They are known as the *Four States of Experience*: (1) the waking state; (2) the dream state; (3) the deep-sleep state and (4) he state of blissful absorption. Each of these categories highlights a particular type of appearance we can potentially encounter. When taken as a set, they cover the full range of possible appearances from the most coarse level to the most subtle.

The Waking State

The first state consists of the sensory appearances of form, sound, smell, taste and tactile sensation. Together they form the objective reality of the universe as experienced from the perspective of a single sentient being. As these appearances are dominant when we are awake, they are referred to as *appearances of the waking state*.

Sensory appearances are considered the coarsest type of appearance as they are heavily conditioned by the physical sense faculties. As long as the mind remains attached to the physical aggregates of the body, these faculties will produce a relatively stable stream of appearances in the mind. It is primarily this stability that leads us to believe in the inherent existence of external phenomena. For even though their nature is a constant state of flux, they appear to be substantial and permanent.

Through the practice of meditation, it is possible to withdraw awareness from the sense faculties and to temporarily cause the waking state appearances to become dormant, as if we were turning our back on them. Although we may no longer pay attention to them, the sense faculties still cause shifts in energy and continue to have an indirect effect on the mind. The only way to fully stop waking state appearances from arising is to sever the energetic influence between the body and mind—a process that happens naturally at death or when induced through advanced yogic techniques.

The Dream State

The second state refers to the range of gross and subtle mental appearances such as thoughts and memories. While these appearances are still objective in nature, they are usually only experienced by a single person and therefore provide the basis for the internal reality of an individual. As these types of appearances are most dominant during our dreams, they are collectively known as *appearances of the dream state*.

Mental appearances are considered more subtle than sensory appearances as they represent the many layers of conceptual imputations we project onto the world. To understand this process, consider the appearance of a dog. This seemingly simple appearance is actually made up of many appearances arising simultaneously. We begin with the sensory appearance of a form. When our mind recognises the pattern these appearances makes, it immediately projects the concept of "dog". At the same time, it also projects other concepts such as "animal", "brown", and "friendly". This collection of conceptual overlays are all gross mental appearances. There are also subtle imputations such as "separate", "permanent", and "inherently existing". Together they form a network of concepts that determine how we as individuals relate to sensory appearances.

Dream state appearances arise as a result of habituation to a particular conceptual view. Through the conditioning of our karma, we associate specific patterns of appearances with specific networks of concepts. In order to purify this type of appearance, we need to break our habits. Unfortunately, due to the interdependent nature of imputations, unravelling the layers of concepts can be quite a complex process. We can bypass this complexity by temporarily dissolving our ordinary view through meditation and consciously projecting a pure view that accords with how reality actually exists. By habituating ourselves to such a view, we effectively "rewire" the associations in our mind and weaken the influence of our karmic conditioning. When the mind is less dominated by karma, it becomes easier to release our grasping and stop the proliferation of concepts.

The Deep-sleep State

The third state consists of the subtle subjective appearances that function as a basis for our conception of self. These appearances act as the glue which binds together all coarser forms of conceptual imputation. As they manifest to a lucid mind during deep-dreamless sleep, they are referred to as *appearances of the deep-sleep state*.

The ordinary self is comprised of basically two types of appearance—the appearance of "me" and the appearance of "mine". The first is an extremely subtle appearance that manifests as the feeling that we exist as a separate, substantially existing entity. It acts as a fixed reference point that establishes the relative perspective of a sentient being. The second is the feeling that a particular phenomenon belongs to or is included within that entity. This feeling forms a conceptual boundary that distinguishes our identity—the sense of who we think we are.

When we are either awake or dreaming, our attention is usually focused outward towards different objective appearances. At these times, the appearance of the subject is largely implicit. It is not until we dissolve objective appearances that the experience of the subject becomes more obvious. We can do this by withdrawing the mind through the practice of single-pointed concentration. As we approach the foundational consciousness, objective appearances go dormant and the subjective qualities of bliss, stillness and lucid presence become manifest. If the mind is stabilised in this experience, it is possible to observe the empty nature of the self and thereby cut the grasping onto its appearance.

The State of Blissful Absorption

The fourth state refers to the very subtle non-dual appearances which arise when the mind becomes absorbed in its own nature. At such a time, the explicit dualism of subject and object is dormant and the mind experiences a non-conceptual experience of suchness. Because these experiences manifest as an extraordinarily intense feeling of bliss, they are known as the *appearances of the state of blissful absorption*.

For most people these appearances are rare and tend to last for only a very short period of time. In normal experience, they manifest when we sneeze, faint or experience orgasm. In each of these situations there is an accumulation of energy that functions to concentrate the mind and dissolve the sense of self. As this concentration of energy usually happens in an uncontrolled manner, as soon as the conceptual mind ceases, the experience of bliss becomes increasingly intense, giving rise to grasping which re-establishes the dualistic mind and releases the energy. This process happens so fast, we don't even notice the actual moment of bliss. While this type of experience is technically a non-conceptual experience of suchness, due to the lack of awareness it doesn't constitute a realisation of suchness.

In order for an experience of suchness to function as an antidote to our karmic conditioning, we need to be able to abide in that experience without grasping. This requires training our mind to approach suchness in a very controlled way which we can do gradually by first achieving a direct experience of suchness through meditation and then mixing that realisation with pure appearances over time. Through this process, our grasping is weakened to the point where we can abide in suchness for greater periods of time. A faster way to achieve this result is to combine meditation with yogic postures that manipulate the subtle energetic body to produce highly concentrated states of non-dual awareness.

The Path to Experience the Enlightened Reality

With the appearances of the four states as our ground, we get a sense for how the Kalachakra Path approaches practice. After cultivating the two outer preliminaries and the first four inner preliminaries, we are now ready to meditate on the ultimate nature of reality. Our immediate aim is to achieve a non-dual awareness of sublime emptiness that is completely free from all dualistic appearances.

Doing this requires a shift in our awareness, away from the ordinary appearances of the conceptual mind and towards the enlightened appearances of primordial wisdom. This process can be divided into four steps: (1) establish a pure view of the guru; (2) extend that view to all appearances; (3) establish a non-conceptual awareness; and (4) abide in suchness.

Establish a Pure View of the Guru

The essence of all Vajrayana practice is to recognise the fully-established nature as the basis of all experience. This realisation is known as *establishing a pure view.* When mastered, everything in our experience will be directly perceived as suchness. Unfortunately, as we are not currently habituated to seeing reality in this way, we must train our mind to interpret our experience.

When we begin this process, we only see the appearances projected by our ignorance. In order to see the world through the eyes of wisdom, we need to concentrate on the appearance in our lives where wisdom is most manifest, namely the Guru. In the previous book, we emphasised the importance of following a spiritual guide. That relationship now forms the basis for recognising the radiance of our own Buddha-nature.

This practice has two components: (1) first we work with the external manifestation of our Guru by practicing *devotion to the vajra master*; training our mind to see the Guru as an enlightened manifestation of the Buddha; (2) we then meditate on *Guru Yoga* in order to dissolve the separation between the external and internal, recognising that the Guru is nothing other than a manifestation of our own Buddha-nature. By making supplications to this inner Guru, we invoke his blessings and create a strong connection to our sacred truth which provides a support for the realisation of suchness.

Extend that View to All Appearances

Through training with the Guru, we develop our pure view to the extent that whenever we see our Guru, we are reminded of our Buddha-nature. While this is an excellent foundation, there is considerably more that we need to do. We can think of our mind as being like a house with many windows. When the windows are clean, the sun can be clearly seen and the darkness in the house is dispelled. The pure appearance of the Guru is like a single clean window. In order to let more light in, we need to clean the other windows.

We do this through reliance on the skilful means of the Kalachakra generation stage which consists of two practices: (1) with reliance on the Guru we receive empowerment and take the *tantric vows and commitments* to help us maintain our pure view at all times; and (2) we then familiarise ourselves with the enlightened mandala of Kalachakra through the practice of *Deity Yoga*. Both of these trainings emphasise the purification of our relationship with different types of phenomena so we can eventually abandon the deluded view of karma. While everything continues to manifest in the same way, we no longer believe they exist as they appear and instead appearances seem illusory in nature, taking on a dream like quality.

Establish a Non-Conceptual Awareness

Once all the windows in our house are clean, no matter where we stand, the light of the sun comes pouring in. When this occurs we can turn our attention from the glass to what lies beyond the house. Seeing the shining sun, we can choose to stay indoors or we can go outside. If we stay where we are, we run the risk of the windows becoming dirty again and we will have to clean them once more. If however we decide to step outside, nothing will stand between us and the radiant warmth of the sun.

Similarly, as long as we continue to see the world through the conceptual imputations of a dualistic consciousness, we will never directly experience our sublime nature. There will always be a veil that blocks our awareness of reality. Even though the thickness of the veil may fluctuate, it is still a veil—an artificial barrier that we need to dissolve in order to allow ourselves the opportunity to experience our Buddha-nature directly.

To step out of our house, we first need to be shown where the doorway is. In practice, this is done through receiving the profound *pointing-out instructions* from our vajra master. During the completion stage empowerments, the vajra master introduces us to the aspects of our definitive nature. This experience provides the basis for developing familiarity with this state.

Through the non-conceptual practice of the *Three Isolations*, we then bring ourselves to the very edge of our dualistic limitations. By dissolving our grasping onto concepts, we create an opening for the pure manifestations of suchness to arise. This is like standing in an open doorway where all we have to do is step over the threshold.

Abide in Suchness

Moving from consciousness to primordial awareness may not seem like a huge transition as once we arrive at the door, all we have to do is step outside. But unfortunately, this is not the case. Since beginningless time we have been habituated to experiencing reality from the perspective of a dualistic self. Due to the karma we have accumulated, we have formed a very strong bond between the mind and the physical body. While this bond exists, our mind will continue to be influenced by the constant movement of subtle energy in that body. This means that even after we sever the explicit grasping that supports consciousness, an implicit layer of residual grasping still remains.

To understand this problem, imagine that in your entire life you have never been outside your house; inside is all you have ever known. Standing in the doorway you look out at a world you have only seen from a distance. If you were to run outside, you would be hit by a wave of new experiences, just like a blind person perceiving colour and form for the very first time. When faced with something so foreign, so different from what we have known, our mind naturally becomes overwhelmed. It recoils and returns to what is familiar and to what feels safe.

Similarly, when we experience suchness for the first time, our mind can become overwhelmed and have difficulty taking it all in at once. If we go too strongly and too quickly, we trigger our grasping and are snapped back into our dualistic default. To overcome this problem, we train in the *first five Vajra Yogas* to skilfully reveal our Buddha-nature in a gradual manner. By working progressively with the various subtle energies that course through the body, we dissolve their influence on the mind, allowing us to integrate more of our experience as suchness. Through this training we unify appearances, awareness and energy in such a way that we can rest in a fully qualified, non-dual experience of the sublime emptiness endowed with all aspects.

As long as our mind is karmically linked with a body, this realisation of suchness will only manifest during meditation. The moment we arise from our session, dualistic appearances will arise once again. These are known as cognitive obscurations and while our mind may no longer grasp onto these appearances with ignorance, they still limit our capacity. Until that bond is completely dissolved, we cannot achieve the state of a fully-enlightened Buddha.

This leaves us with two choices. We can either wait until our lifespan ceases and our body and mind naturally separate, or we can use our realisation of sublime emptiness as a method to burn up the remaining karmic residue. This is the function of the *sixth Vajra Yoga*, which effectively dissolves our physical body and establishes what is known as a *Great Transference Rainbow Body*.

The Resultant State of the Four Vajras

Freed from the limitations of a gross physical body, our mind achieves the very pinnacle of the Bodhisattva path—the state of a *Dharma King of Shambhala*. With mastery of the Six Vajra Yogas we achieve the Dharmakaya truth body of a Buddha. All that remains is to complete our accumulation of merit in order to spontaneously manifest the Rupakaya form-bodies of a Buddha. Fortunately this is relatively easy for a tenth level Bodhisattva who can effortlessly manifest in whatever way is needed to bring benefit to sentient beings. This approach to enlightenment is known as *Arousing Bodhicitta that is Beyond Compare*. It is the method that is exemplified by the three great Bodhisattvas Vajrapani, Manjushri and Avalokiteshvara.

In the Kalachakra System, this resultant state is described as the *Four Vajras:* (1) Vajra-Body; (2) Vajra-Speech; (3) Vajra-Mind and (4) Vajra-Wisdom. Each represents a specific dimension of enlightened experience that is the result of purifying the appearances of the four states respectively.

Vajra-Wisdom

The most subtle dimension is that of *Vajra-Wisdom* which is the blissful nature of a mind that abides immovably in ultimate truth. This is known as the Buddha's nature body or the *Svabhavikakaya*. This dimension of experience naturally manifests when we remove all gross and subtle obscurations from the mind.

Vajra-Mind

Vajra-Mind is the pervasive awareness that remains undistracted from its own ultimate nature and is known as the Buddha's wisdom-truth body or the *Jñana-Dharmakaya*. It manifests in the aspect of the primordial wisdoms of the *Six Buddha Families* and is the result of completely habituating the mind to recognising the aspects of Buddha-nature.

While we speak of Vajra-Wisdom and Vajra-Mind as two separate dimensions, we must always remember that they are inseparable. Everything that arises in the mind of an enlightened being is perceived as suchness and is experienced as immutable bliss. As sentient beings cannot experience this level of reality directly, we need to manifest the remaining vajras of Vajra-Speech and Vajra-Body.

Vajra-Speech

To understand how a Buddha manifests to sentient beings, we can think of the enlightened mind as being like a sun that radiates light in all directions. These rays of light represent the natural expression of a Buddha's enlightened qualities and arise from the perfection of all virtuous qualities through the accumulation of merit. As a Buddha has completely removed all obscurations; nothing prevents these qualities from manifesting simultaneously and continuously. This constant radiance of the Buddha's qualities is known as *Vajra-Speech*.

Even though the sun can shine, not everyone can feel the warmth of its rays. To experience Vajra-Speech directly, a sentient being's mind must be thoroughly purified of afflicted obscurations. For such a highly realised Bodhisattva these qualities are experienced as a host of enlightened deities, collectively called a Buddha's enjoyment body or the *Sambhogakaya*. The deities which appear to the Bodhisattva depends on the specific karmic connections present in their mind. For instance, if they are habituated to seeing their Buddha-nature in the aspect of Kalachakra, they will experience the Sambhogakaya as the enlightened mandala of Kalachakra.

Vajra-Body

Vajra-Body refers to the way Vajra-Speech is experienced by sentient beings who have not yet purified their mind of afflicted obscurations, like seeing the sun through an overcast sky. Depending on the thickness of the cloud cover, more or less of the sun's light will be visible. Similarly, the thickness of a being's obscurations determines whether they experience more or less of a Buddha's enlightened qualities. The form these qualities take in the experience of a sentient being is a Buddha's emanation body or *Nirmanakaya*.

Whether the qualities of a Buddha manifest in the mind of a sentient being depends on the existence of karmic connections between that being and the Buddha. If there are no connections, there is no way for a Buddha to bring them benefit. It is for this reason that the accumulation of merit is so important.

REVIEW OF KEY POINTS

- The Buddha taught two vehicles for achieving the state of full enlightenment: (1) the Causal Vehicle of Sutra which focuses on cultivating the causal conditions needed to manifest Buddhahood; and (2) the Resultant Vehicle of Tantra which focuses on recognising the pure nature of all phenomena in this present moment.

- There are many synonyms used to refer to the practice of tantra: (1) it is known as the Tantrayana to emphasise the presence of the sublime continuum of Buddha-nature within every moment of our experience; (2) it is known as the Mantrayana to emphasise how it protects our mind from ordinary perception; (3) it is known as the Vajrayana to emphasise the indestructible nature of our sacred truth; (4) it is known as the Path of the Vidyadharas to emphasise that it transforms its practitioners into "awareness holders"; and (5) it is known as the Quick Path because it is capable of producing Buddhahood within a single lifetime.

- The common features held between Sutra and Tantra are that: (1) both have the same intention of Bodhicitta; (2) both hold the view of sublime emptiness to be the ultimate nature of reality; and (3) both are capable of producing the attainments of full enlightenment.

- The uncommon features of Tantra are that: (1) it is suited for those with sharp faculties; (2) it is vast in nature; (3) it has an abundance of methods; (4) the clarity of view that is presented and (5) its lack of hardship when practicing.

- The features specific to the Kalachakra Tantra are its: (1) expansive scope, (2) clear presentation and (3) profound methods of empty-form and immutable bliss.

- Secrecy in Tantra is used in two ways: (1) the teachings are naturally secret in that only those whose mind has ripened can understand their incredibly profundity; and (2) the practices are protected through secrecy in order to ensure they are not misunderstood or used in a way that harms the practitioner.

- There are three approaches used to remove obscurations: (1) abandonment of afflicted states of mind through the use of antidotes; (2) transformation of impure afflictions into pure appearances; and (3) recognition of the enlightened nature of all phenomena.

- The ground that is purified by the Kalachakra Path is the dualistic appearances which are imputed on our experience of suchness. We can divide these appearances into four levels of subtlety based on four separate states: (1) the sensory appearances of the waking state; (2) the mental appearances of the dream state; (3) the subtle appearances of self-grasping in the deep-sleep state and (4) the appearance of non-conceptual awareness in the state of blissful absorption.

- The process of purification provided by the Kalachakra Path involves four steps: (1) establish a pure view of the Guru; (2) extend that view to all appearances; (3) establish a non-conceptual awareness; and (4) abide in suchness.

- The result of the Kalachakra Path is the state of a Dharma King of Shambhala. This is equivalent to a Tenth Level Bodhisattva. Having completely removed all afflictive and cognitive obscurations, we are free to manifest countless emanations that allow us to complete the accumulations of merit and wisdom in a very short period. This produces the Four Vajras: (1) Vajra-Body; (2) Vajra-Speech; (3) Vajra-Mind and (4) Vajra-Wisdom.

CHAPTER TWO

Cultivating Devotion Towards a Vajra Master

The Vajrayana has one purpose, to produce the state of enlightenment as quickly as possible so as to effectively relieve the suffering of all sentient beings. In accordance with these teachings, the key to achieving this result is correct devotion to a guru. As stated by Vajradhara in the Tantras:

> *Enlightenment can not be found anywhere.*
> *Only by practising the methods taught by the guru,*
> *can you find enlightenment.*

In essence, enlightenment means to know reality as it is. As we currently see the world from the perspective of ignorance, there is nowhere we can look to find enlightenment. The only way we can transcend our ignorance is for someone to show us how and this is the role of the guru. Without them, there is no enlightenment. Recognising the central role the guru plays in our spiritual development, we will now explore the specific ways to cultivate a vajra relationship with a guru from the perspective of the Vajrayana.

WHO IS THE GURU?

For most of us, the term *guru* refers to our spiritual guide who teaches us the Dharma and directs us along the path. The guru is our spiritual father or mother, who cares for us and does whatever they can to support us in our practice of virtue. They hold the lineage, transmit the teachings, bestow on us the vows and commitments, bless our mind and instruct us in our practice.

In our lifetime, we may have the good fortune to encounter many teachers who we come to call guru. One teacher may introduce us to the foundational topics, while another bestows the vows, and yet another may teach us philosophy. We can find many examples in the past of great masters who have relied on many teachers. Jamyang Khyentse Wangpo, for instance, is known to have had more than one hundred teachers, and the Jonang master Bamda Gelek Gyatso also had a similarly impressive number of gurus. In my own experience, I feel very fortunate to have been able to study and practice with twenty-five masters who opened the door to many different levels of Dharma knowledge and awakened in me a profound appreciation of the various traditions.

Whether we have one or many gurus depends entirely on our karma. Of the wide variety of people we encounter throughout this life, our capacity to learn from them is determined by our karmic propensities which establish our attitudes towards them, and our receptivity for what they have to share. As only an enlightened being can know exactly how karma will play out over time, I recommend keeping an open mind to what others have to offer, for we never know the impact they may have on our life. If we close ourselves off with scepticism and bias, we greatly limit the benefit we could potentially receive.

No matter how many relationships you may form with gurus, it is natural to feel a stronger connection toward some teachers over others. For you, the teachings you receive from them are particularly clear and penetrating and their qualities are obvious. As such, developing a sense of respect and devotion towards them is extremely easy and such a teacher often comes to be our *root guru*. As a primary role model, they are very special and carry a great deal of influence in our lives. There is no rule that states you can have only one root guru, it all depends on how much impact the guru has on your life.

It is said that our root guru is more precious and spiritually beneficial than our mother, as although she has shown us immeasurable

My most precious root guru—Kyabje Lama Lobsang Trinlé

kindness and provided us with every possible worldly benefit, unlike our root guru, she was unable to give us the Dharma. Similarly, we can consider our root guru to be even higher than all the Buddhas of the past, present and future. Since we lacked the karma to meet these Buddhas physically, we could not directly benefit from their inconceivable wisdom, compassion and other sublime qualities. Instead, it is our root guru who appears to us right now, transmitting to us the authentic Dharma.

From the perspective of the Vajrayana, our root guru specifically refers to the vajra master who bestows on us the tantric empowerments, making it possible for us to attain realisations on the tantric path. Through the use of incredibly skilful means, he helps us remove our limitations and clarifies our view, enabling us to experience our most sacred truth through the uncommon practices of the generation and completion stages. With infinite kindness, our root guru creates the conditions for us to achieve Buddhahood within a single lifetime and for this reason, there is no one who will bring us greater benefit.

CULTIVATING A PURE VIEW OF THE GURU

If we hope to experience the full range of benefit that comes from correctly following a vajra master, it is necessary to make a significant effort to establish the right attitude as a support for our practice. As a vajra master is a very special type of guru, building a relationship with them requires an approach different from that of working with a spiritual guide.

An authentic vajra master has diligently trained in the discipline of the Three Vows and the profound practices of the Vajrayana, achieving a level of realisation where they can use a vast array of methods to guide their students towards enlightenment. Empowered by the flexibility of their view, they are often seen to act in ways that challenge social norms and preconceived notions of how a spiritual guide should behave. As they are only concerned with helping their students remove obscurations, vajra masters can take whatever form is needed to bring the most benefit. While this can sometimes lead the general public to misunderstand their intentions, if we as students can cultivate a pure view of our guru, we open ourselves to receiving their full blessings.

With this in mind, we can begin developing our view by considering the differences between the way the guru is understood in the sutras and tantras. For practitioners of the Sutrayana, the guru is seen as a highly realised sentient being and although we are encouraged to venerate them as a Buddha, they are generally regarded as a Bodhisattva on the path. This reflects the causal nature of the Sutrayana approach, where the term Buddha is reserved for those who manifest as a Buddha, such as Buddha Shakyamuni.

In accordance with the resultant nature of the tantras, the guru *is* the Buddha. They are not seen as separate entities but considered to be of the same nature, therefore whenever we encounter the guru, we also encounter the Buddha. In this way, the Buddha is not an historical figure we respect and venerate from afar; he is an active presence in our lives, with whom we interact directly. It is this immediacy which makes the vajra master such a powerful influence on our mind.

Why We Should Think of the Guru as Buddha

We do not follow a guru to generate more problems in our lives. We follow them because they can provide us with the most skilful ways to achieve the results we seek, and training to view the guru as Buddha is the best way to gain the most from that relationship. As we are aiming for the ultimate goal of full enlightenment, significant changes in the way we see the world are required. We need to be willing to let go of our habitual ways, and while the guru can undoubtedly help us do this, lacking the correct attitude will limit their effectiveness.

To provide an illustration, consider how our attitude can alter the impact a person has on our mind. Let's say you meet a complete stranger at a party, who you know nothing about. During your conversation, they offer some advice, but as you don't particularly care what this person thinks, chances are you will not pay much attention, nor be willing to change. This would be especially true if their opinion was contrary to your own.

Now imagine you find out this person was an expert in the subject you discussed. They had won many awards and were highly respected in their field. You receive the same advice from them but this time, you would probably be more inclined to listen to what they had to say. Depending on the degree of respect you have for this person, you may even be inclined to change your opinion.

What this demonstrates is that our attitude towards someone determines how receptive we are to their influence. Viewing our guru as just an ordinary person closes our mind, making transformation difficult. If, however, we see our guru as the manifestation of a fully enlightened Buddha, our mind becomes inspired and open to whatever advice they offer us. Being more receptive to what the guru has to say increases the probability of putting their advice into practice and we are therefore more likely to receive the intended benefits of the Dharma.

How to See the Guru as Buddha

To the sceptical mind, the practice of viewing the guru as Buddha may appear as though we are projecting extraordinary qualities onto something that is ordinary and just fooling ourselves into seeing something which is not there. The truth, however, is the exact opposite. Right now, we project ordinary faults onto something that is perfect. We look at the appearance of the guru whose nature is sublime emptiness and we see the aspect of an ordinary human being. Instead of recognising how reality actually manifests, we place all our faith in a projected fantasy and take that as our truth.

Training to see the guru as Buddha involves reducing our faith in the appearances of delusion and cultivating faith in the appearances of wisdom. We do this by focusing our attention on the virtuous qualities we can perceive, while transforming apparent faults into qualities. In this way, by looking at how the guru is Buddha, we come to see the guru as Buddha.

Meditating on the Guru's Qualities

To see the Buddha's qualities in our guru, we need to be familiar with what those qualities are. By studying the teachings, we can identify specific virtuous minds and then look for those qualities in the guru. For instance, love and compassion are the very essence of a Buddha. In what ways does your guru exhibit these qualities? How do they care for their students and what actions do they take to reduce their suffering? Reflect on your personal experience of the guru to find examples that demonstrate the presence of these qualities and strengthen them in your mind by reminding yourself that this is how the Buddha manifests in your life.

As our guru manifests to us in accordance with our karma, we may not necessarily find every quality of the Buddha. The appearance of the guru's qualities matches the level of purity of our mind and as we presently see the world from the limited perspective of a human being, our gurus will also appear to us as human, with all the corresponding human qualities, including imperfections.

For this reason, we should not expect our guru to exhibit the superhuman capacities of enlightened beings such as reading minds or knowing the future. This is not to say these qualities are not present, but due to our current stage of development, we simply cannot see them. Rather than focusing on the qualities we can't see and regarding their absence as a fault, we should focus on the qualities we can see. If the only quality you perceive in your guru is diligence, allow this to inspire you to also be diligent in your practice. As you apply this quality to your own life, you will purify your mind and the purer your mind becomes, the more qualities you will be able to see.

In this way, we slowly build an inventory of qualities that we aspire to replicate in ourselves. No matter what qualities we perceive, they each become an inspiration for our practice and this is what will bring us the greatest benefit.

How to Work with the Appearance of Faults

Because we experience everything through the lens of our karma, when we start to look at the guru, we will inevitably see a mixture of qualities and faults. If we only focus on the faults, we can quickly develop a negative attitude towards our guru, causing us to lose faith in their capacity to guide us. We therefore need to be skilful with these appearances so we can use them to our advantage.

We can classify a fault as a characteristic or an aspect of the guru's behaviour that we see as being negative or disturbing, such as if our guru appears to have an explosive temper or seems to be attached to things like food or material comforts. Encountering such faults can form the basis for us to disparage our guru and if we allow ourselves to be overly critical, it becomes difficult to see them as a Buddha. Consequently, the relationship loses its potential benefit.

When a fault appears to us, we should reflect on the nature of a Buddha's enlightened mind. A Buddha has completely purified all negativities and actualised all enlightened qualities and as such, they constantly emanate these qualities, like a sun emanates rays of light. When the light of the sun reaches a pool of water, a reflection arises, just as when the Buddha's qualities meet the mind of a sentient being, an appearance arises. If the water is disturbed by the wind, the light becomes broken up and the image of the sun is distorted. When the water is still, the reflection of the sun can be clearly seen. Similarly, when the mind is dominated by the winds of karma, the qualities of the Buddha are distorted and ordinary appearances manifest, but when the mind becomes still, the qualities of the Buddha become visible.

Understanding this, we should avoid believing that any faults we see come from the side of the guru. We should instead recognise that even though the guru's qualities constantly shine, due to the distortions created by our karma we experience those qualities as faults. If our mind was purer, the fault would not arise.

The effect of thinking in this way is that we don't lose faith in the underlying purity of the guru. Rather than immediately trusting in the reality of what appears to us, we learn to trust in the reality of Buddha-nature. In doing so, we use the manifestation of faults as a reminder of our own obscurations and the need to practice the Dharma to purify our mind.

Another beneficial way of working with faults is to think of the guru as a mirror. The function of a mirror is to create a reflection and reflections can show us things we would not normally be able to see. If we look into a mirror and see the reflection of our face with dirt on it, we can take steps to clean it off. Without the reflection however, we would never know our face was dirty to begin with.

Similarly, the guru offers us a reflection of our own Buddha-nature. When we look at the guru, we not only perceive our potential qualities, but also our present obscurations. For every fault that arises, we should reflect deeply on our reaction. What is it about the behaviour we find offensive? What is the problem and how does the behaviour make us feel? What is our response telling us about our mind?

As a result of focusing on the qualities of our guru and working constructively with the appearance of faults, we can transform every moment of our relationship with the guru into a profound Dharma teaching, bringing us closer to enlightenment. Remembering this incredible kindness gives rise to deep feelings of appreciation and respect towards the guru, which is the root for our practice of devotion.

Remarking on the great importance of this type of devotion, the Jonang master Jetsun Taranatha writes:

When you truly see the guru as a Buddha you are so consumed with intense devotion that all conventional perceptions vanish and you dwell in your natural primordial awareness. At this time the blessings of the guru instantly melt into you, all your mental afflictions suddenly cease and you reach your natural mind. If you lack this kind of devotion, even if you have great love towards the teacher, this will not necessarily lead to true realisation unless it is completely free from afflictions such as bias and attachment.

What this passage highlights is that with genuine respect and devotion towards your guru, you will swiftly attain the signs of tantric realisation. Without relying on devotion, there is no chance to achieve these attainments. Only when the mind is filled with an intense uncontrived devotion towards the guru, will the blessings of the lineage be directly transmitted, allowing true realisation be born. Lacking this devotion means your meditation will be dry, your practice will produce few results and you will encounter many more obstacles. For these reasons, it is essential to cultivate devotion as much as possible.

Maintaining Pure View of the Guru

To illustrate the challenges that can arise when cultivating a pure view of the guru, I would like to share a few stories with you. The first demonstrates how the great masters of India cultivated devotion, while the second shows us how lacking a pure view can lead to obstacles. As the scriptures are full of these types of stories, if we want our devotion to be pure, there is much we can learn from their examples

Tilopa and Naropa

During his study at Nalanda, the highly learned and accomplished scholar, pandita Naropa, was told by his personal deity that his teacher from previous lives was the great Tilopa and that in order to find him, he should travel to eastern India. Naropa set off immediately, but had no idea exactly where to look for his precious master. When he asked the local villagers, no one seemed to know of a great master named Tilopa. Eventually he came across a man known as "Tilopa the Outcast", who lived by a ruined wall, from where smoke would often billow.

Naropa found Tilopa seated in front of a wooden bucket full of fish, some of which were dead and others that were still alive. Tilopa would take a fish from the bucket, grill it in the fire and bite its head off while snapping his fingers. Seeing this, Naropa prostrated before him and asked Tilopa to accept him as a disciple. "What are you talking about?" Tilopa responded, "I'm just a beggar!" But Naropa insisted, and eventually Tilopa accepted him as his student.

While everyone in the village saw Tilopa as nothing more than a crazy old beggar, Naropa saw him skilfully practicing the Dharma of the Vajrayana. As the fish were completely dominated by their ignorance, Tilopa would eat their flesh to create a karmic connection with their mind and with the snap of his fingers, he used his extraordinary realisations to direct their mindstream to a pure Buddha-realm.

In ancient times the pure Vajrayana practitioners of India would never display or discuss their practice with anyone other than their guru or closest disciples. Often pretending to be ordinary people, they would travel to remote villages where they were unknown and disguise themselves as outcasts, while secretly practising Vajrayana. Shavaripa for instance lived as a hunter and Saraha lived as an arrowsmith. Almost all of the Mahasiddhas of India adopted lowly lifestyles, such as prostitutes or beggars.

What these examples illustrate is the importance of not jumping to conclusions regarding your teacher's actions. As we can never tell whether someone is an enlightened being or a thief, we should train ourselves to maintain pure perception at all times. Sadly, many people ignore this point and continually misinterpret and criticise their teacher. Such people are likely to even find fault in the Buddha himself.

The Buddha and Sunakshatra

An example of how *not* to follow a teacher, is the story of the Buddha's cousin, Sunakshatra. Ordained by the Buddha, Sunakshatra served as his attendant for twelve years. Although he knew all twelve categories of the Buddha's teachings by heart, he did not see any of Buddha's excellent qualities. He instead saw all the Buddha's actions as being deceitful, coming to the mistaken conclusion that apart from a halo of light that surrounded the Buddha's body, there was no difference between himself and the Buddha. In time he lost his desire to serve the Buddha and gave up his duties as attendant. When the noble Ananda replaced him, the Buddha predicted that Sunakshatra's life would come to an end one week later and that he would be reborn as a hungry ghost.

Ananda visited Sunakshatra and told him what the Buddha had foreseen. Although Sunakshatra considered Buddha's words to be lies, he conceded that sometimes what he said came true, so he resolved to spend the week fasting and decided to be very careful. On the evening of the seventh day he drank some water to quench his thirst and suddenly died when he was unable to digest the water properly. Just as the Buddha predicted, Sunakshatra was reborn as a hungry ghost in a flower garden.

What this shows is that when we allow our mind to become dominated by the faults we perceive, we completely cut ourselves off from any benefit we can receive from our guru. For this reason, it is crucial to strengthen our faith and pure view of the guru as much as we can.

Whenever we see fault in our teacher's actions, we should acknowledge that it is our own faults that determine our perception. Recognising our failings gives us the opportunity to learn from them, so that if your teacher seems to be furious with you, rather than responding with anger, consider that they saw a fault in you that required correction. When his anger has abated, go to him and acknowledge your shortcomings with humility. As followers of the Vajrayana path to enlightenment, we should aspire to see his actions as utterly flawless, while it is our own mental vision that is impure.

The many qualities of Buddha's divine activities can only be comprehended gradually, just as a pot cannot hold all rainfall at once. In order to gain this understanding and actualize such qualities, we must practice devotion by completing the accumulations of merit and wisdom.

HOW TO PRACTICE DEVOTION TO A VAJRA MASTER

According to the Vajrayana, the training in devotion is divided into two types: (1) the external training of devoting oneself through action and (2) the internal training of devoting oneself through thought. For the remainder of this chapter our emphasis will be on the external training as presented in the classic text *Fifty Verses of Guru Devotion* written by the great Indian master Ashvagosha. The internal training forms the subject of the next chapter.

Ashvagosha was a first century philosopher-poet and tantric practitioner who used his vast understanding of the Buddha's esoteric teachings to establish a comprehensive guide to skilfully devoting oneself to a vajra master. Through the study of this text, we will learn which activities should be avoided and which should be adopted. Some of the aspects will be familiar from our discussion of devotion in Book Two, but it is important to understand how they specifically relate to our practice of tantra. For the sake of completeness, I have included commentary on all fifty verses from the opening introduction to its conclusion.

Introduction

Bowing in the proper way to the lotus feet of my guru, who is the cause for me to attain the state of a glorious Vajrasattva, I shall condense and explain in brief what has been said in many stainless tantric texts about guru devotion. [Therefore] listen with respect.

The text begins by paying homage to the guru by bowing down at his lotus feet. Placing the highest part of one's own body at the lowest part of another's, namely the feet, is a traditional way of showing respect. This is done by Ashvagosha because he recognises that devotion to the guru is the main cause for attaining enlightenment—the state of glorious Vajrasattva who is the pure essence of our Buddha-nature. The purpose of this text is to condense the expansive teachings presented in the many tantric texts and explain their essential meaning so we can learn to devote ourselves correctly to the guru.

All the buddhas of the past, present and future, residing in every land in the ten directions, have paid homage to the tantric masters from whom they have received the highest empowerments.

The next verse states that practicing devotion towards a vajra master is the same skilful method used by all Buddhas of the three times in order to achieve their ultimate aim. As such, it is only fitting that we follow in the footsteps of the Buddhas by also practicing devotion towards a qualified guru. Ashvagosha specifically refers to the teachers from whom we have received the highest empowerments, which is to say our vajra master.

In this context there are three types of empowerments which a vajra master can bestow: (1) a causal empowerment that is used to ripen the mindstream, (2) a pathway empowerment that provides the actual practices leading us to enlightenment and (3) a resultant empowerment that is the direct experience of ultimate truth. Anyone who empowers our mind in this way is a valid object for the practice of devotion.

The Essential Practice of Devotion

Three times each day with supreme faith you must show the respect you have for your guru who teaches you [the tantric path] by pressing your palms together, offering a mandala as well as flowers and prostrating [by touching] your head to his feet.

No matter how realised we become, we must never forget the infinite kindness our guru has shown us by bestowing us with the empowerments. Even when we achieve enlightenment, we should continue to revere our guru and show him every respect. A good way to do this is by prostrating to the guru and offering him a universal mandala at least three times each day—morning, noon and night.

If you hold ordination vows and [your guru] is a layman or your junior, [in public] prostrate while facing such things as his scriptural texts in order to avoid worldly scorn but in your mind [prostrate to your guru].

The vows of full ordination prohibit monks from prostrating towards lay people. This is a way of encouraging lay people to revere and respect the Sangha. A monk prostrating to a lay guru would send mixed signals to the public, therefore to prevent the development of wrong views, the text recommends that ordained practitioners physically prostrate in the direction of holy objects, such as sacred texts, while mentally understanding they are in fact prostrating before the guru. If we are lay practitioners, we should openly prostrate towards the guru regardless of whether he is lay or ordained.

As for serving [your guru] and showing him respect, such as obeying what he says, standing up [when he comes in] and showing him to his seat—these should be done even by those with ordination vows [whose gurus are laymen or their juniors]. But [in public] avoid prostrating and unorthodox actions [such as washing his feet].

While ordained practitioners should avoid obvious displays of devotion to lay gurus, this does not mean they should act with disrespect. Regardless of our status, we should always behave in a respectful manner that is culturally appropriate and do whatever we can to serve them with our body, speech and mind.

The Need for Mutual Investigation

In order for the tantric commitments of neither guru nor disciple to degenerate, there must be a mutual examination beforehand [to determine if each can] brave a guru-disciple relationship.

A vajra relationship is formed between a vajra master and student during an empowerment ceremony in which the master bestows the tantric vows and commitments on the student. For these vows to have any power, we must be aware we are entering into a relationship and that we must do whatever we can to avoid degenerating or breaking that connection. If we are careless with these commitments, it will lead to serious karmic consequences for us as the student and for the guru as the master.

One of the biggest challenges related to a vajra relationship is that we are essentially asking the guru to use whatever means necessary to help us remove our obscurations. From his side, this means taking the responsibility to push us to our limits so we can rapidly progress along the tantric path. Such a relationship requires an enormous degree of faith to ensure we can maintain a pure view of whatever the guru does. Without the necessary faith, we may react negatively to the guru's actions which can lead to abandoning the relationship. If this occurs, it will be very difficult to work with another guru in the future and we therefore cut ourselves from the benefits of practicing tantra.

To avoid this problem, Ashvagosha recommends spending time investigating the vajra master before requesting vows from him. This is why it is better to develop a relationship with a teacher in a gradual manner by first receiving teachings from them as a Dharma friend, then as a spiritual guide and finally as vajra master. Giving yourself a chance to build familiarity and develop your relationship means entering into the relationship with significant trust and this will give you the strength needed to face the ups and downs you may experience.

A disciple with sense should not accept as a guru someone who lacks compassion or is prone to anger, or who is vicious, arrogant, possessive, undisciplined or boastful of his knowledge.

This verse presents us with a list of traits we should avoid in a potential guru. If after spending time with the teacher we find such traits are dominant, we should not enter into a vajra relationship with them. Of particular importance is the quality of compassion. Guiding students in the Vajrayana is hard work, and like taming a wild horse, it requires considerable patience with the behaviour of the student. If the guru lacks compassion he may abandon us when we repeatedly cling to our afflictions. We need a teacher who will always look out for us and is willing to stick by us on both the good and bad days.

[A guru should be] stable [in his actions], cultivated [in his speech], wise, patient and honest. He should neither conceal his shortcomings nor pretend to possess qualities he lacks. He should be an expert in the meanings [of the tantra] and in its ritual procedures [of medicine and turning back obstacles]. He should also have loving compassion and a complete knowledge of the scriptures.

As the Vajrayana is part of the Mahayana, a vajra master should fulfil all of the criteria for a spiritual guide (for more details see Book Two):

1. Maintains ethical discipline
2. Mind is tamed by meditation
3. Afflictions are thoroughly pacified
4. Has more qualities than the student
5. Has enthusiasm for the Dharma

6. Has a strong spiritual education
7. Honestly cares about others
8. Has some degree of realisation
9. Is skilled in communication
10. Has unwavering perseverance.

These qualities will ensure that the guru's motivation is pure and that he can be trusted to guide you to enlightenment.

He should have full expertise in both ten fields, skill in the drawing of mandalas, full knowledge of how to explain the tantra, supreme pure faith and his senses fully under control.

In addition to the general qualities of a Mahayana guru, a vajra master also needs to be an expert in the tantric path he teaches. Traditionally there are twenty qualities, presented in two sets of ten. The first set concerns the skills needed to perform rituals related to tantric practice:

1. Skill in visualising, drawing and constructing mandalas of deities.
2. Skill in single-pointed concentration on meditation deities.
3. Knowing how to perform mudras correctly.
4. Skill in performing ritual dances.
5. Skill in sitting in both the vajra posture and the half lotus.
6. Skill in mantra recitation.
7. Skill in making fire offerings.
8. Skill in all the other offering ceremonies.
9. Skill in the rituals for subduing enemies of the Dharma, the teacher and sentient beings; those enemies who always harm sentient beings.
10. Skill in concluding ceremonies.

The second set is the skills specifically needed to bestow empowerments in accordance with Highest Yoga Tantra:

1. The ability to visualise protection wheels and to eliminate interferences.
2. The ability to tie protection knots.
3. Skill in conferring the vase and secret empowerments.
4. Skill in conferring the wisdom and word empowerments.
5. Skill in separating enemies of Dharma from their protectors.
6. Skill in making sculpted tormas and conducting offering ceremonies.
7. Skill in reciting mantras both verbally and mentally.
8. Skill in the wrathful rituals.
9. Skill in consecrating holy objects.
10. Skill in self empowerment, offering mandalas and so forth.

Having these skills is more than simply knowing what to do. An authentic vajra master must be able to generate the corresponding states of mind that accompany these actions so they function as genuine supports for spiritual practice.

If you are fortunate enough to find a guru who fulfils all of these qualities and that guru accepts you as their student, you should do whatever you can to maintain your relationship by devoting yourself fully to that master. This practice can be broken into two main groups of conduct: (1) abandoning disrespect towards your guru and (2) cultivating respect towards your guru.

Abandoning Disrespect Towards Your Guru

The first group of conduct involves avoiding actions that damage the relationship with our guru. Generally speaking, we need to maintain mindfulness of our body and speech whenever in the guru's presence to ensure we do not create the causes to one day abandon the relationship. Ashvagosha presents this training in three sections: (1) giving up deriding your guru, (2) giving up disturbing your guru's mind and (3) the consequences of disrespecting your guru.

Giving up Deriding Your Guru

Having become the disciple of such a protecting [guru], should you then despise him from your heart, you will reap continual suffering as if you had disparaged all the Buddhas.

When we choose to enter into a vajra relationship, we are essentially promising to see our guru as inseparable from the Buddha. Once we do this, the guru becomes an incredibly powerful object for our spiritual practice. Through the enormous blessings we receive from the guru, it is possible to clear oceans of negative karma in a fraction of the time it would take on other paths. This increased power, however, comes with a price. Just as the effects of any virtuous actions are multiplied by the nature of the relationship, so too are the effects of any non-virtuous actions. Recognising this, we should completely abandon the act of verbally criticising the guru, whether to his face or behind his back. Rather than allowing our mind to dwell on the faults we perceive, we must strive to maintain our pure view.

If you are foolish enough to despise your guru, you will contract contagious diseases and those caused by harmful spirits and will die [a horrible death] caused by demons, plagues or poison.

To have an overtly critical attitude towards your guru is like having a poison work its way through your body, weakening your defenses until eventually your whole system collapses. Not only will your good karma be inhibited from ripening, you will also create the conditions for negative karma to manifest. These karmas take the form of serious obstacles to your spiritual practice, preventing you from progressing any further and destroying everything you've worked so hard to create.

You will be killed by [wicked] kings or fire, by poisonous snakes, water, witches or bandits, by harmful spirits or savages, and then be reborn in a hell.

When we turn away from the guru, we also turn away from the Buddhas and from virtue. In such a situation, we are incredibly vulnerable to the influence of negative forces. Using intense imagery, Ashvagosha illustrates the suffering result of abandoning the guru. Knowing that no good can come from it, we must never despise the guru for even a moment.

Giving up Disturbing Your Guru's Mind

Never disturb your guru's mind. Should you be foolish enough to do so, you will surely boil in hell.

The guru's only desire is for you to be completely free from all forms of suffering through the achievement of enlightenment. Knowing that you are actively creating the causes for your own suffering is the only thing that will disturb the guru's mind. Showing disrespect towards the guru does them no harm, but it does create extensive negativity in your own mind. This is the negativity that will ripen in the form of future suffering, such as experienced in the hell realms. For this reason, avoid any behaviour you think would displease your guru.

The Consequences of Disrespecting Your Guru

Whatever fearful hells have been taught, such as Avici, the Hell of Uninterrupted Pain, it is clearly explained that those who disparage their guru will have to remain there [for a very long time].

If you cut the root of a tree, you cut the very lifeblood that keeps it alive. As the guru is the living manifestation of your own Buddha-nature, he is the root of all blessings and the source of all realisations. By damaging that relationship, you are essentially cutting yourself off from your absolute nature and therefore removing any chance you may have to achieve enlightenment. As long as the connection remains severed, you will be isolated by an intense ignorance that is the cause for unimaginable pain and torment.

Therefore exert yourself whole-heartedly never to belittle your tantric master, who makes no display of his great wisdom and virtues.

In summary, Ashvagosha exhorts us to give up all disrespectful behaviour that belittles the guru and causes us to despise him. We must always remember the faults we perceive are nothing other than manifestations of our own karma and therefore it is part of our practice to work with them and bring them into the path.

Cultivating Respect Towards Your Guru

We now move to the practices that help us strengthen our devotion towards the guru and allow us to receive the greatest benefit from our relationship. In total, Ashvagosha recommends eight activities: (1) offering material gifts; (2) perceiving him as Buddha; (3) acting according to his word; (4) looking after his materials and entourage; (5) purifying temporal behaviour; (6) offering body, speech and mind; (7) abandoning pride and (8) not acting according to your own wishes.

Offering Material Gifts

[If, out of lack of awareness, you have shown disrespect] to your guru, reverently present an offering to him and seek his forgiveness. Then in the future such harm as plagues will not befall you.

Even though the act of disrespecting a guru can lead to many negative effects in the future, it is never too late to make the effort to repair the damage done. One of the most skilful ways to do this is through the act of making offerings to the guru and seeking his forgiveness. From the side of the guru, he does not need your gifts nor does he hold any grudge towards you. From the side of the student however, making the effort to present an offering and asking the guru for forgiveness demonstrates remorse for your actions and a sincere desire to heal the rift in the relationship and re-establish your connection.

It has been taught that for the guru to whom you have pledged your word of honor [to visualise as one with your meditation deity], you should willingly sacrifice your wife, children and even your life, although these are not easy to give away. Is there need to mention your fleeting wealth?

This verse highlights the attitude we should have towards the things we normally view as our possessions. When entering a vajra relationship, we should abandon any sense of ownership or attachment to things like wealth and relationships. This does not mean we literally give everything we own to the guru, simply that we should be *willing to give* them, if that is what is most beneficial.

A significant part of practicing devotion is the idea of surrender. The more we cling to the concepts of "me" and "mine", the harder it is to realise ultimate truth. For this reason, by mentally giving your possessions to the guru, you reduce your attachments and create a space for realisation to grow. A good starting point for this training is to think that instead of owning things, you take care of them on behalf of your guru, so that any benefit you receive from them becomes an opportunity to generate appreciation for the guru's kindness.

[Such practice of offering] can confer even Buddhahood on a zealous [disciple] in his or her very lifetime, which otherwise might be difficult to attain even in countless millions of aeons.

By mentally offering everything we own to the guru, we practice an extraordinarily pure form of devotion. This practice is so powerful it is capable of generating the same merit that would normally take countless aeons to produce. It is this power that makes enlightenment possible within a single lifetime.

Always keep your tantric commitments. Always make offerings to the enlightened ones. And always make offerings to your guru, for he is the same as all the Buddhas.

The foundation of our practice of devotion is keeping the tantric commitments we have received from our vajra master. The essence of these commitments is to maintain our pure view of the guru as being inseparable from our Buddha-nature. We strengthen our connection to that nature by making extensive offerings to both the guru and the enlightened beings who are the manifestations of that nature.

Those who wish to [attain] the inexhaustible [state of a Buddha's wisdom body] should give to their guru whatever they themselves find pleasing, from the most trifling objects to those of best quality.

In order to clear all traces of attachment and craving from our mind we should joyfully offer to our guru any experience we find pleasing. The size, quality or value of the offering is not important; it is the avoidance of grasping that you should focus on. It is good practice to always imagine the guru at the crown of your head, so that throughout the day, you can offer him all the pleasant appearances you encounter.

Giving [to your guru] is the same as making continual offerings to all the Buddhas. From such giving much merit is gathered. From such collection comes the supreme powerful attainment [of Buddhahood].

When we see the guru as Buddha, any offering made to the guru is considered an offering to all the Buddhas and therefore generates enormous quantities of merit. When this merit is combined with the profound wisdom of sublime emptiness, they become the direct causes for full enlightenment.

This approach to making offerings is for those who have already investigated the guru and entered into an authentic vajra relationship. From within the context of such a relationship, we can trust that there is no attachment towards the offerings from the side of the guru. We should also know that there is no specific form these offerings need to take as the most important aspect of an offering is not what it is but how it is offered. The vastness of merit is generated by the attitude with which the offering is given.

Perceiving Him as Buddha

Therefore, a disciple with the good qualities of compassion, generosity, moral self-control and patience should never regard the guru and Buddha Vajradhara as different.

As we have previously discussed at length, the primary practice of guru devotion is to see the guru as inseparable from the Buddha. We do this because of the strength of our Bodhicitta. If we are sincerely determined to achieve enlightenment, we should strive to bring the experience of the Buddha into every moment of our lives and devotion to the guru is the first step towards doing this.

If you should never step on even [your guru's] shadow because the fearsome consequences are the same as destroying a stupa, is there need to mention never stepping on or over his shoes or seat, [sitting in his place, or riding] his mount?

This particular piece of advice was given in the tantras and points to the degree of reverence we need to cultivate towards every aspect of how the guru appears to us. We should honour and respect everything about the guru, including his shadow, so we can preserve our pure view and avoid accumulating the unwanted karmic propensities that result from attitudes of arrogance and pride.

Acting According to His Word

[Disciples] having great sense should obey the words of their guru joyfully and with enthusiasm. If you lack the knowledge or ability [to do what he says], explain in [polite] words why you cannot [comply].

By entering into a vajra relationship, we are explicitly requesting the guru to guide us to enlightenment and consequently need to be willing to accept the advice he gives us. If we refuse his advice due to an individualistic sense of pride, we act contrary to the nature of the relationship. Therefore, whenever the guru asks us to do something, we should do whatever we can to fulfil his request.

If we believe we are incapable of completing the task, with respect and sincerity, we can feel free to approach the guru and explain why. Through open communication, the guru can help us develop a beneficial attitude and ultimately overcome the obstacles we are facing.

> It is from your guru that powerful attainments, higher rebirth and happiness come. Therefore make a wholehearted effort never to transgress your guru's advice.

By putting the guru's advice into practice, we can actualise the Dharma in our mind and manifest all the results of the path. If we don't act in accordance with his words however, we cannot achieve the results. It is that simple.

Looking After His Materials and Entourage

> [Guard] your guru's belongings as you would your own life. Treat even your guru's beloved [family] with the same [respect you show] for him. [Have affectionate regard for] those closely around him as if they were your own dearest kin. Single-mindedly think [in this way] at all times.

A very powerful way to extend the benefit we receive from our practice of devotion is to consider everything related to the guru as an extension of the guru. This includes the guru's belongings, like his clothes and home, as well as his relationships, such as his family and students. Such people and things are known as the *pores of the guru*. By showing them the same reverence you show your guru, you strengthen your mindfulness of the guru and increase the opportunities you have to generate merit. When practiced correctly, you can transform almost any action into an offering to the guru.

Purifying Temporal Behavior

The following verses focus on establishing a mode of conduct conducive to maintaining pure devotion towards the guru. While many of these behaviours are rooted in the customs of ancient India, we should still try to understand the essence behind the advice so we can apply them to our own context.

> *Never sit on the [same] bed or seat [as your guru], nor walk ahead of him. [At teachings do not] wear your hair in a top-knot, [a hat, shoes or any weapons. Never] touch a seat [before he sits down or if he happens to sit on the ground. Do not] place your hands [proudly] on your hips or wring them [before him].*

This verse concerns what to do when in the presence of your guru and mainly emphasises actions of the body. In general, avoid any situations in which you place yourself in a position of greater importance than the guru. We should always act with humility and restraint.

> *Never sit or recline while your guru is standing [or lie while he is sitting]. Always be ready to stand up and serve him skilfully in an excellent manner.*

We should also remain attentive and ready to respond to the needs of the guru. Reclining and lying down are restful postures and carry with them a sense of dullness. We must be as alert as possible and therefore should adopt postures that reflect this state of mind.

> *In the presence of your guru never do such things as spit, [cough or sneeze without covering your head. Never] stretch out your legs when at your seat, nor walk back and forth [without a reason before him. And never] argue.*

Out of respect for your guru, any time you spend together should be treated as precious and important. Avoid behaviour which demonstrates a lack of mindfulness or a sense of disregard and while some situations are more formal than others, we should always maintain an appropriate degree of restraint.

Never massage or rub your limbs. Do not sing, dance or play musical instruments [other than for religious purposes]. And never chatter idly or speak in excess [or too loudly] within range of [your guru's] hearing.

Again, the intention behind this advice is to avoid activity which encourages the loss of mindfulness. As the guru is the embodiment of the Buddha in our lives, we try to make every moment with them count and if we allow ourselves to become distracted from this, we waste our opportunity.

[When your guru enters the room], get up from your seat and bow your head slightly. Sit [in his presence] respectfully. At night or at rivers or on dangerous paths, with [your guru's] permission you may walk before him.

Do whatever you can to show your guru respect in a manner suited to the cultural norms. In most cultures, it is customary to stand when an important person enters the room and in Asian cultures, it is also customary to bow your head and prostrate towards the lama. This behaviour is about demonstrating our respect by adopting the customs of our guru. The last part of this verse highlights an exception to the previous advice of never walking in front of the guru. This shows that we must adjust our conduct in accordance with the context of the situation.

In the direct sight of the guru, [a disciple] with sense should not [sit] with his or her body twisted around or lean [casually] against a pillar and so forth. Never crack your knuckles, [play with your fingers or clean your nails].

The essence of this whole section is that our behaviour in the presence of the guru is a reflection of our attitude towards him. By paying attention to our external behaviour, we create an environment that is supportive of the type of mind we are trying to cultivate. These behaviours also have the effect of elevating our relationship with the guru, separating it as being unique and special when compared to our worldly relationships. This helps us to maintain our pure view of the guru.

Offering Body, Speech and Mind

The next set of verses concern how to behave when offering service to the guru or directly interacting with him. They represent specific actions we can do to emphasise our respect for the guru.

When washing [your guru's] feet or body, drying, massaging or [shaving] him, precede such actions with [three] prostrations and at their conclusion do the same. Then attend [to yourself] as much as you like.

Offering prostrations is a formal way of showing respect that was common in ancient India. While this verse recommends offering three prostrations at the beginning and end of every action, in practice this can be difficult. We therefore need to be aware of the context of a given situation and whether physically offering prostrations is something beneficial. If a teacher specifically asks us not to offer them, we should respect his wishes. Of course there is nothing stopping us from offering the prostrations in our mind.

Should you need to address [your guru] by name, add the title "Your Presence" after it. To generate respect for him in others, further honorifics may also be used.

This is another practice we need to be skilful with. In Tibetan, many titles are given to names to show honour and respect, such as *Rinpoche* which means "precious one", or *Kyabje* which means "lord of refuge". In English, we can use terms like *venerable* or in some cases

His Holiness or *His Eminence*. Which titles we use depends on the type of relationship we have and the preferences of the guru. Ashvagosha also mentions that this particular practice is good for generating respect in the minds of others.

Abandoning Pride

Pride is one of the greatest obstacles to developing devotion. It is the mind that holds our own view as superior, closing us off to receiving guidance from our guru. To counteract this affliction, Ashvagosha identifies a number of behaviours which cultivate humility when working with the guru.

> *When asking for your guru's advice, [first announce why you have come]. With palms pressed together at your heart, listen to what he tells you without [letting your mind] wander about. Then [when he has spoken] you should reply, "I shall do exactly as you have said."*

If we are considering offering our service to the guru or requesting his advice, we should first reflect to make sure we are willing and able to follow through with what we are asking. For instance, if we offer our service and the guru gives us a task, we should not abandon that task until it is complete. Even if our conditions change, we should cultivate the determination to finish what we start, but if we find we do not have the capacity to follow through, it is better not to start in the first place.

Likewise, if we request advice from the guru, we need to be willing to put that advice into practice. There is no greater waste of the guru's time than to ask him for advice only to disregard it completely and resort to doing what we think is best. At the very least, you should try to follow the guru's advice as much as possible, even if you know you will not be able to do so perfectly.

After doing [what your guru has told you], report [what has happened] in polite, gentle words. Should you yawn or cough, [clear your throat or laugh in his presence], cover your mouth with your hand.

Any path, whether spiritual or otherwise, is accomplished one step at a time. With every practice you complete in accordance with the words of the guru, you take one step closer to your goal. It is important to mark these occasions by reporting the completion of a task to the guru. This proves to them that you are serious and it will also help you develop the confidence needed to achieve your aims.

If you wish to receive a certain teaching, request three times with your palms pressed together while kneeling before him with your [right] knee. [Then at his discourse] sit humbly with respect, wearing appropriate clothing that is neat [and clean, without ornaments, jewelry or cosmetics].

A guru should only give teachings to those who request it, as the purpose of teaching is to benefit those who are listening. If a student has not cultivated a desire to learn, they will not be receptive to what the teacher has to offer. Therefore, if we wish to receive teachings, we should humble ourselves before the guru and make the effort to request them repeatedly. If the guru accepts, we should recognise the incredible kindness he is showing us and act accordingly.

Whatever you do to serve [your guru] or show him respect should never be done with an arrogant mind. Instead you should be like a newly-wed bride, timid, bashful and very subdued.

No matter what conduct of body and speech we adopt, we should never allow our mind to be tarnished by arrogance. Ashvagosha recommends we adopt a humble demeanour in all our actions, placing ourselves in a lowly position. To the best of our ability, we should put our desires and needs to one side and devote ourselves completely to the guru.

In the presence of [the guru] who teaches you [the path], stop acting in a conceited, coquettish manner. As for boasting to others what you have done [for your guru], examine [your conscience] and discard all such acts.

Whenever you interact with the guru, be wary of the mind that thinks it knows everything. Try to be mindful of your thoughts and examine them closely to ensure you are acting in a way that is sincere and honest.

Not Acting According to Your Own Wishes

The following verses are related to four activities which should only be done with permission from your guru. Failing to do so will cause these activities to create the conditions for us to develop pride and thereby weaken our devotion.

If you are [requested] to perform a consecration, [an empowerment into] a mandala or a fire offering ceremony or to gather disciples and deliver a discourse, you may not do so if your guru resides in that area, unless you receive his prior permission.

The first verse involves performing rituals or giving teachings. In these situations you are taking on the role of teacher which may lead you to feel equal to or more important than your own teacher. To avoid this pride, always request permission from your guru before engaging in these activities. This shifts the focus from you and transforms it into an offering of service to the guru.

Whatever offerings you receive from performing such rites as [the consecration known as] "opening the eyes," you should present all these to your guru. Once he has taken a token portion, you may use the rest for whatever you like.

This verse looks at the danger of receiving offerings as a result of engaging in virtuous practices. If we are not careful, the offerings we receive can swell our sense of importance and feed attachment. To avoid this, we should always offer whatever we receive to our lama, who will often keep a small portion and return the rest to us. This practice helps us cut our attachment while also reinforcing our appreciation for the kindness of the guru.

> *In the presence of his guru a disciple should not act [as a guru] to his own disciples and they should not act towards him as their guru. Therefore [before your own guru] stop [your disciples] from showing you respect, such as rising [when you come] and making prostrations.*

Whenever we are in the presence of our guru, we should see ourselves as a student. As such, we should not accept any demonstrations of devotion from our own students. This helps to remind us that our role as teacher is dependent on the situation and that there is nothing which makes us inherently important or superior to others.

> *Whenever you make an offering to your guru or whenever your guru presents you with something, a disciple with sense will [present and] receive this using both hands with his or her head slightly bent.*

Finally, whenever we are giving or receiving an offering, we should make sure to show an appropriate degree of reverence with our physical body. This helps us avoid the pride of thinking we are an important benefactor or the pride of thinking we are favoured by the guru.

Additional Points of Advice

Having completed the main advice for practicing devotion, Ashvagosha now draws our attention to a few additional points we should keep in mind.

> *Be diligent in all your actions, [alert and] mindful never to forget [your tantric commitments]. If fellow disciples transgress [what is proper] in their behaviour, correct each other in a friendly manner.*

This verse specifically reminds us that we should be diligent in maintaining our tantric commitments at all times. Part of this practice is to always show respect towards those who share a guru with you. These people are known as your vajra brothers and sisters and it is our duty to do whatever we can to live in harmony with them. If a member of our vajra family is acting in a way that contradicts their training or actively goes against the wishes of the guru, we should take steps to help that person correct their behaviour. This should be done in a friendly manner out of a motivation of love and compassion.

If because of sickness you are physically [unable] to bow to your guru and must do what normally would be prohibited, even without [his explicit] permission, there will be no unfortunate consequences if you have a virtuous mind.

Under normal circumstances we should uphold all the practices of devotion to the best of our abilities. The only exception to this rule is when we are sick and temporarily unable to practice with our body. Just remember that external demonstrations of devotion are always secondary, the primary practice is in the mind. As long as we maintain our attitude of respect and devotion towards the guru, we should be able to adapt to whatever situation we find ourselves.

Summary of How to Practice

What need is there to say much more? Do whatever pleases your guru and avoid doing anything he would not like. Be diligent in both of these.

To summarise, the essence of practicing devotion is to make the guru happy by practicing virtue and avoiding non-virtue.

"Powerful attainments follow from [doing what] your guru [likes]." This has been said by [the Buddha] Vajradhara himself. Knowing this, try to please your guru fully with all the actions [of your body, speech and mind].

As a result of dedicating yourself to the practice of virtue, all realisations on the path will ripen in your mindstream. Therefore, make this your heart practice.

After disciples have taken refuge in the Triple Gem and developed a pure enlightened motive, they should be given this [text] to take to heart [how to abandon their own arrogant self-will and] follow in their guru's footsteps [along the graded path to enlightenment].

Ashvagosha recommends that we study this text after taking refuge and generating Bodhicitta. In the context of the Kalachakra Path, we generally introduce this topic as part of the preliminary practice of Guru Yoga.

[By studying the prerequisite trainings of guru-devotion and the graded path common to both sutra and tantra,] you will become a [suitable] vessel [to hold] the pure Dharma. You may then be given such teachings as tantra. [After receiving the proper empowerments,] recite out loud the fourteen root vows and take them sincerely to heart.

Once we have established a strong foundation in the sutras and have trained in devotion to the guru, we are ready to enter the tantric path by taking empowerment. It is during the empowerments we actually receive the tantric vows and commitments.

Conclusion

As I have not made the mistake [of adding my personal interpretation] when writing this work, may this be of infinite benefit to all disciples who would follow their guru. By the limitless merit that I have gathered in this way, may all sentient beings quickly attain the state of Buddha.

Ashvagosha completes his text by dedicating the virtue he generated from writing the text towards the enlightenment of all sentient beings.

REVIEW OF KEY POINTS

- The term guru is generally used to refer to the spiritual guide who teaches you the Dharma and guides you on the path.

- There is no limit to the number of gurus we can have. Whether we have one or many will depend on our personal karmic connections.

- Your root guru is the teacher who has had the most impact on your mind. In the context of the Vajrayana, the root guru is usually the vajra master who has bestowed on you the empowerments and instructions for practicing tantra.

- The main practice of devotion to a vajra master is to cultivate the attitude that sees the guru as inseparable from the Buddha. This pure view protects our mind from developing misconceptions about the guru and allows us to receive the most benefit from the guru-disciple relationship.

- We can cultivate a pure view of the guru by (1) focusing our attention on the virtuous qualities we can perceive while (2) transforming apparent faults into qualities.

- Devotion is the root of all tantric realisations. When it is uncontrived, the blessings of the lineage enter our mind and we achieve a direct realisation of suchness. Without it, our practice will be dry, produce few results and will be plagued by obstacles.

- There are two types of training used to develop devotion towards the guru: (1) the external training of devoting oneself through action and (2) the internal training of devoting oneself through thought.

- The external training of devoting oneself through action

includes a range of conducts that can be practiced in order to strengthen one's appreciation of the guru and heighten one's mindfulness of the guru's presence.

- The essential practice of devotion is to honour one's guru with body, speech and mind at least three times each day.

- In order to ensure we are able to uphold an authentic vajra relationship, we should spend time investigating ourselves and the guru to determine if we are ready to take on the commitments of the relationship.

- The actual conduct of devotion to a vajra master is broken into two groups: (1) abandoning disrespect and (2) cultivating respect.

- There are two things we should abandon completely: (1) disrespecting your guru by criticising his behaviour and (2) acting in ways that displease his mind.

- There are eight activities we should undertake to cultivate devotion towards the guru: (1) offering material gifts; (2) perceiving him as Buddha; (3) acting according to his word; (4) looking after his materials and entourage; (5) purifying temporal behaviour; (6) offering body, speech and mind; (7) abandoning pride and (8) not acting according to your own wishes.

The Dharmakaya Guru—Guru Vajradhara

CHAPTER THREE

Guru Yoga
Gateway to Tantric Realisation

When we began our study of the Dharma, the guru was a Dharma friend who introduced us to the teachings of the great being known as Shakyamuni Buddha. As we learnt about his incredible wisdom and qualities, we developed faith in him as a valid source of refuge. At this time, the guru was a wise source of information and the Buddha was an inspirational figure from our past; the two were seen as separate entities

As our relationship with the guru matured, he took on an increasingly more important role in our lives to become our spiritual guide. Although the Buddha and his stories were inspiring and motivational, as a great being in history, accessible only through texts, statues and holy objects, he remained distant to us. The guru, however, was someone we could talk to and interact with directly and through his activities, the teachings of the Buddha came alive. This immediacy has made our relationship with the guru one of the most important we will ever have.

As we approach the path of tantra, we begin training in devoting ourselves to a vajra master. Learning to view the guru as Buddha, we work to recognise that the guru is none other than a manifestation of the Buddha. By effectively merging the two together in our mind we dissolve any feeling of separation. When the Buddha takes on the immediacy of the guru, he is no longer distant to us but instead an active presence in our lives, guiding us directly and demonstrating his incredible qualities.

In many ways this process is like seeing a fire in the distance. While we can easily see the flickering of its light, it is not until we come close that we feel its warmth. Similarly, the blessings of the Buddha are difficult to feel so long as he remains separate from our present experience. When he is brought closer by working with the guru, these blessings manifest more clearly. We may experience a feeling of increased clarity where once we were confused, or perhaps we find it is easier to develop virtuous qualities such as compassion and patience. However they manifest, when blessings are present, the Dharma ceases to be a mere collection of concepts and is brought to life in our experience.

Although we may be able to identify when blessings are present in our lives, what exactly are they? The answer lies in the relationship between our ordinary mind and our innate Buddha-nature. Our ordinary mind is like a person standing outside and our Buddha-nature is the sun in the sky, hidden behind the gathered clouds. Blessings are this person's experience of feeling the warm rays of sun when the cloud cover parts. They are the manifestation of our Buddha-nature from the perspective of our ordinary experience.

Blessings are especially important because they allow us to directly experience aspects of our nature, and provide us with the opportunity to recognise that nature. In this way, blessings are the basis for achieving realisations of ultimate truth. The more blessings we receive, the more realisations we can establish. According to the Tantrayana, the guru is the source of all blessings and therefore devotion to the guru is the root of all realisations.

OPENING TO THE FLOW OF BLESSINGS

To maximise the benefit we receive from our relationship with the guru, it is necessary to understand how the mind affects the flow of blessings. While the afflictions in general function to block blessings from manifesting, the primary obstacles are:

1. **Self-grasping:** This is the mind that sees the dualistic appearances of the five aggregates as being a self. When we grasp onto these appearances, we create a separation between who we appear to be and our actual nature. If that grasping is strong, the metaphoric distance between the self and its nature is large, weakening the blessings.

2. **Pride:** In this context, pride is the mind that believes that the way we currently see reality is correct and therefore there is no need to change. In relation to blessings, this mind stops us from shifting our focus to our true nature, preventing the flow of blessings from increasing.

In practice, tantra dissolves self-grasping by shifting our pride away from a gross conception of self, to progressively more subtle conceptions. With each step, we move closer to our pristine nature, allowing us to experience an increase of blessings. Eventually, as we abandon the self completely, our experience is filled with the sublime blessings that are free from all limitations.

This process is encapsulated within the training of devotion to the guru, where we extend our conception of the guru to represent increasingly more subtle layers of reality. By devoting ourselves to the guru, we weaken our grasping onto different aspects of reality and surrender our pride so we can experience the blessings that our Buddha-nature has to offer. This method works with four levels of guru: (1) the outer guru; (2) the inner guru; (3) the secret guru and the (4) the most secret guru. We will now examine each in detail.

The Outer Guru

The *outer guru* is the physical being we usually associate with the word guru. He is the teacher who shows us the path and guides us in its practice. In the previous chapter, we spoke at length about practicing devotion in relation to the outer guru. In essence, the training involves viewing the guru as inseparable from the Buddha and acting accordingly in his presence.

A central theme of this practice is to humble ourselves before the master in order to surrender the pride that thinks we are always right. Looking back on our life, we can see that we have constantly listened to our deluded view and made decisions based on ignorance. The result of such pride is the creation of an endless stream of negative karma that only perpetuates our suffering. By devoting ourselves to the outer guru, we are basically telling ourselves, "enough is enough", and instead of listening to our ignorance, we choose to follow the wisdom of the guru.

The Root Guru

The blessings we receive from this type of guru are primarily in the form of inspiration to practice. As we relate to the guru as separate from ourselves, his function is limited to demonstrating qualities and showing us how to develop them through teaching the Dharma. As long as this separation exists, we cannot see the guru as a way to connect with deeper layers of our reality.

The method for bridging the gap between guru and self is to recognise that the sensory appearances that form the basis for what we call "the outer guru" are inseparable from the mind. If we investigate these appearances closely, we find that there is nothing to point to other than the collection of visual forms, sounds and so forth, all of which arise within our consciousness. With this realisation, the guru ceases to be something "out there" and is transformed into something "in here".

The Inner Guru

This transition from external to internal reveals a different type of guru called the *inner guru*. From the perspective of this guru, the outer guru is merely a collection of appearances we use to recognise the manifestation of enlightened qualities. If we compare the nature of these appearances with other appearances we experience, we are unable to find a substantial difference. This understanding opens the door to using all appearances as a foundation for recognising qualities.

In tantric practice, the totality of our experience is represented symbolically in the form of an enlightened mandala, which is filled with meditational deities such as Kalachakra. By familiarising our mind with these deities, we learn to see different types of appearances as pure manifestations of our own Buddha-nature. It is the same principle as that used to see the outer guru as Buddha, only now extended to all appearances.

Guru Kalachakra

Training with the inner guru helps us overcome the pride that holds the guru to be pure and the self to be impure. Rather than seeing them as two separate entities, they are integrated together to then see everything as pure. This process clears our grasping onto ordinary appearances, allowing us to identify more with our enlightened nature.

The blessings of the inner guru manifest in a wealth of inner qualities. As the mind is purified of its gross conceptions, it becomes increasingly more subtle and flexible. Such a mind can use different states of concentration to manifest miraculous abilities. While these qualities can be extraordinary, they are still conditioned by the conceptual view used to generate them and therefore the blessings are still limited.

The Secret Guru

In order to remove the subtle conditioning of our nature, we need to rely on an even subtler type of guru known as the *secret guru*. Instead of working directly with appearances, we focus on the awareness that experiences the nature of those appearances. In a way, we can think of the inner guru as the objective aspect of our nature, whereas the secret guru is the subjective aspect of the mind itself.

When awareness operates from the perspective of a dualistic consciousness, appearances are perceived with many characteristics. If the mind grasps onto these characteristics as separate entities, they form the foundation for the subjective experiences of samsara and nirvana.

Investigating the relationship between these two extremes with meditative techniques, we

Guru Vajradhara

find their primary difference lies in the degree of grasping present. When the mind is dominated by grasping, there is considerable conceptual movement and an experience of suffering. When that grasping subsides, concepts dissolve and the mind settles into its natural state, manifesting an experience of bliss. The implication of this observation is that the nature of the mind is blissful.

Training with the secret guru is essentially working with grasping to cultivate the experience of bliss regardless of what appearances arise. Initially, the bliss is only experienced when entering into the stillness of single-pointed concentration, but through the use of skilful means we can develop the same blissful pliancy when the mind is in motion. In this way, we effectively remove the pride that holds the extreme of nirvana to be supreme by integrating the experience of bliss with the appearances of saṁsara.

The blessings we receive from the secret guru manifest in the form of blissful absorption. As the bliss becomes pervasive across all of our experience, appearances take on a single flavour where there is no longer any basis for subjectively distinguishing between one phenomenon and another. This allows awareness to hold its own ground and rest in a natural state of absorption. At this point, the blessings are like a magnet, drawing us closer to our Buddha-nature.

The Most Secret Guru

The final guru represents the natural ground upon which the other three gurus arise. It is the Primordial Buddha—the sublime emptiness that is endowed with all enlightened qualities and completely free from all forms of conceptual fabrication. This is the most secret guru that is the basis for completely eradicating all karmic obscurations and ultimately manifesting the state of a fully enlightened Buddha.

Up to this point, we have been working with pathway gurus in that they are provisional methods for bringing us closer to a direct realisation of our definitive nature. To summarise this path, we can identify three steps: (1) the outer guru helps us to dissolve our grasping between external and internal; (2) the inner guru helps us dissolve our grasping between the impure and pure; and (3) the secret guru helps us dissolve our grasping between samsara and nirvana. When the practices of all three gurus are mastered, the definitive meaning of reality naturally manifests, and there is nothing additional that needs to be done.

To train in the most secret guru means to abide in suchness. From this enlightened perspective, we recognise that the experience of conventional reality has never actually existed as anything more than mere illusion. Through practicing the path, we establish a primordial wisdom that never strays from its recognition of the definitive

The Primordial Buddha

meaning. Such a mind will never again experience the delusion of cyclic existence and will be free to bring benefit to sentient beings in whatever way is required.

While we may have to exert effort on the path to manifest this ultimate blessing, we can still use our understanding of the most secret guru as a guide. We do this by recognising that the four gurus are not separate. The Primordial Buddha is our most sacred truth; that truth is the basis for the blissful awareness that knows reality as it is—the Sublime Guru Vajradhara; the infinite qualities of Vajradhara are inseparable from the enlightened mandala of Kalachakra; and Kalachakra is inseparable from our own Root Guru. In this way, the four gurus represent an unbroken continuum that leads from the grossest level of reality to the most subtle.

THE PRELIMINARY PRACTICE OF GURU YOGA

The internal training of devotion towards the guru is known as *Guru Yoga*. The word *yoga* is a Sanskrit word meaning "to join", so that literally speaking, the term Guru Yoga refers to the process of joining our mind with the mind of the guru. In practice, this method is primarily used to take us beyond our rational thoughts and prepare us for the authentic practice of tantra.

Before engaging in the practice of Guru Yoga, it is important to spend time cultivating a meaningful motivation through the preliminary practices of Refuge and Bodhicitta. The only valid reason for undertaking the path of devotion is to achieve enlightenment. If we fail to nurture this motivation, we run the risk of becoming lost in our desire for attention, influence, prestige or other emotional attachments. All too easily our devotion can be derailed if our expectations are not met, but with a true renunciation towards samsara and a dedication to attaining Buddhahood, we can have confidence in the process.

For those who have grown up in very individualistic societies there can be an aversion to the idea of devoting oneself to the guru. This can create the temptation to go straight to higher tantric practices without first cultivating a close connection with the guru and the lineage. Such an attitude however will only create obstacles along the path and while the occasional meditative experience may occur, any benefit will only be short-term and will quickly fade. On the other hand, by generating genuine devotion to a qualified teacher, even if it does not appear that we are making significant progress, we are undoubtedly on a steady course for achieving our ultimate aim.

According to the early Jonang-Shambhala Tradition of Kalachakra, each stage of the preliminaries should be practiced until mastery, without the limitation of time. This approach ensured the achievement of all the prerequisite realisations needed to authentically practice the advanced techniques of the Six Vajra Yogas.

Since the 19th century this format has been modified as the nature in which instruction is received has changed. Under the newer system, practitioners are introduced to all practices of the Kalachakra Path over the course of a single three-year retreat. Although this retreat does not allow enough time for most practitioners to establish mastery of the practices, they are able to achieve enough familiarisation with the techniques so that they can continue their practice at their own pace as part of a solitary retreat. This approach enables a greater number of people to be introduced to the complete path and therefore is instrumental in laying the karmic foundations for practice of this path in the future.

In such a three-year retreat, practitioners spend approximately three weeks focusing specifically on the practice of Guru Yoga. Since the 19th century, three traditional texts have been relied on: (1) *Rain of Blessings for the Six Yogas of the Vajra Lineage* by Dolpopa Sherab Gyaltsen; (2) *The Anchor for Collecting Siddhis Guru Yoga* by Jetsun Taranatha; and (3) *The Foundation Guru Yoga* which is included in Taranatha's practice manual *The Divine Ladder*. One week would be spent on each text, allowing the practitioner to build a strong connection with Dolpopa, Taranatha and one's Root Guru respectively. Through the practices of Guru Yoga passed down from guru to disciple for centuries through the Jonang lineage, practitioners are therefore able to discover the enlightened mind.

Once familiarity with each individual text is attained, Guru Yoga is used as a preliminary for all subsequent practices of the Kalachakra generation and completion stages. By practicing in this manner, we are reminded of the different levels of the guru and the importance that devotion plays in our path. When practiced as a preliminary, it is common to rotate the texts, using one per session. Usually we start with Dolpopa's text, followed by Taranatha's and finally the Foundation Guru Yoga. Once one cycle is completed, we start again with Dolpopa.

When Guru Yoga is our main practice, we should briefly recite all the preceding preliminary practices to establish the correct state of mind. This includes the outer preliminaries of renunciation and devotion to the lineage, as well as the inner preliminaries of refuge, Bodhicitta, Vajrasattva purification and mandala offering. With a mind that has been properly prepared, we can engage in the six stages of Guru Yoga practice: (1) establishing the visualisation; (2) accumulating merit with a seven-limb prayer; (3) making supplications; (4) receiving the blessings of the four empowerments; (5) merging your mind with the guru; and (6) dedicating your merit.

Establishing the Visualisation

The first stage of the practice is to bring to mind the qualities of the guru by visualising him in the space before you. This visualisation acts as a support for cultivating devotion and receiving blessings.

Similar to our practice of Vajrasattva, before manifesting a visualisation it is important to consciously release dualistic grasping by reminding ourselves of the empty-nature of appearances. We do this by reciting a mantra such as:

OM SVABHAVA SHUDDHA SARVA DHARMA SVABHAVA SHUDDHO HUNG
All existence including oneself enters into the true state of emptiness.

Alternatively, we can simply rest our mind for a few moments without grasping in a feeling of empty spaciousness. Imagine that all ordinary appearances dissolve and we sit in the centre of a sublime Buddha field.

Although the descriptions will vary slightly between each text, the essence is to visualise in the space in front of you a jewel encrusted throne supported by eight snow lions. On this throne is a lotus seat stacked with four cushions consisting of a white moon, red sun, black rahu and yellow kalagni. These represent the four states that are purified through the path, and the four vajras of body, speech, mind and wisdom which are the result.

In this practice, our root guru appears on top of this throne in the Dharmakaya aspect of Guru Vajradhara. His body is dark blue in colour, with one face and two arms. He is seated with legs crossed in the vajra posture and holds a vajra and bell crossed at his heart. His body is adorned with the thirty-two major marks and eighty minor signs of a Buddha as well as an array of jewelled ornaments and silks. His voice possesses the sixty melodic qualities of enlightenment: deep like thunder, soothing and comfortable to the ear, pleasant, delightful, lucid, articulate, suitable and consistent. His mind possesses the ten powers, such as knowledge of the capacities and temperaments of beings and the path by which each can be liberated. In this way, Guru Vajradhara has the glorious, majestic and completely perfect characteristics of a fully enlightened Buddha. He gazes in your direction with a loving smile.

From the heart of the guru radiates light, manifesting in the profound merit field of Lineage Masters, Yidams, Buddhas, Bodhisattvas, Pratyekas, Shravakas, Dakinis and Dharma Protectors. It is more important to feel the presence of this field than to have a clear appearance of the visualisation. Having generated the field of merit, take a moment to remind yourself that each of these beings is an enlightened manifestation of Guru Vajradhara's infinite qualities. You should feel as though they are all of one essence.

Even though the visualisation is the same regardless of the text you recite, when using Dolpopa's Guru Yoga, try to see Vajradhara as being inseparable from Dolpopa. You may choose to visualise the human form of Dolpopa and place Guru Vajradhara at his heart, emphasising that the outer guru is an emanation of the inner guru. Whichever way you visualise him, the main point is to have the impression that the two are inseparable in nature. The same technique can be used when reciting Taranatha's text or the Foundation Guru Yoga, where we visualise Taranatha or our Root Guru with Guru Vajradhara at their heart.

Accumulating Merit with a Seven-Limb Prayer

Having established Guru Vajradhara as our field of merit, we move to the main practice of making supplications. As is customary in most cultures, before asking our guru for blessings, it is auspicious to first make an offering. As our achievement of enlightenment is what the guru desires most, and knowing this requires the accumulations of merit and wisdom, out of devotion to our guru and the wish to please him, we generate merit through the offering of a *seven-limb prayer*.

This extraordinarily skilful practice was originally presented in the *Prayer of Samantabhadra* as a means to accumulate vast quantities of merit. As the name suggests, there are seven limbs to this practice: (1) homage; (2) offerings; (3) confession; (4) rejoicing; (5) requesting the teachings; (6) beseeching the guru to stay and (7) dedication. Of these seven, homage, offerings, requesting and beseeching are designed to generate merit. Rejoicing is used to increase that merit while confession is used to purify negativities. Dedication is used to ensure the merit generated becomes a cause for enlightenment. While some texts may focus more on particular limbs, try to include all seven in your practice.

Homage

The first limb is to pay homage to the enlightened beings of the field of refuge, particularly the guru and the lineage masters. We do this by simply joining our palms together and bowing our heads or more elaborately by making prostrations. The purpose of paying homage is to generate a feeling of veneration and respect towards the guru and all of his manifestations.

In some texts, this limb takes the form of a lineage prayer or collection of verses that highlight the enlightened qualities of the guru. In *The Rain of Blessings*, the following verses are used:

> *Precious lama, I pay homage to your body, speech and mind.*
> *Your body is adorned with unchanging, perfect marks and signs.*
> *Your uninterrupted Brahma-like speech pervades the ten directions.*
> *You abide in the unmistaken mind of the great seal.*
>
> *I prostrate to you who is the embodiment of the thirty-six Tathagatas,*
> *Unveiled when the thirty-six aggregates are perfectly purified*
> *through the withdrawal vajra yoga and the rest of the six vajra*
> *yogas*

As you recite this passage, develop a sense for the guru's marvellous qualities, feeling as though your guru is the most precious being in your life. Allow your heart to be filled with admiration and respect. To make the merit of this practice truly vast, imagine multiplying your body into innumerable copies with each prostrating alongside you as you pay homage to the guru.

Offerings

> *I offer with joy and pure intention an inconceivable ocean of Samantabhadra offerings, Including all virtue of body, speech and mind gathered during the three times!*

The second limb is to make extensive offerings. While there is nothing wrong with making physical offerings, in the context of Guru

Yoga, visualised offerings are usually made so the flow of the practice is not interrupted. The main purpose of making offerings is to generate vast quantities of merit by practicing generosity, as this reduces our attachment to the pleasures of this life, and strengthens our devotion by imagining we are giving everything to the guru.

To make your offerings truly extensive, the *Twelve Offering Goddesses* from the Universal Mandala can be useful to visualise (see Book Two):

Goddess	Colour	Symbol
Perfumed Water	Dark-Blue	Vase
Flowers	Dark-Blue	Flower garland
Incense	Red	Burning incense
Light	Red	Butter lamp
Food	White	Offering cake (torma)
Fruit	White	Bowl of fruit
Alluring Beauty	Yellow	Silk ribbons
Laughter	Yellow	Crown
Music	Green	Drum
Dancing	Green	Vajra
Singing	Blue	Flute
Desire	Blue	Lotus

Table 3-1: *The Twelve Offering Goddesses of Kalachakra*

For each goddess, imagine emanating a single goddess carrying the corresponding symbol. This goddess then emanates two more goddesses from her heart and those goddesses each emanate two more goddesses and so on until the space is filled with goddesses. The goddesses then melt into light and dissolve into the guru and the merit field. This style of offering is known as an *Offering of Samantabhadra*. If time is limited, an extensive offering can still be made by imagining a single group of twelve goddesses which multiply to fill the space.

Confession

I openly confess all my negativities amassed through body, speech and mind, And pray that they be purified.

The third limb is the confession of all negativities in order to purify the mind and remove obstacles to your practice. The easiest way to do this is to bring to mind the four powers of (1) regret, (2) reliance, (3) remedy and (4) resolve. As you have already performed a Vajrasattva purification as part of your preliminaries, it is sufficient to recall the four powers through a simple meditation.

Regret is first developed by reflecting on the actions of body, speech and mind, performed while under the influence of afflicted minds such as hatred, attachment and ignorance. If you cannot remember specific actions, try to feel remorse for the countless negativities you have created since beginningless time, particularly those related to your vows. Once you have established a feeling of sincere remorse, bring to mind your guru as the source of your refuge and refresh your aspiration to actualise the guru's wisdom in your mind, ridding yourself of all obscurations. Reflect on the empty-nature of the illusory actions you have committed in an illusory world and imagine all your negative karma dissolves away, leaving your mind completely pure. Cultivate the resolve to always act in accordance with your guru's wishes and to avoid committing negative actions again in the future. Spend a few moments at the end of this meditation resting in the certainty that your mind is pure.

Rejoicing

I rejoice in all virtue!

The fourth limb is to rejoice in one's own virtue and the virtue of others, to increase the strength of the merit in your mind. The practice of rejoicing simply involves generating a sense of delight toward any actions of virtue.

To make this practice more extensive, think of the vast merit generated by the enlightened beings of the merit field, especially the guru, the merit created by all sentient beings and finally the merit created by yourself. By remembering the incredible benefit resulting from these actions, nurture the feeling of joy that arises in your mind.

Requesting Teachings

I wholeheartedly request that you turn the wheel of Dharma without ceasing!

The fifth limb requests the guru to continue teaching the Dharma to all sentient beings throughout the three times. This request is made out of a recognition of the interdependent nature of phenomena. In order to achieve enlightenment, we must practice the Dharma; to practice the Dharma we must be taught the Dharma; for the Dharma to be taught, a guru must teach it and for a guru to teach, a student must be willing to receive the teachings and therefore must request them. In this way, by making heartfelt requests for the guru to teach, we create the causes for the Dharma to flourish and for sentient beings to ultimately achieve enlightenment.

In particular, we should make our request as we bring to mind the desire for the complete teachings of the Kalachakra to flourish. Develop the aspiration for this world to always be filled with authentic lineage holders and for all sentient beings to meet with the extraordinary path of the Six Vajra Yogas.

To make the merit of this request vast, imagine multiplying your body to fill the space around you and visualise them offering a golden Dharma wheel to the guru and the field of merit. Imagine the guru happily receiving your offering and promising to turn the wheel of Dharma for the benefit of all sentient beings.

Beseeching the Guru to Stay

I implore you to remain forever in samsara for the sake of all beings!

The sixth limb beseeches the guru to continue manifesting in samsara for the sake of sentient beings. This reminds us that the guru has already passed beyond all suffering to abide in the continual bliss of the Dharmakaya truth body. As we do not have the good fortune to experience this state, we rely on the Rupakaya emanations of the guru to interact with him. While these emanations are completely free from all faults, we still experience them as ordinary beings who are born, live for a time and then pass away.

Technically, we do not need to request the guru to stay as he will manifest spontaneously for our benefit as a result of his perfection of compassion. Our request is therefore made to strengthen our awareness of the guru in our lives and acknowledge the incredibly precious opportunity his presence provides us. More than anything, this limb is about generating appreciation for the kindness of the guru and developing our desire to never be parted from him.

Dedication

As it says in *The Anchor for Collecting Siddhis*:

I dedicate all my virtue so my mind may become inseparable from yours, O holy lama. May all beings attain supreme enlightenment!

The final limb dedicates the merit generated through the offering of the seven-limb prayer towards the attainment of supreme enlightenment. As with any virtuous practice, we use dedication to form a karmic connection between our present actions and a desired result, uniting the two aspects and ensuring the virtue will not be lost. The more merit we dedicate to the same intention, the stronger the intention becomes, increasing the power it has in our lives.

As we complete the dedication, imagine the guru smiles lovingly at you and is thoroughly pleased by your actions. Although we don't want to chase after the guru's approval, we can still delight in the fact that we have done something very beneficial.

Making Supplications

Having created a mind that is ripe for realisations through the accumulation of merit, we now move on to making supplications to the guru, which is a request for him to grant us his blessings. When we make this request we need to cultivate a fervent and uncontrived sense of devotion towards the guru that is completely free from self-cherishing or grasping. This attitude arises from a place of humility and is based on a total surrender of what we think we need or want. We should make ourselves as open and receptive as possible for whatever blessings the guru has to bestow on us.

As you hold the visualisation of the guru in the mind, recite the supplication prayers as they are presented in the text. When Guru Yoga is your main practice, repeat each verse over and over until they evoke an emotional response. As you recite, try not to fabricate anything, but simply open yourself to whatever feelings arise.

Just as your finger will get wet if put in water or will burn if put in fire, so too will your mind transform into the enlightened mind of the Buddha as you connect to the blessings of the lineage. Through this process your ordinary dualistic mind will gradually dissolve as the pristine nature of your mind is revealed.

You can choose to either recite the prayers once or repeatedly before receiving the four empowerments. While each of the three Guru Yoga practices contains different prayers, the following come from the *Foundation Guru Yoga* practice, in which one's root guru is visualised as Guru Vajradhara:

I pray to my precious glorious lama, lord of Dharma
and embodiment of all the Buddhas.
I pray to my precious glorious lama, lord of Dharma
possessing the four Buddha-kayas.
I pray to my precious glorious lama, lord of Dharma,
my unequalled ultimate refuge.
I pray to my precious glorious lama, lord of Dharma,
my unequalled ultimate rescuer.
I pray to my precious glorious lama, lord of Dharma,
who teaches the supreme path to liberation.
I pray to my precious glorious lama, lord of Dharma,
the source of all sublime attainments.
I pray to my precious glorious lama, lord of Dharma,
who clears away the darkness of ignorance.

Please bestow empowerment upon me!
Please bless me with the power to engage in the practice with complete
dedication!

May all obstacles be cleared away so I may dedicate my life to the practice!
May I experience the essence of the practice!
May my practice reach the ultimate perfection!
May I naturally emanate love, compassion and Bodhicitta!
May I unite perfect concentration and insight!
May I attain true experience and supreme realisation of the Dharma!
May I perfect the practice of the profound vajrayoga path!
May I be empowered with the siddhis of the great seal in this single lifetime.

Receiving the Blessings of the Four Empowerments

The next stage of the practice is to receive the blessings of the four empowerments which generate the causal seeds for achieving the enlightened body, speech, mind and primordial wisdom of the guru. The following visualisations are not the same as the actual empowerments we receive in later stages of the path. They function on an aspirational level to prepare our mind by establishing a strong connection between ourself and the guru who is the source of the empowerments. This is like cultivating a patch of soil so we can one day plant it with seeds.

May I see the four syllables at the chakras of the lama's body as the four Buddha-kayas.
May I receive the four empowerments by focusing upon them.
May my glorious lama bless me so that this is accomplished!

After reciting these supplication prayers, visualise your guru smiling in your direction with great love and compassion, ready to bestow the empowerments upon you. At the guru's forehead, visualise a white syllable OM (ཨོ) symbolising the vajra-body of the guru. At his throat, visualise the red syllable AH (ཨཿ) symbolising his vajra-speech. At the heart, the dark-blue syllable HUNG (ཧཱུྃ) symbolising his vajra-mind and at the navel the yellow syllable HO (ཧོཿ) symbolising his vajra-wisdom.

The Blessing of the Vase Empowerment

From the OM at my lama's forehead, a white OM streams forth and dissolves into my own forehead chakra.
Through this power may I receive the vase empowerment.
May my glorious lama bless me so that this is accomplished!

The first blessing is received from the OM syllable at the guru's forehead. Imagine white light streaming from his forehead into your own forehead and completely filling your body with radiant white light. As you receive this blessing, develop a strong aspiration to receive the vase empowerment which is capable of purifying all negativities and obscurations of the body, as well as the appearances of the waking state. Through this blessing, imagine you have created the cause to one day actualise the guru's vajra-body and manifest the Nirmanakaya emanation body of a Buddha. Rest your awareness in this experience, without concepts and without grasping.

The Blessing of the Secret Empowerment

From the AH at my lama's throat, a red AH streams forth and
dissolves into my own throat chakra.
Through this power may I receive the secret empowerment.
May my glorious lama bless me so that this is accomplished!

The second blessing is received from the AH syllable at the guru's throat. Imagine light streams out of his throat and into your own throat, completely filling your body with radiant red light. This time develop the aspiration to one day receive the secret empowerment which is capable of purifying all the negativities and obscurations of speech, as well as the appearances of the dream state. Through this blessing, imagine creating the causes to actualise the guru's vajra-speech and manifest the Sambhogakaya enjoyment body of a Buddha. Again, rest in your awareness for a time.

The Blessing of the Wisdom Empowerment

From the HUNG at my lama's heart, a black HUNG streams forth and
dissolves into my own heart chakra.
Through this power may I receive the primordial wisdom empowerment.
May my glorious lama bless me so that this is accomplished!

The third blessing is received from the HUNG syllable at the guru's heart. Imagine light streams from his heart and into your own heart, filling your body with radiant dark-blue light. Develop the aspiration to one day receive the wisdom empowerment which is capable of purifying all the negativities and obscurations of the mind as well as the appearances of the deep-sleep state. Through this blessing, imagine you have created the causes to actualise the guru's vajra-mind and manifest the Jñana-Dharmakaya wisdom-truth body of a Buddha. Again, rest in your awareness.

The Blessing of the Word Empowerment

From the HO at my lama's navel, a yellow HO streams forth and dissolves into my own navel chakra.
Through this power may I receive the sacred fourth empowerment.
May my glorious lama bless me so that this is accomplished!

The fourth and final blessing is received from the HO syllable at the guru's navel. Imagine light streams from his navel and into your own navel, filling your body with radiant yellow light. Develop the aspiration to one day receive the word empowerment which is capable of purifying all latent traces of attachment and conceptuality, as well as the appearances of the state of blissful absorption. Through this blessing, imagine you are creating the causes to actualise the guru's vajra-wisdom and manifest the Svabhavikakaya nature body of a Buddha. Once again, rest in your awareness for a time.

Empowerment	Syllable	Colour	Location	Purifies	Attainment
Vase	OM	White	Forehead	Waking State	Nirmanakaya
Secret	AH	Red	Throat	Dream State	Sambhogakaya
Wisdom	HUNG	Dark-blue	Heart	Deep-sleep State	Dharmakaya
Word	HO	Yellow	Navel	Blissful Absorption	Svabhavikakaya

Table 3-2: The Four Empowerments

Merging Your Mind with the Guru

The lama at my crown melts into light and dissolves into me.
He abides in the centre of an eight-petalled lotus at my heart.
May my glorious lama bless me so that this is accomplished!

When practising Guru Yoga it is crucial to have unshakable faith, and believe you have actually received the primordial wisdom mind of your vajra master. After receiving the four empowerments and praying to your guru repeatedly with intense devotion, dissolve the visualisation and become one with the guru's enlightened mind.

First dissolve the field of merit into the central figure of Guru Vajradhara, including the throne and cushions. Visualise Vajradhara coming to the crown of your head, melting into blissful nectar, and dissolving into your central channel. Imagine that the guru's body, speech and mind become inseparable from your own body, speech and mind, and rest your awareness in the certainty that you and your guru are of one nature.

Hold this non-conceptual state for as long as you can. If you become distracted by thoughts, you can either end your session or repeat the practice from the beginning by re-establishing the visualisation, reciting supplications and again merging your mind with the guru.

Dedication of Merits

When you are ready to finish the practice, be sure to dedicate the merit:

In all my future lives may I remain inseparable from my perfect Guru and never be separated from the true Dharma. May I gradually discover all my natural qualities and finally reach my true natural mind, the state of Vajradhara.

May I and others come to have bodies similar to yours, root and lineage lamas. May our entourage, life-span and field of merit become like yours and may we emulate your noble, supreme name. Through the power of my prayers to you, may disease, poverty and conflict be pacified and may Dharma and auspiciousness increase wherever I and others abide.

Kind and precious lama, everything good and virtuous in samsara and nirvana has arisen from the strength of your compassion. My protector, source of every conceivable benefit, I pray to you from the depths of my heart.

ADVICE FOR THE PRACTICE
OF GURU YOGA

Guru Yoga is the very heart of the tantric path. When mastered, it has the capacity to strengthen your connection to your Buddha-nature and open the way for using devotion to achieve enlightenment. To maximise the benefit from this practice, I would like to offer the following advice:

All Tantric Practice is a Form of Guru Yoga

The Vajrayana is essentially concerned with making the resultant state of Buddha-nature manifest in our present experience through the use of many skilful methods and while the individual techniques may change, the purpose is always the same. This means that all tantric practices function to converge the mind on a single point—the sublime emptiness of suchness.

Rather than thinking of the practices as separate from one another, I recommend viewing them as part of the same essential process. Remember each one provides an opportunity to recognise the way that Buddha-nature manifests in your life and although the object of focus and the level of reality will shift between practices, we always need to connect it back to Buddha-nature.

One way to contextualise this process is through embedding it within the relationship we have with our guru. We can think of the practices of the generation and completion stages as a way of practicing Guru Yoga with the more subtle levels of guru, with our ultimate aim being to mix our mind inseparably with the most secret guru. Devotion then becomes a common thread that binds everything together, allowing us to rapidly progress towards our definitive nature. This perception enables us to simplify the process of tantra and integrate our actions to avoid becoming sidetracked by spending too much time on provisional activities.

Make Supplications Personal

Making supplications is an extremely important part of practicing Guru Yoga in that it is an experiential method for releasing our self-grasping through the act of surrender. The key to making this practice truly effective is to generate our supplications from deep within our heart, nurturing the emotional connection behind them so that they are not merely words we recite.

An ideal way for supplications to be heartfelt is to make them personal. Rather than reciting words written by someone else, bring to mind your own aspirations or the obstacles you currently face. With the guru present before you, formulate a request in your own words that expresses your desire for help. The more personal your requests are, the more powerful the effect will be on your mind.

If you find it hard to put your feelings or your needs into words, you can of course rely on the vajra words of the great masters. When doing so, try to spend time connecting the supplication back to your own experience. Additionally, it is not necessary to only use the supplications in the practice text. If you find other verses you particularly connect with, these can absolutely be brought into your practice. The most important thing is that they come from the heart.

Be Aware of the Guru at All Times

Whether or not Guru Yoga is your main practice, try the best you can to integrate the awareness of the guru into every moment of your daily life. Before sleeping, visualise a white eight-petalled lotus flower at your heart-centre with your guru seated in the centre, the size of the tip of your thumb, smiling at you with great love and affection. Concentrating single-pointedly on this image as you fall asleep will eventually bring you clear light dreams. When waking in the morning, immediately visualise your guru rising from your heart along the central channel to above the crown of your head, where he stays to guide and watch over you throughout the day.

When you are seated, remind yourself that the guru is above the crown of your head and whenever you are walking, visualise him above your right shoulder. This symbolises circumambulating or walking clockwise around the guru, which is both a sign of respect and a means of accumulating merit. When you eat and drink, try to visualise your throat expanding to a vast size to include the presence of the guru and offer him nourishment as you eat and drink.

If you have difficulty with these visualisations, rather than being concerned with building up a picture in your mind, simply try to imagine these incidences occurring as offerings to the guru. Also, simply being aware of his presence is still an effective practice. Remember that focusing on the feeling or meaning of the words of the practice is an aspect which not only applies to Guru Yoga but to any practice involving visualisation. It is important not to be overly worried or discouraged with your efforts, but instead be aware of your abilities and strengths and carry out the practice in a way that uses these abilities to your best advantage.

Repeatedly Merge with the Guru

The essence of Guru Yoga is recognising the inseparable nature of the guru with our own mind. It is this experience which will bring us closer to our definitive nature. For this reason we should repeat the process of merging with the guru as often as we can.

During the day, with the guru visualised above your crown, take a moment to imagine receiving the blessings of the four empowerments and allow the guru to dissolve into your heart. Rest in your awareness for as long as you like, then visualise the guru manifesting at your heart, rising up the central channel and taking his place again above your crown.

If you don't have time to perform the visualisation, try recalling the presence of your guru and rest non-conceptually in the awareness that he is inseparable from your nature. Try to scatter these essential meditations throughout the day so you are constantly reminded of this sacred truth.

REVIEW OF KEY POINTS

- Practicing devotion to the guru as Buddha brings the Buddha close to us so we can receive his blessings. These blessings are the manifestation of our Buddha-nature from the perspective of our ordinary experience and provide us with an opportunity to realise that nature.

- The primary obstacles to receiving blessings are: (1) self-grasping which separates our mind from its nature and (2) pride which prevents us from dissolving our grasping and prevents our blessings from increasing.

- To dissolve self-grasping, we shift our pride from gross to subtle conceptions of self using four types of gurus as support: (1) the outer guru who helps us dissolve external appearances into internal appearances; (2) the inner guru who helps us dissolve impure appearances into pure appearances; (3) the secret guru who helps us dissolve the suffering of samsara into the bliss of nirvana; and (4) the most secret guru who helps us to dissolve the deluded ground into the enlightened result.

- The preliminary practice of Guru Yoga is used to take us beyond our rational thoughts and prepare us for the authentic practice of Tantra by joining our mind with the mind of the guru.

- Since the 19th century, three texts have been used for the cultivation of Guru Yoga: (1) Rain of Blessings for the Six Yogas of the Vajra Lineage by Dolpopa Sherab Gyaltsen; (2) The Anchor for Collecting Siddhis Guru Yoga by Jetsun Taranatha; and (3) The Foundation Guru Yoga that is included in Taranatha's practice manual The Divine Ladder.

- There are six stages in Guru Yoga practice: (1) establishing the visualisation; (2) accumulating merit with a seven-limb prayer; (3) making supplications; (4) receiving the blessings of the four empowerments; (5) merging your mind with the guru; and (6) dedicating your merit.

- The seven-limb prayer consists of seven practices which help us to generate merit, increase that merit and clear away negativities. They are: (1) homage; (2) offerings; (3) confession; (4) rejoicing; (5) requesting the teachings; (6) beseeching the guru to stay and (7) dedication.

- It is helpful to think of all tantric practices as being different forms of Guru Yoga that allow you to merge your mind with the different levels of guru. Our aim should be to ultimately practice Guru Yoga with the most secret guru—the ultimate nature of reality.

- To make supplications truly effective, they need to come from the heart. Therefore, make the effort to connect with the supplications on an emotional level so that they are relevant and sincere.

- By visualising the guru at your heart or above the crown of your head, you can develop mindfulness of the guru's presence throughout the day and night. This feeling of constant connection will help you strengthen your devotion and increase your awareness of Buddha-nature.

- The essence of practicing Guru Yoga is to merge your mind with the guru's mind. For this reason, we should take every opportunity we can throughout the day to remind ourselves of our inseparable nature.

PART TWO

Generating the
Enlightened Mandala

CHAPTER FOUR

Ripening the Mind Through Tantric Empowerment

Before we are qualified to practice the *Kalachakra Generation Stage*, our mind must be empowered by an authentic vajra master. Participating in an empowerment ceremony gives us the opportunity to establish a close bond with the lineage and enables us to gather the conditions needed for our Vajrayana practice to be successful.

To understand the role of empowerment, consider a patch of land we would like to use to cultivate crops. If the land is not fertile, it will be unable to sustain any plants. Therefore skilful methods are needed to fertilise the soil, providing it with the capacity or power to give rise to a bountiful harvest.

Similarly, through different types of empowerments, we fertilise our mind so that new ideas and qualities can arise within it. While there are many ways to empower the mind, specifically designed ceremonies are used to bring about particular effects that are relevant to the path. These ceremonies are given the name "empowerments".

The basic principle common to all forms of Vajrayana practice is that through shifting our internal state of mind, we also shift the way we perceive and experience our external reality. This principle is used during an empowerment to help us transform our experience into something that is both unique and ultimately meaningful.

This principle can be seen at work in many situations and is not restricted to the highly ritualised setting of an empowerment ceremony. Imagine for instance staying in a cave to practice, free from external distractions. We may think this would be a fantastic experience, but as we become bored, frustrated, uncomfortable or depressed, we find ourselves being challenged. With perseverance and by focusing on the practices, we may become completely engaged with this reality, and a genuine sense of devotion and love arises. All of these conditions, both the external and internal obstacles that come up, contribute to giving rise to particular qualities.

The shift or transformation that allows these qualities to arise is the actual empowerment. Whatever the conditions, experiences of empowerment generally manifest in three ways:

1. **Actual Experience:** The most potent form of empowerment comes in the form of a direct realisation of the specific aspect of reality that is being pointed-out by the empowerment. This type of experience alters the way we perceive reality, preventing different forms of ignorance from arising again in the future.

2. **Experience of Signs:** Depending on the karmic propensities in our minds, an empowerment may trigger a wide variety of signs such as visions or spontaneous behaviours that you cannot explain. While not as powerful as actual experiences, they do provide indication that the empowerment has had some effect on your mind.

3. **Feeling or Understanding:** At the very least, we may experience some form of non-conceptual feeling such as increased joy, contentment, peace or love. This may also arise as a conceptual understanding where we are aware of the intention of the empowerment.

In this way, empowerment can really be anything that catalyses these sorts of internal transformations. It is a shifting of one's view to see things differently and although sometimes this can be an intense experience, it doesn't necessarily have to be. It does however always involve a transformation in the mind. This means that empowerment can be an ongoing process, occurring throughout the day and night.

THE KALACHAKRA EMPOWERMENT CEREMONIES

An empowerment ceremony is essentially a very skilful means to introduce aspiring practitioners to the states of mind required for engaging in tantric practice. They are like guided meditations in which the vajra master introduces you to different aspects of your reality, creating the conditions for specific experiences to arise. In the Jonang-Shambhala Tradition, there are two ceremonies used as preliminaries to enter into the generation and completion stages of Kalachakra:

1. **The Seven Empowerments of a Growing Child:** The main purpose of this ceremony is to bestow the *tantric vows and commitments* which are the foundation for all Vajrayana practice. Within the context of this ethical discipline, we are also introduced to the *enlightened mandala* which will be used as the basis for purifying the mind through the generation stage practice of Deity Yoga.

2. **The Four Higher Empowerments:** The purpose of this ceremony is to *introduce us to the nature of our mind* in accordance with the Kalachakra Tantra, by demonstrating how to establish the union of immutable bliss and empty-form. This is the view used for engaging in the non-conceptual meditations of the Kalachakra completion stage.

Of these two, the first set of empowerments are generally given in public enabling people from all walks of life to participate in the ceremony and receive the blessings of joining the vajra family of Kalachakra. The second set are only given to those who have ripened their mind through the practice of the generation stage and are committed to practicing the completion stage.

RECEIVING THE SEVEN EMPOWERMENTS OF A GROWING CHILD

To develop a clear understanding of the ceremony for the *Seven Empowerments of a Growing Child*, we will take a look at a general overview of its distinct features. The ceremony can be divided into six parts: (1) preliminaries; (2) receiving the tantric commitments; (3) introduction to the enlightened mandala; (4) the actual empowerments; (5) additional transmissions and commitments and (6) the conclusion.

The first two are concerned with bestowing the different vows and commitments which form the foundation for practicing Kalachakra; the third and the fourth are the introduction which bestows permission for us to practice the Kalachakra Generation Stage; while the fifth provides additional vows and commitments that enhance our practice.

Preliminaries

The ceremony is structured in a step-by-step manner to ensure participants are properly prepared for the stages to follow. Before we are ready to receive the tantric vows and commitments, it is important to generate a conducive attitude and motivation. This is done by (1) removing external and internal obstacles and (2) generating refuge and Bodhicitta.

Removing Obstacles to Receiving the Empowerments

Throughout the ceremony, the vajra master introduces us to methods for familiarising ourselves with the different aspects of our enlightened nature. As many of these aspects are subtle phenomena, it is easy to become confused by the process. To help us develop confidence and focus, we need to remove the potential sources for obstacles to arise. There are two types of obstacles we should consider:

1. **External Obstacles:** This includes obstacles arising as a result of the negative influence generated by the environment or the beings present. Being unaware of the unseen beings that inhabit a particular place does not mean their behaviour cannot affect our mind. If their attitudes are not in harmony with our own, they can try to obstruct our practice. To avoid this, the vajra master performs a number of rituals designed to bring harmony into the environment and to pacify any beings who could be a disturbance.

2. **Internal Obstacles:** This includes any obstacles arising from the negative karmic propensities present in our mind. If our mind is dominated by afflictive obscurations, connecting with our Buddha-nature in a meaningful way will be very difficult. For this reason the vajra master guides us through various visualisations designed to purify our mind and give us a clean foundation to work from.

As a result of consciously removing these obstacles, our mind should be at ease with faith in the vajra master and our innate capacity. With the confidence of having the support we need, nurture the feeling of being free of any sense of fear or worry.

Generating Refuge and Bodhicitta

Once we have cleared away negativities, the next stage is to establish a meaningful motivation, ensuring the merit we generate becomes the cause for enlightenment. As the Kalachakra belongs to the Vajrayana, the only valid motivation for entering this path is Bodhicitta. This mind is generated in two steps:

1. **Taking the Refuge Precepts with Aspirational Bodhicitta:** For our aspiration to achieve enlightenment to carry any weight in our mind, we need a firm conviction that enlightenment is actually possible. We can do this by strengthening

our faith in the Three Jewels who are the source of our refuge and the means through which all sentient beings will achieve enlightenment.

2. **Generating Engaged Bodhicitta:** Not satisfied with a mere aspiration, we must be willing to work towards achieving our goal. Only through removing all obscurations and actualising all enlightened qualities can we truly bring benefit to sentient beings, but more than this, we also need to recognise that the longer we take to achieve our aim, the longer sentient beings suffer and therefore we must use the incredibly skilful means of Tantra to progress along the path as quickly as possible.

In addition to establishing our motivation, in the context of the empowerment ceremony, taking refuge and generating Bodhicitta provide us with an opportunity to renew our *Vows of Personal Liberation* and our *Bodhisattva Vows*. Both of these forms of ethical conduct are considered prerequisites for receiving the *Tantric Vows and Commitments*. If we have never received these vows before, this stage establishes them in our mind for the first time.

The Tantric Commitments According to Kalachakra

Having gathered the preliminary conditions, we are now prepared to receive the tantric commitments from our vajra master. In the Kalachakra system there are three sets of commitments which encapsulate the essence of the Kalachakra training of ethical discipline: (1) *The Common Pledges of the Five Buddha Families* which establish the view; (2) *The Uncommon Pledges of Kalachakra* which establish how to meditate; and (3) *The Twenty-Five Conducts of Kalachakra* which establish our external behaviour.

When receiving these pledges we are committing ourselves to upholding the precepts to the best of our ability until we achieve enlightenment. While we are not expected to uphold them perfectly, we should nonetheless develop a strong aspiration to maintain them as purely as we can. Understanding the essence of each pledge helps us practice skilfully without the fear of being overwhelmed.

Regardless of which set of commitments we may be emphasising, the essence of all tantric commitments can be summarised by the following passage from the *Kalachakra Root Tantra*:

> *Holding the vajra and bell, with supreme compassion,*
> *teaching the supreme Dharma.*

The words "Holding the vajra and bell", refer to the practice of maintaining awareness of one's pure and definitive nature; "with supreme compassion" refers to maintaining the supreme motivation of Bodhicitta; and "teaching the supreme Dharma" refers to constantly working for the benefit of sentient beings. If we can be mindful of these three points at all times, we can easily uphold all our vows as everything else is simply an extension or aspect of these three root trainings. Keep this in mind as we examine the specific precepts related to each set of commitments.

The Common Pledges of the Five Buddha Families

The foundation of all tantric practice is the pure view which recognises the definitive nature of ordinary phenomena. To establish this view we need to be introduced to the various aspects of our Buddha-nature so we have an idea of what to focus on. To help us become familiar with these aspects, the Buddha defined nineteen pledges grouped into five Buddha families: (1) the Buddha Family; (2) the Vajra Family; (3) the Jewel Family; (4) the Lotus Family; and (5) the Action Family. By working with these pledges, we strengthen our connection with this nature and thereby maintain our awareness of it at all times. They are considered common in the sense that they are shared across all systems of Highest Yoga Tantra.

The Buddha Family

The Buddha Family manifests as Buddha Vairochana who embodies the *pristine wisdom of basic space*—the pervasive aspect of Buddha-nature in which all phenomena arise. In accordance with this wisdom, everything manifests in dependence on Buddha-nature and therefore everything can be used as a basis for revealing that nature.

This family teaches us to not be satisfied with a superficial understanding of the conventional truth of an object. We should instead always penetrate deeper to connect with its definitive meaning. To exemplify this behaviour, we pledge to uphold the practices of taking refuge and generating Bodhicitta, while maintaining mindfulness of their ultimate nature. This essence is expressed through six pledges:

1. **Take refuge in the Buddha:** We should remember to see the Buddha as the pure ground of absolute reality—the sublime emptiness endowed with all enlightened qualities.

2. **Take refuge in the Dharma:** We should see the teachings as the natural manifestation of pristine wisdom in our mind—the profound realisations that clear all obscurations.

3. **Take refuge in the Sangha:** We should see the infinite array of tantric practitioners as the external display of our Buddha-nature manifesting in order to guide and support us in our practice—the enlightened demonstrations of our innate capacity.

4. **Abandon non-virtue:** From now until we reach Buddhahood, we should hold dear the precious Bodhicitta, just as the Buddhas and Bodhisattvas before us have done, and refrain from unethical conduct, upholding the precepts we have taken. Even though sentient beings have never existed from the perspective of primordial wisdom, we recognise that due to the temporary obscurations of a dualistic consciousness, suffering

has arisen. Therefore, we strive to eradicate this illusory suffering by abandoning the afflictive states of mind.

5. **Cultivate virtue:** As much as we can, we should engage in wholesome activities such as studying the Dharma and meditating on its meaning. Through striving in our practice, we will manifest our enlightened qualities which are not newly created, but are complete within the infinite capacity of suchness. Rather than developing anything, we merely remove the conditioning that prevents these qualities from manifesting.

6. **Benefit others:** We should serve the needs of other sentient beings according to our capacity. The ultimate nature of reality is the interconnection of love and compassion and from this perspective, there is no separation between self and other. Therefore, in order to truly actualise our own potential, we must strive to help others achieve theirs.

These six pledges encapsulate all the trainings of the Bodhisattva path of the Sutrayana. This includes the two ethical disciplines of the *Vows of Personal Liberation* and the *Bodhisattva Vows*. What makes these pledges tantric is that they are practiced within the context of our understanding of Buddha-nature. The practices are the same, but the view shifts from a causal to resultant focus.

The Vajra Family

The Vajra Family manifests as Buddha Akshobhya who embodies the *mirror-like wisdom of primordial awareness*—the innate capacity of Buddha-nature to give rise to an infinite array of appearances without limitation. This is the boundless aspect that allows both samsara and nirvana to arise within suchness.

This family teaches us to use specific appearances as symbols for maintaining our mindfulness of the aspects of Buddha-nature as manifested in Kalachakra. In total, there are four pledges corresponding to four symbols:

1. **Vajra:** The pledge of the *enlightened mind* is to keep in one's possession a vajra as an external symbol of immutable bliss—the non-dual awareness that is completely free from all grasping. This mind is in the nature of method and is represented by the masculine aspect of enlightenment, Kalachakra.

2. **Bell:** The pledge of *enlightened speech* is to keep in one's possession a bell, symbolising empty-form—the sublime emptiness endowed with all enlightened qualities. This mind is the nature of wisdom and is represented by the feminine aspect of enlightenment, Vishvamata.

3. **Mudra:** The pledge of the *enlightened body* is to visualise yourself in the aspect of the meditational deity Kalachakra in union with his consort Vishvamata—the inseparable union of method and wisdom.

4. **Guru:** The pledge of the *vajra master* is to always practice devotion towards the guru who shows us the greatest kindness by revealing to us the enlightened mind. He is the symbol of non-referential compassion—the spontaneous manifestation of our own enlightened nature.

Keeping these vows trains us to look past what appears to our ordinary senses and to instead connect those appearances with the definitive meaning of our sacred truth. This is the basic principle behind the practice of pure perception.

The Jewel Family

The Jewel Family manifests as Buddha Ratnasambhava who embodies the *primordial wisdom of equality*—the one flavour of all phenomena, completely free from bias. This is the unified aspect of Buddha-nature that points to the shared purity of all appearances. Although we temporarily perceive phenomena as distinct, ultimately there are no distinctions as everything arises on the basis of suchness.

This family teaches us to release our bias through the practice of generosity. By reminding ourselves of the inherent purity of phenomena, we dissolve the conceptual barriers that we project. This dissolution opens us up and allows our Buddha-nature to manifest freely without limitations. There are four specific pledges related to this family:

1. **Giving Material Wealth:** By giving away physical objects and material wealth, we free ourselves from attachment to external phenomena and create the conditions for resources to manifest in our experience. This dissolves the bias of self-cherishing that tries to hoard everything for oneself.

2. **Giving Fearlessness:** By offering protection to those who find themselves in situations of danger or fear, we free ourselves from the fear of being harmed by others. This dissolves the bias of self-cherishing that needs to protect the self from external threats.

3. **Giving Dharma:** By offering the sublime gift of the Dharma with a pure motivation, we clear away ignorance and create the conditions for wisdom to ripen. This dissolves the bias that grasps onto the self as existing inherently from its own side.

4. **Giving Loving-Kindness:** By cultivating the wish for others to be happy and to attain the causes of happiness, we free ourselves from the aversion and hatred which are the opposite of our sublime purity. This dissolves the bias of self-cherishing that rejects sentient beings and ultimately separates us from our nature.

These four types of generosity should be practiced six times each day (three times in the morning and three at night). As generosity is the source of joy for ourselves and others, it is likened to a wish-fulfilling jewel from which all enlightened qualities naturally arise.

The Lotus Family

The Lotus Family manifests as Buddha Amitabha who embodies the *primordial wisdom of discrimination*—the awareness which clearly distinguishes between phenomena at a conventional level. This is the manifold aspect of Buddha-nature which realises that even though appearances are rooted in suchness, they still appear to a dualistic mind as a diversity of phenomena. Such an awareness is never confused by the veils of ignorance and therefore can differentiate each aspect with clarity.

This family teaches us to utilise the many teachings given by the Buddha. Some teachings will be personally relevant to our spiritual development, whereas others will allow us to skilfully guide sentient beings. By upholding all teachings without bias, we can clearly distinguish how each should be practiced. This essence is expressed in three pledges:

1. **Sutrayana:** Uphold and preserve the teachings of Sutrayana as presented in the *Foundational Vehicle* of the Hearers and the *Great Vehicle* of the Bodhisattvas.

2. **Lower Tantras:** Uphold and preserve the teachings of the Lower Tantras as presented in the *Action, Performance* and *Yoga* classes of Tantra.

3. **Highest Yoga Tantra:** Uphold and preserve the sublime teachings of Highest Yoga Tantra as presented in the systems of *Father, Mother* and *Non-Dual Tantras*.

The aim here is not to achieve mastery of everything, but to know what the teachings are and how they can be used in different situations. This is done with the recognition that all phenomena are inseparable from our enlightened nature and manifest in accordance with the karmic propensities of sentient beings.

The Action Family

The Action Family manifests as Buddha Amoghasiddhi who embodies the *all-accomplishing wisdom*—the spontaneous aspect of Buddha-nature which manifests in whatever form is needed to bring benefit to sentient beings. This wisdom is the natural perfection of compassion and is the basis for accomplishing the two aims of self and others.

This family teaches us to be mindful of our actions so we can fully integrate them into our view of the ultimate nature of reality. The training is to familiarise ourselves with the conduct that supports achieving enlightenment, as the greater our familiarity, the more spontaneously the conduct will arise. Specifically there are two pledges related to this family:

1. **Maintaining the Discipline of the Three Vows:** Although the Three Vows are included within the pledge to abandon non-virtue, within this context we adopt the determination to keep them purely. This means we commit ourselves to studying the vows so we can clearly distinguish what actions to perform in any given situation.

2. **Making Extensive Offerings:** The most skilful way to accumulate merit is through making offerings to the Buddhas and Bodhisattvas. We do this by focusing on the three types of offerings: (1) external offerings of various offering substances whether real or visualised; (2) internal offerings of our dualistic experience of conventional reality; and (3) secret offerings of our non-dualistic experience of suchness.

These practices help us develop our ability to accomplish anything we wish by uniting the wisdom that knows what to do with the merit that is able to manifest whatever is needed.

If we summarise the five groups of pledges, we can say they consist of: (1) taking refuge in the ultimate nature of reality; (2) remembering its aspects; (3) removing the temporary obscurations that limit that reality; (4) clearly distinguishing how it manifests; and (5) acting in accordance with that reality. If we do these five things, we strengthen our connection with our Buddha-nature and open ourselves to experiencing its infinite blessings.

The Uncommon Pledges of Kalachakra

While the view of the ultimate nature of reality is common across all systems of Highest Yoga Tantra, the methods used to work with that nature are different. In the Kalachakra system the uncommon pledges specific to the Kalachakra Tantra are grouped into *Six Buddha Families*: (1) the Akshobhya Family; (2) the Ratnasambhava Family; (3) the Vairochana Family; (4) the Amoghasiddhi Family; (5) the Amitabha Family; and (6) the Vajrasattva Family. This six-fold division emphasises the way Kalachakra specifically works to purify the six chakras, establishing an immutable realisation of one's ultimate nature. Of these six, as Vajrasattva represents the non-dual nature of the mind, he is considered the king of the mandala and is the main focus of this system.

The Six Buddha Families can be seen as an overview of the specific methods used in the Kalachakra System to produce the result of enlightenment. For each set of vows there are two levels to be considered; a provisional level and a definitive level. The first is a skilful means for orientating the mind to working with the definitive meaning, whereas the second is a skilful means for working with that nature. In this way, the provisional pledges correspond to the generation stage practices and the definitive pledges correspond to the completion stage.

The essence of these vows involves committing ourselves to the practice of the Kalachakra Path, taking it as our primary focus and pledging to work towards achieving each stage. We are not promising to do everything right now but acknowledging the strong aspiration to complete the Kalachakra Path. Recognising our level of spiritual development, we concentrate our energy on the practices suited for our present capacity. As this capacity develops, our aspirations are realised and we progress to the next step.

Akshobhya Family

The essence of the Buddha Akshobya is to establish a pure perception of reality through the unification of our body, speech and mind. At the provisional level, this is accomplished through meditating on the great compassion of Bodhicitta as method, the nature of sublime emptiness as wisdom and the enlightened mandala of Kalachakra as their unity. All these practices are included within the skilful means of *Deity Yoga.*

On the definitive level, the pure perception to be established is the very subtle awareness that arises as a result of practicing the *Six Vajra Yogas.* This non-dual state is produced when the subtle winds and essences converge and are held at the lower opening of the central channel, thereby giving rise to the ultimate Mahamudra which is the union of immutable bliss and empty-form. From this perspective, the purity of all phenomena can clearly be seen.

Ratnasambhava Family

The essence of the Buddha Ratnasambhava is to realise the equality of all phenomena. At the provisional level, this is achieved through the practice of making extensive offerings to the enlightened beings within the Kalachakra mandala. Traditionally there are ten objects of offering used, including things that ordinary people are attached to such as material possessions, loved ones and one's own body. By recognising that these things are ultimately pure in nature, they can be considered suitable offerings for the Buddhas and Bodhisattvas. This practice of generosity is usually performed through offering rituals such as *Tsok Feasts*.

On the definitive level, this equality can be directly realised by bringing your ten subtle winds into the central channel and making them abide there. As more of these winds are drawn inwards, your dualistic perceptions are correspondingly reduced. Once all the winds have been gathered, everything you experience arises with the single flavour of empty-form.

Vairochana Family

The essence of the Buddha Vairochana is to realise the blissful nature of all phenomena. At the provisional level this is accomplished through working with ten substances known as the five meats and the five nectars. These are substances which are normally considered as disgusting and a source of suffering. By realising their underlying purity however, they become a profound basis for the experience of bliss. Because this practice requires an enormous degree of realisation, most practitioners work with meat and alcohol in a symbolic way to remind themselves of this underlying purity.

On the definitive level, the ten substances each represent the ten types of subtle essences that are distributed throughout the subtle body and provide the basis for the experience of great bliss. By working with the completion stage practices, the winds are stopped at key points within the central channel, activating the corresponding chakras and drawing the essences into them like a magnet.

Amoghasiddhi Family

The essence of the Buddha Amoghasiddhi is the absence of grasping onto the blissful nature of reality. At the provisional level, this is accomplished through the practice of making offerings of everything that gives you joy. The focus here is to recognise ordinary bliss as a sign of the more profound ultimate nature of bliss. By offering it to the enlightened mandala, you symbolically let go of your grasping onto the experience.

On the definitive level, this mind of non-grasping is achieved through the practice of *Inner Fire* (tummo). As you develop greater familiarity with this practice, a greater intensity of bliss is experienced. Learning not to grasp onto this experience in a dualistic way enables you to abide continually in a state of blissful, non-dual awareness.

Amitabha Family

The essence of the Buddha Amitabha is to clearly distinguish the unified nature of reality through relying on a consort. At the provisional level, for those who have attained a high degree of realisation and can maintain their pure perception at all times, this practice involves entering into sexual union with a physical consort. For most practitioners, however, this practice is performed with a visualised consort. Either way, the purpose is to unify one's experience of bliss with the wisdom that realises sublime emptiness.

On the definitive level, this unity is achieved when all the subtle essences are gathered and held at the lower tip of the central channel, producing the highly concentrated mind of immutable great bliss. By allowing the mind to abide in this non-dualistic experience, one is said to be in union with the Great Consort of Empty-Form.

Vajrasattva Family

The essence of the Buddha Vajrasattva is to abide in the union of immutable bliss and empty form. At the provisional level, this means maintaining mindfulness of the sexual organs as the basis for bliss, which in turn is the basis for realising the sublime emptiness that is the ultimate nature of reality. Therefore, with the aspiration to free all sentient beings from suffering, one develops the strong determination to abide in that union.

On the definitive level, enlightenment is achieved through abiding in the vajra-like samadhi that is produced by the union of immutable bliss and empty-form. For each moment that one remains absorbed in this state, the winds of karma are dissolved and the conditioning of cyclic existence is severed forever.

Through the Six Buddha Families we can identify twelve pledges, six for the generation stage and six for the completion stage. The provisional pledges of the generation stage are: (1) unify the body, speech and mind through the practice of Deity Yoga; (2) make extensive offerings through the practice of Tsok Feasts; (3) maintain mindfulness of the purity of phenomena by working with the ten impure substances; (4) reduce grasping onto ordinary bliss by offering all blissful experiences to the enlightened mandala; (5) recognise the purity of bliss by working with a visualised consort; and (6) cultivate the aspiration to abide in the union of immutable bliss and empty-form by maintaining mindfulness of the sacred aspect of sexuality.

The definitive pledges of the completion stage are: (1) unify the body, speech and mind through the practice of the Six Vajra Yogas; (2) experience all perceptions as empty-forms by bringing the ten winds into the central channel; (3) gather all subtle essences into the central channel; (4) release grasping onto bliss by working with the practice of Inner Fire; (5) gather all subtle essences at the lower tip of the central channel by working with a consort; and (6) abide in the union of immutable bliss and empty-form.

The Twenty-Five Conducts of Kalachakra

The *Twenty-Five Conducts of Kalachakra* are a set of supplementary vows which are specifically designed to help you integrate your tantric commitments with your daily life. They were originally created to counteract the wrong views prevalent at the time. While the context may have shifted, the principles of these conducts continue to hold true, providing a powerful method for reinforcing our connection with Buddha-nature.

The twenty-five conducts are split into five groups of five: (1) the five major negative karmas to abandon; (2) the five minor negative karmas to avoid; (3) the five forbidden killings; (4) the five attitudes of disrespect and (5) the five attachments. If you can understand the essential nature of each group, it becomes much easier to recognise when to apply them in your day-to-day activities.

The Five Major Negative Karmas to Abandon

The first set of conducts is the same as the *Root Vows of Personal Liberation* (pratimoksha). The essence of this group is *non-violence*. This means we do our best to avoid using our body or speech in a way that causes harm to others. The specific actions to be abandoned are as follows:

1. **Taking life:** Generally speaking this refers to inflicting physical or mental harm on a human or animal. This definition of the vow is much broader than usually found in the common lay vows. While it is very difficult to completely abandon all harm, we should still strive to live our lives in non-violence.

2. **Speaking lies:** We should abandon all forms of lying based on afflicted motivations. In particular we must be careful not to give false teachings based on our own misconceptions. We should always strive to communicate our reality as it is and to avoid any form of distortion.

3. **Taking what is not given:** Any time we use something, we should be confident that we have the permission of the person who owns it. It doesn't matter how insignificant it may be, if we do not own it, we need permission. This includes things like using money that has been promised for repayment of a debt.

4. **Inappropriate sexual conduct:** We should avoid any form of conduct that uses sexuality as a means of inflicting harm or encouraging afflicted states of mind. In general, a Kalachakra practitioner should view sex as something very special and highly respected.

5. **Taking intoxicants:** We should avoid all forms of alcohol or drugs that are likely to cloud our judgement, weaken our self-control or influence us to behave in destructive ways. This vow does not prohibit the use of alcohol as a part of our spiritual practice such as in a tsok feast or other tantric ritual. The key factor is that your mind is free from afflictions and that you have the capacity to avoid becoming intoxicated.

These five commitments of restrained action are crucial as they serve as a fundamental basis for all other commitments.

The Five Minor Negative Karmas to Avoid

The next set of conducts is focused on activities that reinforce afflicted states of mind such as the three poisons of attachment, aversion and ignorance. The following activities should be avoided as much as possible:

1. **Gambling:** This includes activities such as playing cards, or board games which cause us to waste time, especially when they involve self-centred and competitive intentions that desire profit for oneself at the expense of others' wellbeing. Such time-consuming activities divert our constructive energy, however there is no fault if they can be used for educational purposes, or as a way to establish a rapport with others if our intention is altruistic.

2. **Eating unseemly meat:** Some belief systems consider it virtuous if the meat they consume is killed by themselves, but from a Buddhist perspective this kind of activity is non-virtuous and

"unseemly". This precept calls on us to avoid eating the meat of an animal which we either know or suspect was killed specifically for our consumption.

3. **Reading ignoble words:** This refers to reading books, articles, or looking at photos, websites or video material that arouses anger or gross desire when we have no control over these afflictive emotional states. Such actions are non-productive and serve to distract us, wasting our precious time. On a deeper level, this precept encourages us to be mindful of anything that comes to our attention which incites anger or increases our attachment and to also refrain from speaking about such topics.

4. **Making offerings to spirits:** The worship of spirits is considered wrong when the sacrifice of a living being such as an animal is involved. This includes making offerings to spirits of the dead, nature spirits or any unseen beings related to prosperity, good fortune and the like. Offerings which do not involve the sacrifice of a living being or use of stolen objects are appropriate if we hold in our hearts the wish to alleviate their suffering or to repay our karmic debts.

5. **Following extremist practices:** Although extreme types of rituals are now rare, some barbaric customs or irrational actions do occur in certain traditions. Examples include adhering to an extreme diet to gain spiritual benefit or making blood offerings. In a more general sense, we should always examine whether our actions sacrifice the welfare of others for our own benefit.

The Five Forbidden Killings

While taking life is one of the *Five Major Negative Karmas to Abandon,* the Buddha chose to emphasise five specific forms of killing accompanied by wrong views, that attempt to legitimise the act of killing. The focus is abandoning the afflicted minds that see killing as a virtuous deed and the essence is to always be aware of your *motivation for killing*, recognising when it is fuelled by any of the three poisons.

1. **Killing animals:** The killing of beings has already been mentioned in a general way, but here we specifically refer to the killing of animals with the aim of personal, material or spiritual gain. Certain religions may condone such killings but in Buddhism it is not supported. Killing with self-centred intentions is completely non-virtuous and will generate heavy negative karma. In the modern age people find it relatively easy to give up hunting, killing cattle or fishing, but much more difficult to stop killing insects. When our automatic reaction is to squash an insect that irritates us, we build a habit of dealing with small annoyances through violent means. This goes against the heartfelt awareness, so crucial to the Buddhist view, that all beings are equal in their wish to be happy and to avoid suffering. If however, for economic or health reasons a pest must be removed, it is important to do so without anger or hatred and try to find a method which spares their life. This also applies to scientific research, where it is important to consider the welfare of animals and to minimise harming or killing them.

2. **Killing children:** The killing of all human beings is forbidden but children are emphasised here because it was once considered acceptable to some belief systems, possibly for economic or health reasons. This action is especially negative when our motivation is governed by emotions such as anger or thinking only of our own convenience. In the present time this precept applies especially to the practice of abortion. Although there may be certain justifiable reasons such as health, this is a delicate issue and depends on individual circumstances. If we are

Monks constructing the Enlightened Mandala with coloured sand.

contemplating abortion our motivation and action should be analysed very carefully, ensuring it does not only serve our personal well-being or convenience.

3. **Killing women and men:** These two negative actions have their origin in the practices of human sacrifice present in many ancient religions. In modern times, it raises the issue of euthanasia, both of people and animals. From the Buddhist perspective, if our motivation is pure, the act of taking another being's life leads to much lighter karmic consequences than ordinary killing. However we can never say that killing is beneficial as it stops the natural human suffering which is the result of one's own individual karma and therefore more suffering may occur in future lifetimes. A person suffering in the worst conceivable way in the human realm may well be experiencing the effects of rapid purification, as they may otherwise be destined to experience the suffering of the lower realms instead. Actions to bring an end to their suffering in this human lifetime could lead to far greater suffering in their next life until that karma has completed.

4. **Destroying representations of enlightened body, speech and mind:** These are the actions of misguided beings who wrongly believe they will inherit the merit of holy people or objects if they destroy them. Holy objects include sacred images, texts or monuments such as stupas. In a modern context this precept calls us to treat Dharma texts and other holy objects with respect and gratitude. If we need to dispose of Dharma texts for any reason, the usual custom is to burn them with respect. We should avoid being disrespectful to holy objects and treating them in the same way as ordinary belongings.

The Five Attitudes of Disrespect

These five conducts are meant to draw our attention to five powerful relationships that concern the creation of particularly powerful karma. As our intention is to achieve enlightenment for the benefit of all sentient beings, damaging our relationship with these people creates obstacles to achieving our aim. The essence is to instead cultivate respect and appreciation for those who are engaged in virtue or are creating the conditions for others to engage in virtue. The five attitudes to avoid are as follows:

1. **Hating friends who benefit Dharma or the world in general:** We may find ourselves looking down upon those who try to benefit others, thinking their actions are not very skilful and even denying that they are bringing any benefit at all. This haughty outlook leads to self-centred thoughts such as "we know what's best"—such an attitude seriously limits our ability to help anyone.

2. **Hating leaders or elders worthy of respect:** We should take care not to let our judgement of leaders be swayed by personal preferences, such as whether or not we like their personality. Our discriminating awareness can be clouded by these concerns and weakens our ability to discern anything correctly. We must remember that our view is limited and that respecting others is always beneficial.

3. **Hating spiritual teachers or Buddhas:** Respect for spiritual teachers is highly beneficial. This not only includes our own spiritual teachers but also extends to other teachers, even if they do not seem properly qualified. Recognising mistakes and shortcomings in teachers does not go against this precept unless there is a negative view towards them as a person.

4. **Hating members of the Sangha, in particular Arya beings:** Although this negative action is mainly concerned with Arya beings (who have directly realised selflessness), the Sangha is conventionally represented by the monastic community. Some people may become monks or nuns with worldly motivation, yet because of what their robes represent, it is inappropriate to show them contempt. Nowadays in the West, the term Sangha also includes members of a Buddhist centre. Enmity within such communities can only jeopardise spiritual growth.

5. **Hating those who trust us:** This negative action includes letting down or deceiving those who depend on our help, as well as abusing positions of power. When people rely on us, we should do everything in our power to keep our word and fulfil our duties.

The Five Attachments

The last five conducts are concerned with attachment to the experiences of the five senses. In order to transcend the conceptual mind, it is necessary to withdraw from the sensory world, but we cannot do this if our mind is attached to sights, sounds and so forth. The essence is therefore to focus on genuine happiness by cultivating a degree of self-control that does not get caught up in the pursuit of sensory pleasure. This doesn't mean we cannot enjoy ourselves, simply that we should not be motivated to specifically seek it out. This is not a promise of asceticism, but rather a pledge to set reasonable limits and exercise self-control.

To summarise the twenty-five conducts we should: (1) avoid any sort of violence towards sentient beings; (2) reduce activities which ignite afflicted states of mind; (3) abandon afflicted motivations for killing; (4) cultivate respect and appreciation for those who are engaged in virtue and (5) focus on genuine happiness by cultivating self-control.

Introduction to the Enlightened Mandala

After establishing the tantric commitments in our mind, the next phase of the empowerment ceremony is for the vajra master to introduce us to the symbolic representation of reality known as the *Enlightened Mandala of Kalachakra*. Through the distinct features of this conceptual model, our attention is directed to aspects of our experience so we can systematically realise their innate purity.

To understand how this works, we need to remember that everything is of one nature in suchness. Even though its nature is inseparable, we can say that Buddha-nature possesses two aspects: (1) a clarity aspect which allows for a limitless variety of empty appearances to arise; and (2) a luminous aspect which is the pristine awareness that knows whatever arises. Through the interplay of these two co-emergent qualities, appearances manifest in a great diversity of ways.

The two aspects of clarity and luminosity are represented in the enlightened mandala as (1) the objective environment that is experienced and (2) the subjective deities that inhabit that environment. As we will explore the extensive details of this mandala in the next chapter, the following is a basic summary of the key features introduced during the empowerment ceremony.

The Enlightened Environment

When referring to the environment, we tend to only think of the external world of mountains, cities, oceans, forests, stars and planets. In the context of the enlightened environment, the term includes a much broader range of experiences, incorporating everything that can potentially be known by the mind, known as objective appearances. These are considered objective as they are taken by the mind as its object.

Within the enlightened environment, these objects are grouped into six mandalas based on their nature and varying degree of subtlety: (1) the universe mandala; (2) the body mandala; (3) the speech mandala; (4) the mind mandala; (5) the great bliss mandala and (6) the essential mandala. While the first represents the purity of the external world formed as a result of the shared karma between sentient beings, the remaining five are related to the aspects of the internal world of an enlightened being.

The Enlightened Deities

For every object we can potentially encounter in our experience, there are two alternative ways we can interpret it. If our mind operates from a dualistic perspective of ignorance, the object will appear as an ordinary appearance, conditioned by karma. However, if our mind operates from the non-dual perspective of primordial wisdom, objects will appear as pure manifestations of suchness. These pure manifestations are represented in the enlightened mandala as a host of wisdom deities.

The Enlightened Mandala of Kalachakra identifies the following sixteen groups of deities: (1) the principal deity of Kalachakra Yab-Yum; (2) the ten shaktis; (3) the four emblems; (4) the twelve Buddhas; (5) the ten vases; (6) the twelve Bodhisattvas; (7) the five wrathful ones; (8) the twelve offering goddesses; (9) the eight female deities with yoginis; (10) the thirty-six desire goddesses; (11) the twelve male deities of the lunar months; (12) the six wrathful guardians; (13) the ten naga kings; (14) the thirty-six detachment goddesses; (15) the ten very-wrathful deities; and (16) the thirty-five million perimeter deities. Of these deities, six hundred and thirty-six are used in the generation stage practices of the Jonang Tradition.

The Actual Empowerments

After introducing us to the general structure of the enlightened mandala, the vajra master bestows on us the actual empowerments using the deities of the mind, great bliss and essential mandalas. These deities collectively represent the Dharmakaya mind of the Buddha and are the source from which we receive the blessings of the empowerments.

In total, there are seven distinct empowerments which correspond to seven phases that a growing child experiences as they approach puberty. Just as a child is born into the world, so too are we introduced to the enlightened reality of Kalachakra. Then, like a child developing a sense for who they are in relation to the world, we train in the generation stage practices so we can develop a pure view of who we are, from the perspective of our sacred truth.

This pure view is established through the purification of the four states of experience, which occurs when the obscurations generated by the four maras are removed. Once these obscurations are removed, our definitive nature is free to manifest as the four vajras of a fully-enlightened Buddha. These correlations can be summarised as follows:

State	Mara	Vajra
Waking	Aggregates	Vajra-Body
Dream	Afflictions	Vajra-Speech
Deep-sleep	Lord of Death	Vajra-Mind
Blissful Absorption	Son of the Gods	Vajra-Wisdom

Table 4-1: Purification of the Four States

Each set of empowerments will be studied individually to identify how they help us purify the aspects of our experience. At this stage, the focus should be on forming a connection between the empowerment deities and the specific purity they represent.

The Empowerments to Achieve Vajra-Body

This first group transforms our experience of gross phenomena from an external and internal perspective. We are specifically seeking to transform our perception of the world "out there" and the person "in here". This class of experiences correlates to the appearances that arise during the waking state.

The Water Empowerment

Beginning with the five elements of space, wind, fire, water and earth, these form the basis for our experience of the external universe. Meditating on the empty nature of these phenomena, we realise they are the five *Female Buddhas*. This phase corresponds to washing a newborn baby for the first time.

Female Buddha	Element
Vajradhatvishvari	Space
Tara	Wind
Pandara	Fire
Mamaki	Water
Lochana	Earth

Table 4-2: Deities of the Water Empowerment

The Crown Empowerment

Having purified the external universe, we turn inwards to the constituents which form our sense of self. In this empowerment, we concentrate on the five aggregates of form, perception, feeling, conceptions and consciousness. By contemplating the empty nature of each aggregate, we realise they are the five *Male Buddhas*. This phase corresponds to when the child receives its first hairstyle.

Male Buddha	Aggregate
Vairochana	Form
Amitabha	Perception
Ratnasambhava	Feeling
Amoghasiddhi	Conceptions
Akshobya	Consciousness

Table 4-3: Deities of the Crown Empowerment

The Empowerments to Achieve Vajra-Speech

The next group of empowerments moves to a subtler level, specifically the subtle structure of our channels and winds. In accordance with the Kalachakra system, the movements of the winds within the channels are the supporting condition for the mental afflictions to arise. This class of experiences correlates to the appearances of the dream state.

Silk Ribbon Empowerment

Every day, ten types of winds circulate throughout the body providing the subtle basis for its many functions. We can think of them as the energetic push and pull keeping the body alive. Meditating on the empty nature of these winds, we realise they are the ten *Shaktis*. This phase corresponds to adorning the child with ornaments.

Shakti	Wind
Krishnadipta	Fire-Accompanying
Raktadipta	Upward Moving
Shvetadipta	All-Pervading
Pitadipta	Naga
Dhuma	Tortoise
Marici	Chameleon
Khadyota	Devadatta
Pradipa	Dhanamjaya
Paramakala	Life-Supporting
Bindurupini	Downward-Clearing

Table 4-4: Deities of the Silk Ribbon Empowerment

Vajra and Bell Empowerment

There are more than 72,000 subtle channels running throughout the body, with two primary channels running parallel to the spinal column on the left and right. As winds pass through them, they stir the mind, giving rise to karmic appearances. By meditating on the empty nature of these channels, we realise they are inseparable from the principal deities of *Kalachakra and Vishvamata*. This phase corresponds to the child enjoying the experience of laughing.

Deity	Channel
Kalachakra	Left
Vishvamata	Right

Table 4-5: Deities of the Vajra and Bell Empowerment

The Empowerments to Achieve Vajra-Mind

Whereas the last two groups worked with our physical reality at a gross and a subtle level, the following two groups focus on our mental reality. This particular group looks at gross level consciousness and the way these consciousnesses motivate our activities. This class of experiences correlates to the appearances that arise during the deep-sleep state.

Conduct Empowerment

There are six types of gross consciousness we use to perceive our world: visual consciousness, aural consciousness, olfactory consciousness, gustatory consciousness, tactile consciousness and mental conscious-ness. Each of these arises when our sense powers comes into contact with six types of sense objects, namely, shape and form, sound, smell, taste, tactile sensation and mental events. When we contemplate the empty nature of these two sets of six, we realise the six sense powers are the six *Male Bodhisattvas* and the six sense objects are the six *Female Bodhisattvas*. This phase corresponds to the child enjoying the sensual experiences of the desire realm.

Male Bodhisattva	Sense Power
Ksitigarbha	Eye
Vajrapani	Ear
Khagarba	Nose
Lokeshvara	Tongue
Sarvanivarana	Body
Samantabhadra	Mind

Female Bodhisattva	Sense Object
Rupavajra	Forms
Shabdavajra	Sounds
Gandhavajra	Smells
Rasavajra	Tastes
Sparshavajra	Tactile Sensations
Dharmadhatuvajra	Mental Phenomena

Table 4-6: Deities of the Conduct Empowerment

Name Empowerment

On the basis of the different types of consciousness that arise in the mind, we form a conceptual interpretation of our world, and on the basis of this interpretation we engage in activities. In this empowerment, we purify these activities and the faculties of the body used to perform them. The five faculties of the mouth, arms, legs, anus, and the supreme faculty, are realised as the five *Male Wrathful Deities*. The corresponding five activities of speaking, taking, going, defaecating, and both urinating and emitting vital fluids, are realised as the five *Female Wrathful Deities*. This phase corresponds to the naming of the child.

Male Wrathful Deity	Faculty
Vighnantaka	Mouth
Prajñantaka	Arms
Padmantaka	Legs
Yamantaka	Anus
Ushnisha	Supreme

Female Wrathful Deity	Action
Stambhaki	Speaking
Manaki	Taking and Holding
Jambhaki	Coming and Going
Anantavirya	Defaecating
Atinila	Urinating and Emitting Vital Fluids

Table 4-7: Deities of the Name Empowerment

The Empowerments to Achieve Vajra-Wisdom

This final group of empowerments works with the subtlest level of the mind. It cuts through the gross conceptual mind and focuses on the very foundation from which all appearances arise. This class of experiences correlates to the appearances arising during the state of blissful absorption.

Permission Empowerment

Underlying every moment of mental activity is a subtle layer or cognition; a mere appearance and a subtle awareness. Within the dualistic mind they appear as subject and object, but ultimately they are inseparable. When contemplating the nature of the subjective aspect of the pristine awareness aggregate and the objective aspect of the consciousness element, we purify them into the non-dual primordial wisdom of *Vajrasattva and Prajñaparamita* in union. This phase corresponds to educating the child.

Deity	Wisdom
Vajrasattva	Aggregate of Primordial Wisdom
Prajñaparamita	Element of Conventional Wisdom

Table 4-8: Deities of the Permission Empowerment

Additional Transmissions and Commitments

After receiving all seven empowerments, we are granted permission to enter the Kalachakra Generation Stage. To help us practice as effectively as possible, the vajra master bestows a number of additional transmissions and commitments to enhance and support our practice. The essence of these commitments was included within the pledges already presented, but is spelled out here in order to strengthen our mindfulness of it.

Transmission of the Kalachakra Mantra

As we will see in the coming chapters, the generation stage focuses primarily on the practice of Deity Yoga. Part of this practice is the recitation of mantras that correspond to different deities in the enlightened mandala. These mantras are used to purify the subtle winds and bring the mind to a more subtle state of consciousness.

Before we recite a mantra, it is traditional to first receive its transmission from our vajra master. This transmission bestows on us the blessings of the lineage, as well as introducing us to the sound of the mantra. During the ceremony we receive the essence mantras which represent the definitive nature of the mandala and by learning them, we are granted permission to work with all the mantras used in the Kalachakra system.

Name	Mantra
Essence Mantra of Kalachakra	OM SHRI KALACHAKRA HUNG HUNG PHAT
Essence Mantra of Vishvamata	OM PHREM VISHVAMATA HUNG HUNG PHAT
Root Mantra of the Universe	OM HA KSHA MA LA VA RA YANG SOHA
Peaceful Mantra of Six Families	OM AH HUNG HO HANG KSHA
Wrathful Mantra of Six Families	OM HRANG HRING HRING HRUNG HRLING HRAH SOHA

Table 4-9: Kalachakra Mantras

The Secret Meaning of the Six Vajra Pledges

Although we are not yet empowered to engage in completion stage practices, it is important to begin developing an awareness of what this process entails. Understanding how the completion stage unfolds gives us insight into how the generation stage prepares us for more advanced practices. This helps the effectiveness of our present practice, as well as strengthening our aspiration to achieve enlightenment through the *Six Vajra Yogas*.

To this end, the vajra master briefly introduces us to the *Six Vajra Pledges*, which are included within the *Uncommon Pledges of Kalachakra*. Their purpose is to highlight the essence of each completion stage yoga. By developing familiarity with these pledges, we lay down the propensities to one day accomplish the final result of the Kalachakra Path. The six pledges are as follows:

1. The vajra pledge of the **Akshobya Family** is to "kill". This means to hold your awareness at the crown chakra, effectively cutting the gross winds of conceptual mind and drawing the subtle winds into the central channel. This pledge corresponds to the *Yoga of Withdrawal*.

2. The vajra pledge of the **Amoghasiddhi Family** is to "speak lies". This means to retain the winds in the central channel where they no longer support the conventional truth as seen by the dualistic mind. In this way, the hidden reality of our sacred truth is revealed. This truth is not known by ordinary consciousness, which is the meaning of speaking untruths. This pledge corresponds to the *Yoga of Stabilisation*.

3. The vajra pledge of the **Ratnasambhava Family** is to "steal". Recognising that Buddhahood is not something that can be given by another, through the power of your own faith and determination, you take hold of the subtle winds so they abide

within your navel chakra. This pledge corresponds to the *Yoga of Wind Control*.

4. The vajra pledge of the **Amitabha Family** is to "take another's partner". This means that in order to achieve enlightenment, you must rely on the union of immutable bliss and empty form. For this reason, you initially rely on a consort that is other than yourself, whether physical or visualised. Ultimately, both of these consorts are provisional and are eventually abandoned in favour of the Great Consort of Empty-Form that is inseparable from your own nature. This pledge corresponds to the *Yoga of Retention*.

5. The vajra pledge of the **Vairochana Family** is to "take meat and alcohol". This means to rely on the sixteen joys that are the result of practicing tummo. Through this practice, you refine your experience of bliss by igniting the inner fire, melting the subtle essences and bringing them to the tip of the central channel. These experiences of bliss are referred to as meat and alcohol. This pledge corresponds to the *Yoga of Recollection*.

6. The vajra pledge of the **Vajrasattva Family** is to "not disparage a woman's sexual organs". Instead of releasing the vital essences, you hold them at the tip of the lower opening. Here, the act of release is considered "disparaging" the immutable bliss generated from the union with a Great Consort of Empty-Form. This pledge corresponds to the *Yoga of Absorption*.

These pledges are metaphoric in nature and so should not be taken literally. When told we must "kill", the meaning is very specific and in no way suggests we should take the lives of sentient beings. When it comes to our external behaviour, we must always follow the *Twenty-Five Conducts of Kalachakra* where we are clearly prohibited from acts of killing, stealing and so forth.

Review of the Tantric Vows in Accordance with Kalachakra

As part of our commitment to the Action Family of Amoghasiddhi, we pledge to uphold the ethical discipline of the three vows. This includes the vows of individual liberation, the vows of a Bodhisattva and the vows of a tantric practitioner. While the essence of the tantric vows is to abandon ordinary perceptions of reality, this practice can be made difficult due to the level of obscurations present in our mind. To help us maintain our discipline, the Buddha defined *Fourteen Root Vows* and *Eight Branch Vows* that provide a more detailed framework for how we should behave.

The Fourteen Root Vows

The following behaviours should be abandoned completely:

1. **Disturbing the mind of one's vajra master:** This root vow is to not disparage or scorn any teacher from whom we have received empowerment, instruction or transmission in any of the classes of tantra. We should not show them contempt, disrespect or impoliteness, and avoid finding fault in them or believe their teachings to be of no benefit. A root downfall occurs if we intentionally act or speak in a harmful manner, we do not think to refrain from doing so during the act, and the master learns of our conduct and shows displeasure.

2. **Transgressing the words of one's vajra master:** This vow calls on us to not transgress or secretly commit one of the ten non-virtuous actions, not to despise the vajra master's teachings or to break a vow after being warned by the vajra master not to do so. A root downfall is committed if, despite knowing the vajra master is a holy being and that such behaviour would displease him, we continue to commit the act anyway, and if the action is motivated by a negative emotion.

3. **Showing contempt towards one's vajra family:** This root vow warns us to refrain from expressing anger towards those who have received teachings from the same tantric master, our vajra brothers and sisters. The teachings do not have to be received at the same time, nor do they need to be in the same class of tantra. This root vow is broken when we intend to harm them with body, speech or mind such as verbally abusing them about faults, mistakes or transgressions they may or may not have committed. The motivation must be one of hostility, anger or hatred. If one doesn't confess after eight hours of committing the downfall, the vow has been broken.

4. **Abandoning the mind of love:** This root vow reminds us to not abandon love and compassion. This is the heartfelt wish for all beings to be happy and attain the causes of happiness, and the wish for them to be free from suffering and its causes. It is considered a downfall if we abandon our love for a sentient being for more than a day. Losing love for someone for a shorter period is not a root downfall.

5. **Damaging one's Bodhicitta:** In this vow we are instructed to not abandon Bodhicitta in either its aspirational or engaged form. In the context of the Kalachakra Path, this vow specifically refers to not discarding the subtle essences that are the basis for actualising enlightenment through the sublime awareness of immutable bliss. Whenever a male or female experiences the uncontrolled release of energy that accompanies an ordinary experience of orgasm, the potency of our subtle essences is reduced. Therefore this vow focuses on shifting our attitude towards sexuality to safeguard our subtle energy so it can be used in the completion stage practices. We should avoid as much as possible intentionally causing the loss of vital fluids.

6. **Criticising philosophical tenets:** This vow instructs us to abandon bias between the teachings of sutra and tantra. We commit a downfall if, out of anger or sectarianism, we fail to accept that the view of sublime emptiness presented in the Third Turning of the Wheel of Dharma is the same as that described in the Tantras. The essential meaning of this vow is to always maintain a non-sectarian approach that incorporates all of the Buddha's teachings into a cohesive system free from contradictions.

7. **Proclaiming secrets to those who are unripe:** This vow is to not disclose the secret and profound teachings to those who would find it difficult to comprehend, such as the teachings describing the practices to produce the blissful awareness of the completion stage. The essential meaning of this vow is to always be mindful of how information could be received so we do not create the conditions for misconceptions to arise.

8. **Despising one's aggregates:** Abuse of the five aggregates (which include our physical body and the factors which make up our mind-stream) occurs when we practice activities such as extreme fasting or asceticism, or subject ourselves to undue mental stress. If we harm or abuse our aggregates we weaken our ability to use them as the path to enlightenment. A root downfall is committed if we purposefully harm our body or mind, knowing full well that our actions will prevent us from practicing the completion stage.

9. **Making others uncertain about the Sacred Dharma:** This vow instructs us to hold a view that accords with the definitive teachings of the Mahayana as presented by the Buddha. While we may use provisional explanations to help sentient beings develop an understanding of the ultimate truth, we must never stop trying to establish a direct realisation of our Buddha-nature.

10. **Holding deceitful love:** This vow refers to speaking loving words to others while cultivating malice or ill-intent in our mind. A root downfall is committed if we are hypocritical in our practice, for example reciting texts and attending rituals without sincere faith, and deceitfully acting in ways contrary to our commitments.

11. **Developing self-fabricated concepts about the ultimate nature of reality:** This root vow is concerned with ensuring we do not rely on a dualistic understanding of sublime emptiness. We should always remember that to directly experience suchness, we must transcend the consciousness and abide in the non-dual awareness of immutable bliss. We commit a downfall if we believe our conceptual understanding of the ultimate truth is the same as the ultimate truth itself.

12. **Speaking about the faults of those who are pure:** This root vow reminds us not to discourage people from tantric practices in which they have faith, as long as they are suitably qualified and have received the appropriate empowerment. A downfall occurs when we specifically deride, judge or speak about the faults of practitioners with some accomplishment in tantric practice out of an afflicted mind of jealousy.

13. **Abandoning the sacred substances:** Here we vow to not refuse the specially consecrated offerings of a tantric activity because of wrong views. Furthermore, we also pledge not to greedily indulge in them either. Some tantric practices involve the tasting of specially consecrated alcohol and meat, substances which symbolise the aggregates, bodily elements and sometimes the energy winds. It is a root downfall to consider these substances as disgusting and to refuse them on the grounds of extreme views such as being a vegetarian. It is also a downfall to overindulge in their consumption.

14. **Disparaging women:** This root vow instructs us to not disparage women, who are considered the nature of wisdom in tantra. The aim of Kalachakra is to attain immutable bliss in order to remove the obstacles to enlightenment and working with a consort is vital for achieving this result. It is a root downfall to belittle or consider a specific woman, women in general or a female Buddha-figure to be inferior in any way. We also commit a downfall if we give a low opinion or direct contempt towards a woman with the intention of putting her down or putting down women in general.

Eight Branch Vows

The following eight behaviours should be avoided as much as possible:

1. **Relying on an unqualified consort:** The first of these branch vows instructs us only to practice with a consort who has three qualities: they must have received empowerment, must uphold tantric vows and must also have trained in tantric practices. Most importantly they should not regard ordinary sex and orgasmic release as something spiritual, or as a path to enlightenment. A downfall also occurs when a partner has been coerced into sexual union either by psychological pressures such as flattery or by force, and also if circumstances are inappropriate such as sickness or obligations to keep other vows restrict such conduct.

2. **Entering into union without maintaining an awareness of emptiness:** This vow states that we should only enter sexual union (whether it be a physical or visualised consort) if we can abide by the three recognitions of regarding our body as the deity, our speech as the mantra of the deity and our mind as primordial wisdom, while maintaining blissful awareness of

emptiness. A downfall occurs if our pure perception falters, especially if we purposefully cause orgasmic release or experience it unintentionally.

3. **Demonstrating tantric implements and practices to those who are unsuitable:** This includes disclosing or showing images of tantric deities, tantric texts, mudras or objects such as one's vajra and bell to people who have not received empowerment when it then causes them to react with a negative view towards tantric practices. Our own practice is greatly hindered if we allow others to deride the practices or improperly use these objects, so it is always better to prevent misunderstanding wherever possible.

4. **Creating conflict during an offering feast or ceremony:** This vow reminds us not to argue during an offering feast or other tantric ceremony. We should be focused on visualising ourselves as deities abiding in the blissful awareness of emptiness so we can make offerings for the benefit of all beings. If we agitate each other during such a ritual, we lose our visualisations and cultivate negative states of mind, making our participation ineffective and potentially harmful to our spiritual path. It is best not to speak at all during a ritual, except for the mantra and chanting of the practice.

5. **Leading astray those with genuine faith:** This vow instructs us to not give false answers to questions asked with sincerity or by those with faith. When someone who is suitable and has the appropriate empowerment asks about tantric practices, a downfall occurs if we avoid the question by either changing the subject or answering on a different level, consciously deceiving the person. However, there is no downfall if we give a mistaken answer out of ignorance.

6. **Spending long periods of time with those who do not believe in the vajra path:** This specifically refers to someone who has contempt for tantra or tantric practice, or anyone who writes it off as a waste of time. Staying for a long time with such persons, who are only focused upon individual liberation, can discourage us from our path. There is no downfall if there is a real need to stay in such a person's abode or if we have no choice about whom we live with, for instance if we have to spend time in a hospital. In this case we should just keep our tantric practices private.

7. **Boasting about your spiritual accomplishments:** This vow tells us to be humble and to avoid boasting about being a highly accomplished practitioner when we have only done a small amount of tantric practice. The downfall occurs when we think of ourselves as a great yogi or yogini, possessing supernatural powers, insights and so forth, and then announce this to other people.

8. **Teaching the Dharma to those who have no faith in the teachings:** This vow specifically refers to giving secret tantric teachings and instruction to those who don't have the appropriate empowerment or who lack faith and respect for the teachings. It is a downfall to disclose teachings to those who have no interest or belief in the teachings, or even to those who have received an empowerment but have no genuine faith.

Conclusion

We conclude the empowerment ceremony by strengthening our commitment to practice devotion to the vajra master and to uphold the vows and pledges they have bestowed upon us. We should feel we have fully entered into a vajra relationship with the master and therefore, from this point forward, we should act in accordance with the advice as presented previously in the text *Fifty Verses of Guru Devotion*.

MAINTAINING AND RESTORING VOWS

The tantric commitments we make during an empowerment ceremony are the lifeblood of our Vajrayana practice. They are what provides us with the pure perception to make the skilful methods of Tantra such powerful causes for achieving enlightenment. Without the vows, our practice will have no long term benefit. Therefore once we receive the vows we should do our best to maintain them as best we can. This involves knowing how to (1) prevent our vows from degenerating, (2) recognise the degree of damage that has occurred and (3) restore our vows through practices of purification.

How to Prevent Vows from Being Broken

Tantric vows are easily broken as most rely on constantly maintaining a pure view. They not only relate to what we do and say, but also how our mind manifests at any given moment, making them very difficult to keep. Even the great tantric master Atisha confessed that his breaches of the tantric vows were as common as the patter of raindrops, whereas he only broke his Bodhisattva vows on rare occasions and never did he break his Pratimoksha vows. As a result, a day and night never passed without him confessing and performing purification. We should therefore realise that taking, breaking and mending vows are the means by which we progress along the path.

How do we then train ourselves not to break vows? As the great scholar-yogi Ngari Panchen stated, we should strive to know and understand the vows, to develop devotion to the guru and to respect all beings with an awareness of their underlying enlightened nature. We should especially strive to maintain constant mindfulness and vigilant awareness.

In particular, there are four doors which lead to downfalls that should be carefully guarded, just as we would guard the doors of a room filled with gold to prevent thieves from stealing it. The four doors are:

1. The door of disrespect
2. The door of ignorance
3. The door of lack of conscientiousness
4. The door of uncontrolled mental afflictions

In order to stop a thief from breaking in, we need to be able to recognise them. Similarly, to guard the second door we must know what the vows are. To guard the remaining doors, we need to realise when our mind is being swept away by disrespect, heedlessness or mental afflictions, and how to combat these afflictive states.

Remembering the vows can be difficult, let alone maintaining them. However we should not let ourselves become overwhelmed with the "duty" of keeping the vows, and instead try to keep in mind their essential points. The essence of the individual liberation vows is to avoid harming others, while the crucial point of the Bodhisattva vows is to try our best to always have undiscriminating love and compassion for all sentient beings. At the same time we should recognise that we are all enlightened in our true nature and everything we perceive is a display of enlightened form. We should always try to recall this kind of pure perception, especially towards the tantric master. This is the essence of tantric vows.

How to Recognise Different Levels of Downfalls

Damaging the higher tantric vows is almost inevitable and is the very nature of the path. We must therefore learn what it means to damage a vow and how to repair it. A breach of a vow has occurred when four factors are present:

1. **Recognition:** You knowingly contradict a vow.
2. **Intention:** You intentionally break it.

3. **Action:** You carry through with the action, whether of body, speech or mind.

4. **Completion:** This action yields a specific result.

The severity of the breach increases once a prescribed time for confession has passed in which you have not generated a sense of regret towards the action. All four factors would be present, if for example you killed an insect with the intention of harming it, knowing you had vowed not to do so, yet you remained unburdened by a guilty conscience. However, whether all four factors need to be present in order for a vow to be broken does vary according to the specific vow.

There are several different levels of breaches, the worst being the defeat of a vow, when all four factors are present and a specific amount of time has passed with no feeling of remorse. A root downfall follows when the four factors are present and one fails to confess before a span of four hours has passed. There are also major and minor faults, when the four factors are incomplete.

How to Restore Broken Vows

There are many methods for restoring broken vows. Tantric purification methods are the most powerful and can be used to purify faults in any of the three vow categories, examples of which can be found in Ngari Panchen's *Perfect Conduct: Ascertaining the Three Vows*. They generally relate to the type of empowerments one has received or the severity of one's transgressions.

Restoration Based on the Four Empowerments

The way to restore vows is generally related to which of the four empowerments you have received. This is especially relevant if we receive the empowerments one at a time before engaging in a particular part of the practice.

If the vows deteriorate after receiving the vase or secret empowerment, we can recite the mantra of the Kalachakra deity related to those specific vows 36,000 times. Other methods are available depending on the individual's capacity and level of practice. We should also be sure to follow our guru's advice regarding the most suitable purification practice.

If deterioration occurs after the wisdom or word empowerment we should confess the fault and engage in purification practice until a sign of purification is seen such as auspicious dreams, visions and increased physical pliancy or clarity of mind. Nothing has the power to repair this other than entering into strict retreat, for example in an isolated place and meditating upon the union of the generation and completion stages. When signs of purification are seen, we should re-enter the mandala and receive the vows and empowerments either from our guru or through self-initiation, taking care not to sit with senior practitioners or receive any offerings for ourselves.

Restoration Based on Time

The conditions required to restore a vow get progressively more involved with time. If a full day has passed, more than just confession is required. A specific tantric purification ritual needs to be performed, such as the Vajrasattva practice or tsok offering. A genuine offering that entails considerable personal sacrifice, financial or otherwise, is also required to show regret for the transgression. If a month passes, in addition to the purification ritual, an offering of even greater personal sacrifice must be made. This may involve offering our possessions to the guru or the Three Jewels, represented by the Sangha community. Confession occurs through the offering.

After a year the requirement is more extensive and costly and you may need to symbolically give up or offer something as precious as your son or daughter to the deities of the mandala and to the guru. After two years, as even your belongings and family are no longer sufficient, you would be required to offer yourself to the service of the guru and the Buddha-Dharma without the slightest concern for one's own life. Complete restoration of the vow is not possible in this lifetime after a period of three years, meaning you cannot possess or repair the complete tantric vows in this lifetime. You can still, however, purify the negative karma accumulated from breaking the vow and avoid being reborn in realms such as the vajra hell.

Other Methods of Restoration

Several other methods of restoration are described in detail in the text Perfect Conduct, for example, using the six syllables that symbolise purification of the six realms of samsaric existence. Another is to visualise the syllable KHAM at the navel-centre while you imagine your negativities and obscurations as a mass of flesh at the heart. By igniting the fire of inner heat at the navel chakra, they are burnt away. We can also perform prostrations and recall our Yidam deity in order to confess and purify our negativities.

An alternative is to invoke Vajrasattva, who represents the essential nature of all tantric deities. His mantra should be recited with faith in Vajrasattva as the support for purification, along with sincere regret and resolution not to commit the fault again. You should be familiar with this practice from the corresponding chapter in Book Two.

ADVICE FOR RECEIVING EMPOWERMENT

In this world, participation in a *Kalachakra Empowerment Ceremony* is an exceedingly rare and precious opportunity. It requires an enormous degree of effort to bring the necessary karmic conditions together to bestow these empowerments authentically. Recognising this, if we are fortunate enough to have the chance arise, we should do whatever we can to attend and to take advantage of the countless blessings that such an event offers. To help you make the most of the experience, I would like to offer the following advice:

Vows are Not a Burden

When attending a Kalachakra empowerment, many Western students have told me that they do not feel "ready" to take the tantric vows.

They have anxiety over receiving them and then breaking them, fearing that they will have to endure immense suffering. As a consequence, they think it is better to reject the vows until a time when they are confident they will not damage them. This type of thinking is however flawed in a number of ways.

While it is definitely good to be serious about one's ethical discipline, we should not let our fear rob us of the incredible opportunity that vows provide. By focusing on the negatives of breaking vows, we forget the limitless benefits that come from keeping them. Even if we can only uphold the tantric vows for the time of the empowerment ceremony, generating them in our mindstream accumulates more merit than billions of lifetimes of virtuous activities undertaken without them. To think that you are somehow doing yourself a favour by not taking the vows is misguided.

Another problem with this attitude is that it is not realistic. The only people who can purely hold tantric vows without damaging them are highly realised Bodhisattvas who are able to rest their mind at all times in a direct realisation of suchness. This means that ninety-nine percent of all tantric practitioners are working with vows that are repeatedly damaged. The only way to achieve authentically pure vows is to first develop the aspiration to hold our vows purely and make effort to continually purify and refresh our vows until we achieve our goal. As long as our aspiration is sincere, it doesn't matter how many times we break the vows. Everytime we fall down, we get back on our feet.

In this way, vows are not a burden but a gift which supports our practice, helping us to actualise our greatest potential. Rather than placing all your attention on whether or not you can uphold a vow, focus on your aspiration to do so. Strengthen your determination by contemplating the benefits of holding the vows and recognise the disadvantages of not holding them. If the opportunity then arises for you to receive them, don't hesitate to take them.

Empowerment is a Private Matter

Kalachakra empowerments are known for attracting many people. Within a particularly large gathering, it is easy to forget that the empowerment process is an entirely individual experience between you and the vajra master. Although there may be two hundred thousand people sitting in close proximity, we can be certain that two hundred thousand different experiences are unfolding.

Understanding this, we need to be very careful not to project onto others our own ideas about what it means to receive the empowerments. Instead of worrying about what those around you are doing, try to focus on what is occurring in your own mind. Do your best to cultivate a pure motivation and try to maintain your awareness of the guru throughout the process. If you can do this, you open yourself to the blessings he has to offer.

Nurture a Child-like Attitude

It is common for students whose minds are intellectually oriented to encounter many obstacles when taking empowerments. Out of an intense desire to understand everything in detail, they can feel uncomfortable with the uncertainty related to a tantric ritual and experience considerable tension and anxiety.

It is certainly beneficial to study the structure of the ritual beforehand, but we must remember that when the time comes to receive the empowerment, we should do our best to release our conceptual fixations. Try to nurture an almost child-like attitude that is free from expectations and feel an openness to whatever may arise. Consider the way a young child is filled with wonder and excitement when experiencing something for the first time. This is the kind of emotion we want to generate when our guru shows us the nature of our mind. Don't worry if you have trouble following every detail, the most important aspect is what you feel, not what you know.

Take the Empowerments as Many Times as You Can

Another common misconception that people have is that an empowerment only needs to be taken once. This idea tends to arise when people view the empowerment ceremony as merely an initiation taken at the start of the path in order to receive permission to practice. This misconception fails to recognise that the nature of empowerment is to strengthen the bond between our present mind and the enlightened reality of our Buddha-nature. The more we strengthen this bond, the closer we come to achieving our goal and for this reason we should take every possible opportunity to receive the empowerments repeatedly from an authentic vajra master.

REVIEW OF KEY POINTS

- Before practicing the Kalachakra generation stage it is necessary to empower the mind. An empowerment is an experiential shift or transformation that allows qualities to arise. They are experienced in three ways: (1) realisation; (2) understanding; or (3) feeling.

- Empowerment ceremonies are designed to create the conditions for specific empowerment experiences to occur. In the Jonang Tradition there are two ceremonies which correspond to the generation and completion stages of Kalachakra: (1) the Seven Empowerments of a Growing Child and (2) the Four Higher Empowerments.

- The ceremony for the Seven Empowerments of a Growing Child is divided into six parts: (1) preliminaries; (2) receiving the tantric commitments; (3) introduction to the enlightened mandala; (4) the actual empowerments; (5) additional transmissions and commitments and (6) the conclusion.

- The preliminaries are designed to help establish the correct attitude and motivation for receiving the tantric commitments. They consist of two parts: (1) removing external and internal obstacles and (2) generating refuge and Bodhicitta.

- The essence of Vajrayana ethics is to: (1) maintain awareness of one's pure and definitive nature; (2) maintain the supreme motivation of Bodhicitta; and (3) always work for the benefit of sentient beings.

- There are three sets of commitments which form the ethical discipline specifically presented in the Kalachakra Tantra: (1) The Common Pledges of the Five Buddha Families which establish our view; (2) The Uncommon Pledges of Kalachakra which establish how we should meditate; and (3) The Twenty-Five Conducts of Kalachakra which establish how we should behave.

- The nineteen pledges related to the Five Buddha Families can be summarised as: (1) taking refuge in the ultimate nature of reality; (2) remembering its aspects; (3) removing temporary obscurations which limit that reality; (4) clearly distinguishing how it manifests; and (5) acting in accordance with that reality.

- The provisional pledges related to the Six Buddha Families of Kalachakra are: (1) unify the body, speech and mind through the practice of Deity Yoga; (2) make extensive offerings through the practice of Tsok Feasts; (3) maintain mindfulness of the purity of phenomena by working with the ten impure substances;

(4) reduce grasping onto ordinary bliss by offering all blissful experiences to the enlightened mandala; (5) recognise the purity of bliss by working with a visualised consort; and (6) cultivate the aspiration to abide in the union of immutable bliss and empty-form by maintaining mindfulness of the sacred aspect of sexuality.

- The definitive pledges of the Six Buddha Families are: (1) unify the body, speech and mind through the practice of the Six Vajra Yogas; (2) experience all perceptions as empty-forms by bringing the ten winds into the central channel; (3) gather all subtle essences into the central channel; (4) release grasping onto bliss by working with the practice of Inner Fire; (5) gather all subtle essences at the lower tip of the central channel by practicing with a consort; and (6) abide in the union of immutable bliss and empty-form.

- The Twenty-Five Conducts of Kalachakra can be summarised as: (1) avoid any sort of violence towards sentient beings; (2) reduce activities which fuel afflicted states of mind; (3) abandon afflicted motivations for killing; (4) cultivate respect and appreciation for those who are engaged in virtue and (5) focus on genuine happiness by cultivating self-control.

- Clarity and luminosity are the two aspects of Buddha-nature. They are represented in the enlightened mandala as (1) the objective environment that is experienced and (2) the subjective deities that inhabit that environment.

- There are seven empowerments used as the basis for purifying the four states of experience and creating the causes for achieving the four vajras: (1) water; (2) crown; (3) silk ribbon; (4) vajra and bell; (5) conduct; (6) name; and (7) permission. The first and second produce Vajra-Body; the third and fourth produce Vajra-Speech; the fifth and sixth produce Vajra-Mind and the seventh produces Vajra-Wisdom.

- The Six Vajra Pledges are to: (1) kill; (2) speak lies; (3) steal; (4) take another's partner; (5) take meat and alcohol; and (6) not disparage a woman's sexual organs.

- The Fourteen Root Vows are to abandon: (1) disturbing the mind of one's vajra master; (2) transgressing the words of one's vajra master; (3) showing contempt towards one's vajra family; (4) abandoning the mind of love; (5) damaging one's Bodhicitta; (6) criticising philosophical tenets; (7) proclaiming secrets to those who are unripe; (8) despising one's aggregates; (9) making others uncertain about the Sacred Dharma; (10) holding deceitful love; (11) developing self-fabricated concepts about the ultimate nature of reality; (12) speaking about the faults of those who are pure; (13) abandoning the sacred substances; and (14) disparaging women.

- The Eight Branch Vows are to avoid: (1) relying on an unqualified consort; (2) entering into union without maintaining an awareness of emptiness; (3) demonstrating tantric implements and practices to those who are unsuitable; (4) creating conflict during an offering feast or ceremony; (5) leading astray those with genuine faith; (6) spending long periods of time with those who do not believe in the vajra path; (7) boasting about your spiritual accomplishments; and (8) teaching the Dharma to those who have no faith in the teachings.

- Once you have received the tantric vows and commitments, you should know how to (1) prevent your vows from degenerating, (2) recognise the degree of damage that has occurred and (3) restore your vows through practices of purification.

- There are four doors that we should be mindful of to ensure that we do not break our vows: (1) disrespect; (2) ignorance; (3) lack of conscientiousness and (4) uncontrolled mental afflictions.

- In order to break a tantric root vow, four conditions must be present: (1) recognition; (2) intention; (3) action and (4) completion.

- Vows can be restored through: (1) confession; (2) making offerings; (3) reciting mantras; (4) practicing Vajrasattva meditation or (5) retaking the empowerments.

CHAPTER FIVE

Purifying Appearances with the Kalachakra Generation Stage

Buddhist Tantra provides a wealth of specialised techniques. They include the visualisation of meditational deities, the recitation of mantras, and physical yogas for working with the subtle body. Many of these practices are not exclusive to Buddhism, as the vast majority can also be found in Non-Buddhist traditions of Tantra. Looking only at their superficial similarities, we may conclude that there is no difference between the two, but this is not the case. Non-Buddhist Tantra has the capacity to produce incredibly refined states of samadhi, but unlike the practices of Buddhist Tantra, they fail to generate the ultimate state of enlightenment.

The type of mind present when practicing is what defines a practice as Buddhist. Without specific and necessary requirements, Buddhist Tantra cannot be practiced authentically and consequently, the result of full enlightenment will be unachievable. Therefore, before we venture into the unique practices of the Kalachakra Path, it is important to conduct a personal inventory to ensure we have gathered together the right conditions.

Our first requirement is the establishment of an authentic Buddhist view through study, reflection and meditation on the common teachings shared with the Sutra Tradition. This foundation creates a strong feeling of *renunciation* towards cyclic existence, accompanied by a powerful desire to abandon suffering. The mind of *Bodhicitta* should be cultivated to such a degree that it has become your primary motivation in life and the teachings of *emptiness* and *Buddha-nature* need to be very familiar to your mind. While a direct realisation of these two aspects is not necessary, you must have a firm belief in their accurate description of conventional and ultimate truth.

The second requirement is a very strong *aspiration to practice Tantra* for the specific purpose of achieving enlightenment. The strength of your aspiration comes from reflecting on the unique characteristics of the Vajrayana and understanding how this path can produce enlightenment within the span of a single lifetime.

Entering into a vajra relationship with an authentic vajra master by receiving the *tantric vows and commitments* is the third requirement. These commitments provide the context for all tantric practice, ensuring that your conduct will lead you to the result you seek. Only through maintaining these vows purely can the transformative power of these techniques be fully utilised.

The fourth and final requirement is to be introduced to the enlightened mandala and granted permission to practice Tantra by receiving the *generation stage empowerments* from your vajra master. This process makes certain that you have all the necessary karmic propensities needed to effectively progress along the tantric path.

With all of these conditions successfully gathered, you are qualified to practice the Kalachakra generation stage. If, however, you feel they may be lacking, I highly recommend concentrating on the common preliminaries. In the meantime, while there is no danger in studying the generation practices to become familiar with their structure, you should refrain from putting them into practice until the four requirements are complete.

THE GENERATION STAGE

To establish a context for the specific practices presented in the following chapter, we will now look at some of the general features of the generation stage. As this is a considerably vast subject, focusing on the essence will help us develop a working model and provide us with a good starting point. If you desire to study this material in greater detail, the extensive writings of lineage masters such as Kunkhyen Dolpopa or Jetsun Taranatha provide a wealth of information.

Although the generation stage is not emphasised by the Jonang tradition, its role in our practice is still vital. The reason for this can be understood by considering the evolution of our view up to this point. Prior to our practice of Guru Yoga, our ordinary perspective looked to the field of refuge for help and guidance. We aspired to emulate their achievement and prayed to them with respect and devotion.

As we moved on to Guru Yoga, this relationship became internalised and we recognised that the guru was ultimately inseparable from our own Buddha-nature. While we no longer looked outwards for salvation, a sense of separation between our ordinary sense of self and the potential of our most sacred truth remained. With our dominant identity still firmly planted in samsara, we made requests to our ultimate guru to bestow his blessings upon us.

Now as we enter the generation stage, our practice seeks to close the gap between who we think we are and who we actually are. Our goal is to shift our sense of identity from the illusory self that is projected by our ignorance, to a concept of self that arises from wisdom. To do this, we use the method of working with the Kalachakra deity as our Yidam.

The Tibetan term *yidam* is often translated as "meditational deity", whereas the actual meaning is much more profound. The first part is derived from *yid* which means "mind" and the second part *dam*, means "to bind". When taken together, they communicate the idea of "a method to bind the mind". Through meditating on the form of Kalachakra, we familiarise our mind with the qualities of our Buddha-nature and by transferring our concept of self onto these qualities, we effectively bind our mind to that nature. We no longer see ourselves as inferior samsaric beings and instead realise that ultimately, we *are* Kalachakra.

The following chapter will examine the actual practice with a Yidam, so for now we need only remember that in a Highest Yoga Tantra such as Kalachakra, there is no separation between self and Yidam; they are experienced as inseparable. Rather than visualising the Yidam in the space before us or above our crown, we generate ourselves as arising in the aspect of the Yidam. Learning to identify with this aspect more than our ordinary appearance of self and maintaining this awareness at all times is the main practice of the generation stage.

However, simply visualising yourself in a different form does not necessarily mean you are practicing the generation stage and therefore does not guarantee the result will lead to enlightenment. For our practice to be authentic, five conditions need to be fulfilled: (1) the practice must come from an *authentic source*; (2) it must be transmitted through an *authentic lineage*; (3) our view must be *rooted in emptiness*; (4) the practice must be *similar to the result* and (5) we must have *faith in its power*. Let's now look at each of these conditions in detail.

Authentic Source

Our minds have an incredible capacity to generate appearances. If I asked you to visualise a pink elephant with tiny white wings, you could do so with little difficulty, but our ability to do this merely illustrates a point and has no particular benefit otherwise. This same mind however, if channelled correctly through the appropriate practices, can bring us to enlightenment. Since it is impossible from our current perspective to know the potential of a specific practice, it is necessary to consider the source of the teachings. When practicing tantra, the source must always be a fully enlightened Buddha, for only a Buddha has realised the ultimate truth of reality and has the capacity to show others how to achieve it.

This means we need to focus our energy on the methods which have a scriptural foundation—the practices specifically described in the teachings by realised beings. In doing so we should be mindful of errors that may have arisen over time and do our best to refer back to the root texts wherever possible. Closely following these texts will give us the greatest confidence of achieving our desired result.

Authentic Lineage

Knowing that a practice has its roots in the words of an enlightened being is important, but scriptural understanding alone is not enough. We must also have received the teachings from an authentic lineage master who has actualised these teachings in their own mindstream. Only such a teacher has the capacity to transmit the blessings of an unbroken lineage, connecting us back to the original source. These are the blessings which create the conditions for realisations to arise in our own mind.

In addition to the blessings bestowed on us, the lineage is also the source of the profound pith instructions which describe exactly *how* we should practice. These instructions have been repeatedly tested over hundreds of years and can therefore be trusted to bring benefit to our mind. By looking at the history of a lineage, we can see the results that the lineage produces. If a practice lacks this sort of proof, then you should investigate further before making it your main practice.

Rooted in Emptiness

Generating oneself as the Yidam is not possible until our conventional view of self is fully dissolved. We do this by meditating on emptiness before we manifest in the aspect of Kalachakra. This single step is often the defining factor which distinguishes a Buddhist practice from a Non-Buddhist practice.

Attempting to practice tantra without an awareness of emptiness is essentially replacing one deluded appearance for another, like imagining oneself as a dog or a chicken. Instead of the practice creating the causes to realise our sacred truth, it only serves to reinforce our self-grasping and perpetuate our suffering in samsara.

Similar to the Result

When we practice in accordance with the sutras, we are training in methods which are distinct from the results we want to achieve. For instance, in order to achieve a wealth of resources, we practice generosity; to achieve beauty, we practice patience; and to achieve a human rebirth, we practice ethical discipline. This is much like a farmer planting seeds with the aspiration to one day grow a bountiful harvest.

In tantra, the approach is quite different. Authentic generation stage practice is always similar in nature to the desired result. This is like an actor rehearsing a play in preparation for a live performance. The rehearsal may lack the full experience of the production, but it mimics the final result, providing a basis for developing familiarity.

To further illustrate this principle we can consider how the Vajrayana leads to the resultant state of a fully enlightened Buddha. Whereas the completion stage emphasises producing the Dharmakaya truth body, the generation stage is specifically modelled on the way a Buddha generates emanations and therefore acts as a cause for producing the Rupakaya form bodies. It does this through the purification of three types of experience:

1. **Birth:** This refers to the way a Buddha manifests in the mind of sentient beings and is the process in which an emanation takes form to bring benefit to others. Determined by our karmic conditioning, we currently experience this process without any control. Through the generation stage practices, we purify birth by learning how to generate our mind in different aspects such

as Kalachakra Yab-Yum or any of the other 636 deities of the Enlightened Mandala. By meditating on these forms, we habituate our mind to manifest in these ways.

2. **Death:** The form bodies of a Buddha are impermanent in nature. They arise spontaneously in dependence on the needs of sentient beings and dissolve back into the enlightened mind when they are no longer needed. This process allows a Buddha to constantly adapt to causes and conditions so they can bring the most benefit to others. In our present experience, this type of dissolution occurs each night when we fall asleep or during the process of death at the end of our lives. However, since we lack awareness when it occurs, we fall into ignorance and cannot control our subsequent manifestation. The generation stage practices purify death by showing us how to dissolve appearances back into emptiness, helping us reduce our grasping onto appearances and allowing us to maintain our awareness at all times.

3. **Bardo:** This represents the period between the formation of an emanation and its dissolution. During this time, an emanation engages in enlightened activities such as generating grosser emanation forms or performing the four activities of pacifying, increasing, magnetising and subjugating. In the generation stage practices we train in these activities by sending out light rays to fulfil the needs of sentient beings. This process purifies the various bardos and habituates our mind to virtue thereby accumulating vast quantities of merit.

Within a single session of generation stage practice, it is common to experience the process of birth, death and bardo as cycles embedded within cycles. For instance, at the beginning of the practice, we dissolve our ordinary self to establish emptiness and then generate ourselves in the form of the principal deity. This deity in turn emanates a range of further deities, each of which engages in enlightened activities. When they are done, we dissolve the secondary deities back into the main deity. This process can be repeated many times within a single session until finally we dissolve the main deity before manifesting our ordinary aspect. Due to this multi-layered approach, the generation stage practices can be highly complex in nature, which serves to refine the state of our mind and provide us with an immeasurable capacity to benefit others.

Faith in the Practice

The last condition that must be present to make your generation stage authentic is strong faith in the power of the practices to lead to the result of enlightenment. Without faith, the act of generating yourself as a deity is similar to daydreaming and while you may become very skilled at it, there is no real belief in the process and therefore it will fail to have an impact on your mind. This would be like an actor playing different roles. They become immersed in each for a time, but they are always aware that they are only acting and therefore they never truly abandon their ordinary sense of identity. This is appropriate for acting, but it defeats the purpose of practicing tantra.

This is why it is important to study and reflect on the theories which inform the practice of tantra. Having greater awareness of the reasoning behind the practices will help you develop the confidence to completely let go of your ordinary view. Although you may continue to manifest as your ordinary self, you stop projecting a sense of reality onto it and instead see your regular life as illusory in nature, like a recurring dream. When this stage is reached, your mind will be ripe to actually experience your enlightened nature.

THE ENLIGHTENED MANDALA OF KALACHAKRA

The heart of the Kalachakra generation stage is the enlightened mandala which describes the pure manifestations of the enlightened mind as seen from the perspective of conventional reality. By familiarising ourselves with the details of this mandala we can transform every aspect of our conventional experience into pure perception. As this view is modelled on the actual nature of reality, it functions as a perfect transition between the illusory nature of conventional truth and the truly-established nature of ultimate truth.

When compared with other systems of Highest Yoga Tantra, the Enlightened Mandala of Kalachakra is easily the most complex mandala with a staggering 636 deities distributed throughout six nested mandalas. Understandably, this intricacy can be daunting for beginners but the key to unlocking its benefits is to concentrate on the essential meaning of each section and slowly build the details over time.

In the sections to follow, we will examine the mandala in a step-by-step fashion. As a full exposition of every detail and their corresponding meaning is beyond the scope of this book, the essence of each element will be introduced to provide enough information to understand the context for the generation stage practices.

The Enlightened Environment

We start our study of the mandala by first dissecting the objective environment which acts as the container for the host of deities. As we discuss each aspect, keep in mind that the Kalachakra mandala as a whole represents the *totality of all experience*—everything we can potentially know is included, without a single exception. This totality corresponds to the pervasive quality of Buddha-nature and while we may experience a seemingly infinite variety of illusory manifestations, there is nothing that is not grounded in this ultimate reality.

Within this context, the enlightened mandala can be divided into two sections: (1) the external support of sentient beings and (2) the internal support of enlightened beings. On the path, we rely on the first to generate great compassion which is the basis of Bodhicitta. Once we establish the mind that seeks enlightenment for the benefit of others, we then rely on the second to help us remove our obscurations and actualise our aspiration. These two supports are represented by the universal mandala and the enlightened mansion.

The Universal Mandala

From the pervasive element of space arises the dark-blue wind element, followed by the red fire element, the white water element, and finally the yellow earth element. These are arranged as discs stacked on top of each other. Upon the foundation of the golden earth arises Mount Meru which has four colours; dark-blue in the east, red in the south, yellow in the west and white in the north. Surrounding the upper portion of Mount Meru is the Celestial Sphere through which the ten planets orbit. For a more detailed description of this universe, you can refer to the mandala offering as presented in Book Two.

From the perspective of a sentient being, this external universe appears to exist objectively from its own side, and is filled with countless types of phenomena. From the perspective of an enlightened being, however, none of these phenomena have ever existed as anything other than a sublime emptiness. Clearly distinguishing the two truths in this way, there are two types of phenomena—conventional and ultimate.

Conventionally there are separate phenomena such as mountains and rivers, which to an enlightened mind, are ultimately perceived as suchness. To refer to this inseparable nature, we can

UNIVERSE MANDALA

BODY MANDALA

SPEECH MANDALA

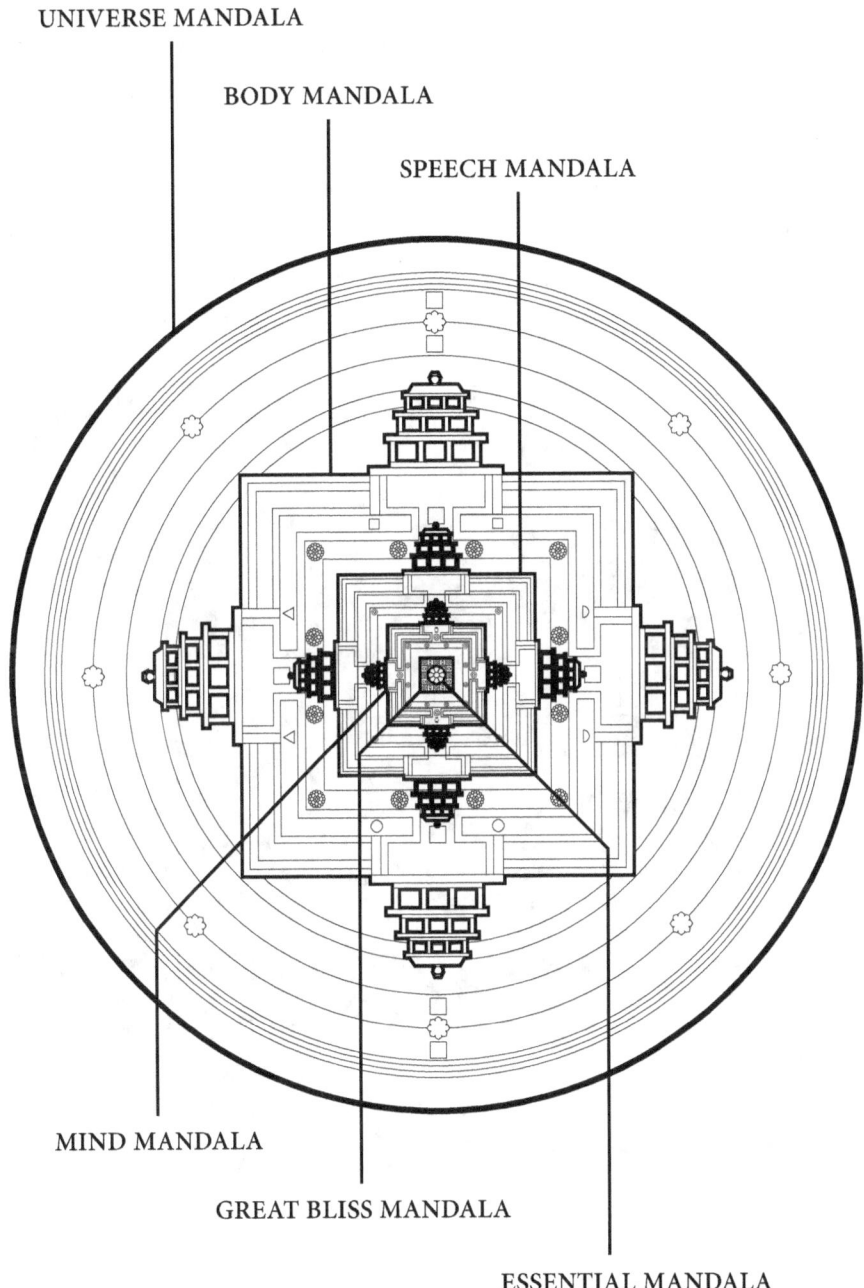

MIND MANDALA

GREAT BLISS MANDALA

ESSENTIAL MANDALA

call them *ultimate phenomena*, for instance, ultimate mountains or ultimate rivers. This naming convention is used as a skilful means to highlight the presence of the two truths in everything we experience.

When we incorporate this way of thinking into our practice, all phenomena become a basis for developing mindfulness of the two truths. If we look at a tree, we can acknowledge the conventional tree that appears to our deluded consciousness and also remember the ultimate tree, which is its true nature. It is this collection of ultimate phenomena that are included within the Enlightened Mandala of Kalachakra.

The Enlightened Mansion

At the top of Mount Meru, resting on the summit of the central peak, is a multicoloured lotus measuring 25,000 yojanas. The centre of this lotus is one-third of the overall size and has four discs corresponding to the moon, sun, rahu and kalagni. On top of this lotus seat rests the vajra ground measuring 50,000 yojanas in diameter. This ground represents the state of absorption of a Fully Matured Bodhisattva within which the Sambhogakaya manifestation of the Enlightened Mandala is actually experienced. This ground is divided into four quadrants in the same way as Mount Meru and as this colour scheme is used throughout the mandala, it is worth memorising the colour associated with each direction:

Direction	Colour	Buddha-Family
East	Dark-Blue	Action
South	Red	Jewel
North	White	Lotus
West	Yellow	Buddha
Centre-Above	Green	Vajra
Centre-Below	Blue	Vajra

Table 5-1: Mandala colour coding

You may have noticed that the directions are not presented in the order that many people are accustomed to. This is due to the symbolic nature of the enlightened mandala. During the process of generating the deities, this pattern of east, south, north then west occurs often. As each deity has a correlation within the subtle energetic body, the order that they are generated has a very subtle effect on the way our energy flows, which allows the generation of the mandala to prepare our subtle bodies for completion stage practice. We should therefore familiarise ourselves with this sequence.

Within the boundary of the vajra ground stands the *Enlightened Mansion of Kalachakra*. This magnificent structure is made of multi-coloured light and is home to the majority of the enlightened deities included within the mandala. The mansion itself is divided into four storeys representing the purification of the four states of experience. Moving from the ground floor upwards, and from the outside in, corresponds to achieving progressively more subtle states of experience. The following table summarises some of the general correlations of the enlightened mansion:

Jewel	Floor	State	Dimension	Mandala
Sangha	First	Waking	Nirmanakaya	Body
Dharma	Second	Dream		Speech
Buddha	Third	Deep-Sleep	Sambhogakaya	Mind
	Fourth	Blissful Absorption	Jñana-Dharmakaya	Great Bliss
			Svabhavikakaya	Essential

Table 5-2: Meanings of the Enlightened Mansion

As a support for practice, the enlightened mansion can be understood to represent the Three Jewels of Buddha, Dharma and Sangha which correspond to the enlightened body, speech and mind of a Buddha. When the enlightened mind is further divided into three aspects, we arrive at a total of five mandalas of deities: (1) the body mandala; (2) the speech mandala; (3) the mind mandala; (4) the great bliss mandala and (5) the essential mandala. We will first review the features of the environment for each of these mandalas before continuing with our presentation of the deities which abide in these environments.

The Body Mandala

The first floor of the enlightened mansion is home to the deities of the Body Mandala which represent the spiritual community that support your practice and help you to reveal your sublime nature. Its shape is a square cube measuring 50,000 yojanas on each side and the walls are made of five layers of light: yellow, white, red, dark-blue and green. The roof is the same colour as the ground it covers.

Four large, ornate gateways are on each side of the building and the outer ledges are adorned with beautiful ornaments and victory banners. In each gateway there is a chariot with a lotus on top, drawn by seven animals.

Animal	Direction	Colour
Pigs	East	Dark-Blue
Horses	South	Red
Snow Lions	North	White
Elephants	West	Yellow
Garuda	Above	Green
Eight-limbed Lions	Below	Blue

Table 5-3: Positioning of the gateway chariots

Inside the walls is a deity plinth with twelve lotuses resting atop twelve beings as mounts. Each lotus has twenty-eight petals organised in three concentric circles. The innermost circle has four petals, the middle circle has eight and the outer circle has sixteen.

Mount	Direction	Colour of Lotus
Hungry Ghost	Right of East	Red
Garuda	Left of East	Red
Deer	South-East	White
Sheep	Right of South	Red
Buffalo	Left of South	Red
Peacock	South-West	White
Sea-Monster	Right of North	Red
Bull	Left of North	Red
Rat	North-East	White
Elephant	Right of West	Red
Elephant	Left of West	Red
Goose	North-West	White

Table 5-4: Positioning of deity mounts in the Body Mandala

On the plinth just outside the walls of the mansion are eight elemental mandalas located to the right and left of the four gateways:

Element	Direction	Shape
Wind	East	Semi-circle
Fire	South	Triangle
Water	North	Circle
Earth	West	Square

Table 5-5: Positioning of the elemental mandalas

Outside the Body Mandala are located *Eight Great Cemeteries*. These charnel grounds are situated in the eight cardinal and intermediate directions with two additional grounds representing above and below. For each ground there is a mount with an eight spoked wheel resting on top.

Name	Direction	Mount
Pierced	East	Rhinoceros
Remainder	South-East	Verundra Bird
Blazing	South	Bear
Unending War	South-West	Crane
Putrid	North	Female Yak
Death of the Foolish	North-East	Bat
Smell of Pus	West	Lion
Magical Food	North-West	Nilika Bird
Emptiness-Above	Beyond West	Garuda

Table 5-6: Positioning of the cemeteries

The Speech Mandala

The second floor of the mansion is home to the deities of the Speech Mandala, representing the teachings of Kalachakra which reveal the yogic path to enlightenment. This floor is half the size of the first floor, measuring 25,000 yojanas and has almost all of the same features, including the four gateways, adornments and walls made from five layers of light. Unlike an ordinary building, the bottom of this floor extends down to the ground, forming a central pillar upon which the structure sits giving it a total height of 75,000 yojanas. Inside the walls is a deity plinth with eight lotus seats resting on top of eight animal mounts. Each lotus has eight petals.

Mount	Direction	Colour of Lotus
Hungry Ghost	East	Red
Garuda	South-East	White
Buffalo	South	Red
Peacock	South-West	White
Bull	North	Red
Lion	North-East	White
Elephant	West	Red
Goose	North-West	White

Table 5-7: Positioning of deity mounts in the Speech Mandala

The Mind Mandala

The third floor is home to the deities of the Mind Mandala and represents the Sambhogakaya enjoyment bodies manifested by the Buddha's enlightened mind for the benefit of fully matured Bodhisattvas. The floor again is half the size of the previous level, measuring 12,500 yojanas and its base extends down to the ground of the previous level, giving it a height of 37,500 yojanas. The walls have three layers of light: dark-blue, red and white.

Throughout this mandala a variety of lotus seats are distributed, ready to receive the various deities of the Mind Mandala. Six are placed in the gateways and twelve on the deity plinth inside the walls. Of those in the gateways, three of the lotuses are white with a red sun disc and three are red with a white moon disc. Similarly, six of the inner lotuses are white with a sun disc and six are red with a moon disc. The placement of each will be covered in the section concerning the deities.

The Great Bliss Mandala

On the fourth floor of the mansion is an open pavilion, half the size of the previous level, measuring 6,250 yojanas. The base of this pavilion extends down to the ground of the previous floor, giving it a total height of 18,750 yojanas. There are twenty columns around the perimeter of the outer edge of the pavilion with sixteen columns forming an inner ring which then opens into a courtyard in the centre. The outer ring of the pavilion has a four-coloured roof similar to the other levels. It is home to the deities of the Great Bliss Mandala and represents the pristine wisdom of the Buddha's enlightened mind.

Within the outer ring of this pavilion are eight lotus seats. In the cardinal directions, there are four white lotuses with red sun discs, while in the intermediate directions there are four red lotuses with white moon discs.

The Essential Mandala

The inner columns of the pavilion extend a further 3,125 yojanas and are covered by a beautiful golden roof, shaped like a pagoda. In the centre of the pavilion's courtyard is a large green eight-petalled lotus and in its centre are four stacked discs: white moon, red sun, dark-blue rahu and yellow kalagni.

This courtyard is home to the deities of the Essential Mandala and is considered the centre of the entire mandala. It represents the non-dual nature of the Buddha's enlightened mind—the perfect union of immutable bliss and empty-form that is the basis for the rest of the mandala.

The Enlightened Deities

Once you have developed familiarity with the general layout of the enlightened mandala, you can move on to studying the individual deities that populate each section. For each group of deities there are many layers of meaning corresponding to each detail. As identifying every meaning is beyond the scope of this book, we will instead concentrate on a few essential concepts to provide a general sense for their correlations.

In total, there are 636 deities counted in the Jonang Tradition. This number is derived from the deities which are visualised as emanating from the womb of Vishvamata and are broken down as follows:

Mandala	Group	Number
Essential (10)	Kalachakra Yab-Yum	2
	Shaktis	8
Great Bliss (18)	Buddhas with Consorts	18
Mind (44)	Bodhisattvas with Consorts	24
	Wrathful Ones with Consorts	8
	Offering Goddesses	12
Speech (116)	Female Deities with Consorts	16
	Surrounding Yoginis	64
	Desire Goddesses	36
Body (428)	Male Deities of the Lunar Months	360
	Six Wrathful Guardians with Consorts	12
	Nagas with Consorts	20
	Detachment Goddesses	36
Universe (20)	Very Wrathful Ones with Consorts	20
	Total	**636**

Table 5-8: How the deities are counted in the Jonang Tradition

The Deities of the Essential Mandala

The Essential Mandala consists of three groups: (1) the Principal Deity of Kalachakra Yab-Yum; (2) the Ten Shaktis and (3) the Four Emblems.

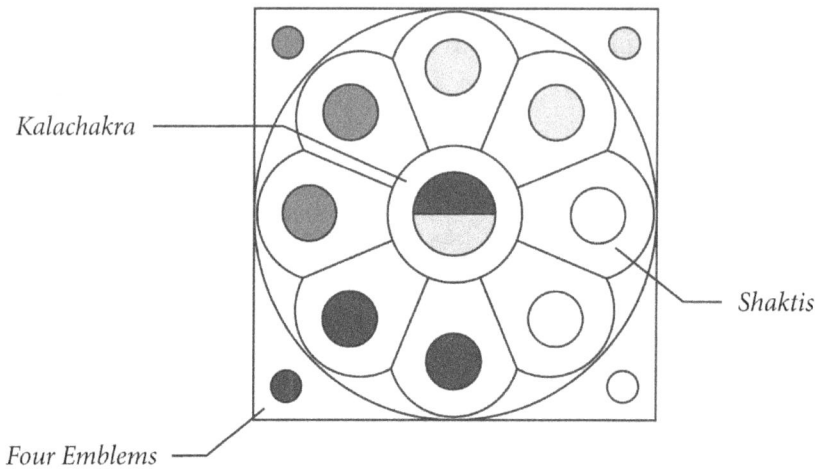

Kalachakra

Shaktis

Four Emblems

The Principal Deity of Kalachakra Yab-Yum

In fully-manifest form, Kalachakra appears as a twenty-four armed deity with four faces, each with three eyes, three necks, one body and two legs. His faces match the colours and directions of the ground—dark-blue, red, yellow and white—while his three necks are dark-blue, red and white.

He wears a Vajrasattva crown with his hair tied in a top-knot and adorned by a crossed vajra and jewel ornament. His body is draped in a vajra scarf and a variety of vajra ornaments, and his waist is wrapped in a tiger-skin loin cloth and vajra skirt.

He has three shoulders on each side of his dark-blue body. The front set is dark-blue, the middle set is red and the back set is white. Each shoulder splits into two creating twelve upper arms and these upper arms split into two at the elbow, creating twenty-four lower arms. Each arm is coloured in accordance with the shoulder it comes from. The outside of each finger is a different colour starting with the thumb—yellow, white, red, dark-blue and green. The inner joints of the hands are coloured from the base joint up—blue, red and white.

Each hand holds a unique instrument which is used to tame the afflictions of sentient beings. Starting with the right side, in the dark-blue hands he holds (1) a vajra, (2) a sword, (3) a trident and (4) a curved knife. In the red hands he holds (5) an arrow, (6) a vajra hook, (7) a damaru drum and (8) a hammer. In the white hands he holds (9) a wheel, (10) a spear, (11) a staff and (12) an axe. Then on the left side, in the dark blue hands he holds (13) a bell, (14) a shield, (15) a khatvanga and (16) a skull-cup. In the red hands, he holds (17) a bow, (18) a vajra noose, (19) a jewel and (20) a white lotus. Finally in the white hands he holds (21) a conch, (22) a mirror, (23) a vajra chain and (24) the head of Brahma.

He stands atop the four discs of the central lotus. With his red right leg outstretched, he tramples the heart of the desire god Kamadeva, while his white left leg is bent and tramples the heart of Rudra. The wives of these worldly gods cling to Kalachakra's feet.

Kalachakra is embraced by his consort Vishvamata who is golden yellow in colour. She has four faces—yellow, white, dark-blue and red—with three eyes on each. She has eight arms branching out from her shoulder. In the right hands she holds (1) a curved knife, (2) a hook, (3) a damaru drum and (4) a rosary. In the left hands she holds (5) a skullcup, (6) a noose, (7) a white-petalled lotus and (8) a jewel. She wears a Vajrasattva crown with half her hair tied in a top-knot and the rest falling loose. Her naked body is adorned by a silk scarf and a variety of bone ornaments. Her left leg is extended and her right leg is bent.

Name	Direction	Colour	Seed	Emblem
Kalachakra	Centre	Dark-Blue	HUM	Vajra
Vishvamata	Centre	Yellow	PHREM	Curved Knife

Table 5-9: The Principal Deities

Of all the deities in the mandala, the principal deity has the most levels of symbolic meaning. In its most essential form, Kalachakra represents the supreme awareness of immutable bliss, and Vishvamata represents the diversity of empty-forms that manifest on the basis of the sublime emptiness endowed with all enlightened qualities. Their union represents the inseparable nature of these two aspects.

When a deity is visualised in union with a consort, it always signifies the union of method and wisdom. If the method aspect is dominant, the masculine deity is visualised as principal and it is referred to as a *yab-yum*. The Tibetan word *yab* means "father", while *yum* means "mother". When the wisdom aspect is dominant, the female deity is visualised as principal and is called a *yum-yab*.

These unions are also used to indicate the balancing of opposing energies. This may refer to the balance between masculine and feminine energies or the elemental opposites such as fire and water, earth and wind or space and consciousness. Through visualising the deities in this way, we harmonise our body and mind bringing the whole system into balance. For this reason, you will often see the following pairing of colours:

Colour	Opposite
Dark-Blue	Yellow
Red	White
White	Red
Yellow	Dark-Blue
Green	Blue
Blue	Green

Table 5-10: Colour relationships

The two worldly deities that are visualised under Kalachakra's feet represent the purification of different obscurations. Rudra and his wife represent the four afflictions: ignorance, attachment, aversion and pride. Meanwhile Kamadeva and his wife represent the four maras: the mara of the aggregates; the mara of afflictions; the mara of the lord of death and the mara of the son of the gods.

The Ten Shaktis

On the eight petals of the central lotus stand eight goddesses of wisdom known as the Shaktis. All these deities stand with legs together with eight arms and four faces with three eyes. They hold a variety of hand implements that tend to be variations on the emblem used to manifest them and their bodies are adorned with bone ornaments similar to Vishvamata. Although there are ten shaktis, two are visualised as being inseparable from Vishvamata herself and therefore only eight are actually counted.

Name	Direction	Colour	Seed	Emblem
Krishnadipta	East	Dark-Blue	A	Incense Holder
Raktadipta	South	Red	AH	Lamp
Shvetadipta	North	White	AM	Food
Pitadipta	West	Yellow	AA	Dharma Conch
Dhuma	South-East	Dark-Blue	HA	Yak-tail Fan
Marichi	South-West	Red	HAH	Yak-tail Fan
Khadyota	North-East	White	HAM	Yak-tail Fan
Pradipa	North-West	Yellow	HAA	Yak-tail Fan

Table 5-11: The Eight Shaktis

The eight Shaktis represent the purification of the eight channels which branch out from the heart chakra. It is from this chakra that the subtle winds originate and distribute to form the subtle body. When taken as ten, the Shaktis represent the subtle winds themselves.

The Four Emblems

In the four corners of the square courtyard of the Essential Mandala are four emblems representing the four vajras which are the result of purifying the four states of experience. As they are not technically deities, they are not counted towards the total. They also correspond to the purification of the four channels which branch out from the crown chakra.

Emblem	Direction	Colour	Seed	Vajra
Dharma Conch	North-East	White	OM	Vajra-Body
Wooden Gong	South-West	Red	AH	Vajra-Speech
Wish-Fulfilling Jewel	South-East	Dark-Blue	HUM	Vajra-Mind
Wish-Fulfilling Tree	North-West	Yellow	HO	Vajra-Wisdom

Table 5-12: The Four Emblems

The Deities of the Great Bliss Mandala

Surrounding the central lotus is the pavilion of columns, between which are sixteen alcoves where two groups of deities reside: (1) the Twelve Buddhas and (2) the Ten Vases.

The Twelve Buddhas

There are two sets of six Buddhas—male and female—of which two are considered inseparable from Kalachakra and two inseparable from Vishvamata. This leaves eight placed in the alcoves of the pavilion. The males are placed in the cardinal directions and sit upon white lotuses with red sun discs, while the female Buddhas are placed in the intermediate directions sitting on red lotuses with white moon discs.

Each Buddha has three faces with three eyes, six arms and is seated in either the vajra posture for males or the lotus posture for females. All the deities sit in union with their corresponding consort, meaning that there are actually two sets of each deity—once as a main deity and once as a consort.

Name	Direction	Colour	Seed	Emblem	Consort
Akshobhya	Kalachakra	Green	A	Vajra	Prajñaparamita
[Vajradhatvishvari]	Vishvamata	Green	AA	Vajra	Vajrasattva
[Vajrasattva]	Kalachakra	Blue	A	Vajra	Vajradhatvishvari
Prajñaparamita	Vishvamata	Blue	AA	Vajra	Akshobhya
Amoghasiddhi	East	Dark-Blue	I	Sword	Lochana
Tara	South-East	Dark-Blue	II	Blue Utpala	Vairochana
Ratnasambhava	South	Red	RI	Jewel	Mamaki
Pandara	South-West	Red	RII	Jewel	Amitabha
Amitabha	North	White	U	Lotus	Pandara
Mamaki	North-East	White	UU	Utpala	Ratnasambhava
Vairochana	West	Yellow	LI	Wheel	Tara
Lochana	North-West	Yellow	LII	Wheel	Amoghasiddhi

Table 5-13: The Twelve Buddhas

The five male Buddhas (the four who are shown plus Akshobhya) represent the purification of the five aggregates, while the five female Buddhas (the four who are shown plus Prajñaparamita) represent the purification of the five elements. If we consider only the outer ring of male and female Buddhas, including their wisdom consorts, we have sixteen Buddhas who represent the sixteen channels of the forehead chakra.

The Ten Vases

Between each Buddha is an offering vase containing the nectar of a purified substance. These vases are considered to be the consorts of the Shaktis. Two vases are placed to the right and left of each male Buddha, and the remaining two are placed in the eastern and western doorways of the Mind Mandala. Although these vases are visualised, they are not counted towards the total number of deities.

Substance	Direction	Seeds
Marrow	East	HI and HII
Blood	South	HRI and HRII
Urine	North	HU and HUU
Excrement	West	HLI and HLII
Semen	Above	HAM
Blood	Below	HAH

Table 5-14: The Ten Vases

These vases represent the blissful nature of all phenomena. Through bringing the primordial wisdom of the Buddhas to bear on these substances, they are transformed into nectar and become the basis for the experience of bliss. In this way, the Buddhas represent wisdom while the vases represent method.

The Deities of the Mind Mandala

Descending to the third floor of the mansion, we find the deities of the Mind Mandala which consists of three groups: (1) the Twelve Bodhisattvas; (2) the Five Wrathful Ones and (3) the Twelve Offering Goddesses.

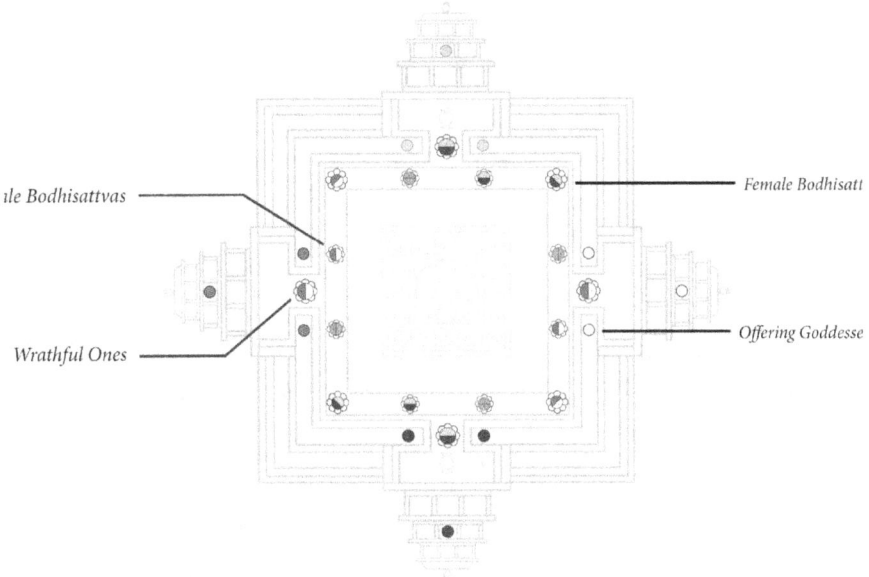

ale Bodhisattvas

Wrathful Ones

Female Bodhisatt

Offering Goddesse

The Twelve Bodhisattvas

As with the Buddhas, there are two sets of six Bodhisattvas—male and female. The Bodhisattvas also have three faces with three eyes, six arms and sit respectively in the vajra and lotus postures. Four of the male Bodhisattvas are placed to the right of each gateway on the deity plinth inside the walls. The two remaining male Bodhisattvas are placed to the left of the eastern and southern gateways. They sit upon white lotuses with sun discs. The female Bodhisattvas are placed in the intermediate directions as well as to the left of the northern and western gateways. All deities sit in union with their respective consorts to make two sets of deities for a total of twenty four.

Name	Direction	Colour	Seed	Emblem	Consort
Kagarbha	Right of East	Dark-Blue	E	Sword	Gandhavajra
Sparshavajra	South-East	Dark-Blue	AI	Cloth	Nivaranaviskambhin
Ksitigarbha	Right of South	Red	AR	Jewel	Rupavajra
Rasavajra	South-West	Red	AAR	Bowl of Flavour	Lokeshvara
Lokeshvara	Right of North	White	O	Lotus	Rasavajra

Rupavajra	North-East	White	AU	Mirror	Ksitigarbha
Nivaranaviskambhin	Right of West	Yellow	AL	Wheel	Sparshavajra
Gandhavajra	North-West	Yellow	AAL	Conch of Perfume	Kagarbha
Vajrapani	Left of South	Green	A	Vajra	Shabdavajra
Dharmadhatuvajra	Left of West	Green	AA	Dharmodaya	Samantabhadra
Samantabhadra	Left of East	Blue	AM	Vajra	Dharmadhatuvajra
Shabdavajra	Left of North	Blue	AH	Vina	Vajrapani

Table 5-15: The Twelve Bodhisattvas

The male Bodhisattvas represent the purification of the six sense powers of the eye, ear, nose and so forth; while the female Bodhisattvas represent the purification of the six sense objects of form, sound, smell and so forth. The union of these deities represents the purification of the moment of contact where the causes and conditions come together and the experience of a dualistic consciousness arises, such as in a visual consciousness.

The Five Wrathful Ones

Of the five Wrathful Ones, four are placed on lotus seats in the four gateways, whereas one is not shown. Each deity stands with the right leg extended and the left leg bent, embracing his consort, their bodies enveloped in radiant flames. They have three faces each with three bulging eyes, six arms and powerful bodies and are adorned by frightening ornaments. The deities in the eastern and northern gates stand on white lotuses with sun discs, while those of the southern and western gates stand on red lotuses with moon discs.

Name	Direction	Colour	Seed	Emblem	Consort
Vighnantaka	East	Dark-Blue	YAM	Sword	Stambhaki
Prajñantaka	South	Red	RAM	Club	Manaki
Padmantaka	North	White	VAM	Lotus	Jambhaki
Yamantaka	West	Yellow	LAM	Hammer	Anantavirya
[Ushnisha]	Above	Green	HAM	Vajra	Atinila

Table 5-16: The Five Wrathful Ones

The Wrathful Ones of the Mind Mandala represent the five powers—the power of concentration, the power of attention, the power of effort, the power of confidence and the power of understanding. When the four Wrathfuls are combined with the twelve Bodhisattvas, we have sixteen deities. As each has a consort, this makes thirty-two deities who represent the thirty-two channels of the throat chakra.

The Twelve Offering Goddesses

The Twelve Offering Goddesses are placed on the plinth outside the walls, with two goddesses to the left and right of the gateways and one goddess above each gate. Each goddess stands in a dancing posture, with one face and two arms holding their corresponding offering substance. These deities represent the purification of the activity of making offerings.

Name	Direction	Colour	Seed	Emblem
Gandha	Left of East	Dark-Blue	CA-CHA-JA-JHA-NYA	Conch of Perfume
Mala	Right of East	Dark-Blue	CAA-CHAA-JAA-JHAA-NYAA	Garland of Flowers
Dhupa	Left of South	Red	TA-THA-DA-DHA-NA	Incense Holder
Dipa	Right of South	Red	TAA-THAA-DAA-DHAA-NAA	Lamp
Naivedya	Left of North	White	PA-PHA-BA-BHA-MA	Vessel of Nectar
Amritaphala	Right of North	White	PAA-PHAA-BAA-BHAA-MAA	Bowl of Fruit
Lasya	Left of West	Yellow	TA-THA-DA-DHA-NA	Crown Ornament
Hasya	Right of West	Yellow	TAA-THAA-DAA-DHAA-NAA	String of Jewels
Vadya	West-Above	Green	KA-KHA-GA-GHA-NYA	Drum
Nritya	East-Above	Green	KAA-KHAA-GAA-GHAA-NYAA	Scarf
Gita	North	Blue	SA-HPA-SA-SHA-HKA	Vajra
Kama	South	Blue	SAA-HPAA-SAA-SHAA-HKAA	Lotus

Table 5-17: The Twelve Offering Goddesses

The Deities of the Speech Mandala

As we descend to the second floor we find the deities of the Speech Mandala divided into two groups: (1) the Eight Female Deities with Yoginis and (2) the Thirty-Six Desire Goddesses.

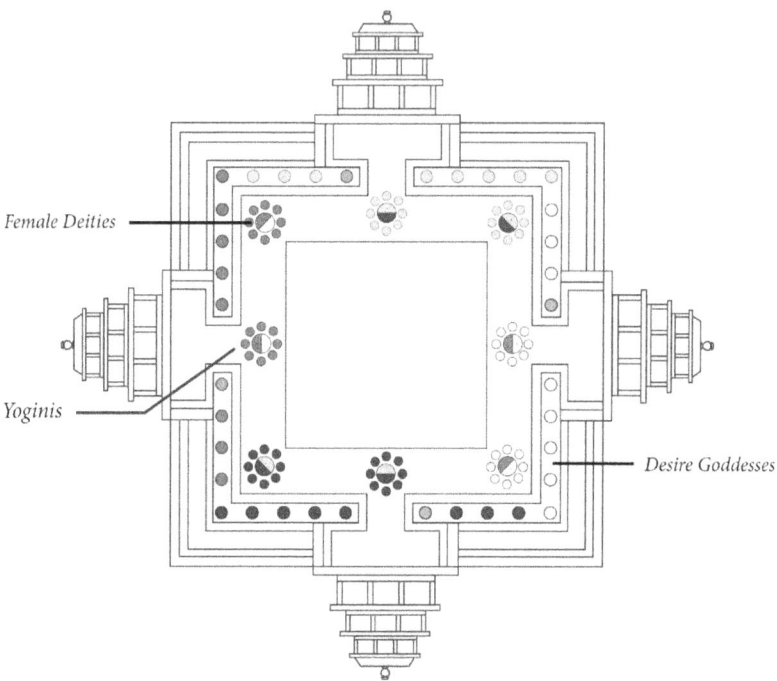

The Eight Female Deities with Yoginis

The principal deities of the Speech Mandala consist of eight Female Deities who stand in the centre of an eight petalled lotus resting on top of an animal mount. Each deity has one face, three eyes, four arms and stands in union with a consort, surrounded by eight yoginis. The yoginis are similar in form to the female deities except they are standing in a dancing posture. Except for bone and jewel ornaments, their bodies are naked.

Name	Direction	Colour	Seed	Emblem	Consort	Mount
Charchika	East	Dark-Blue	HA	Curved Knife	Indra	Hungry Ghost

Name	Seed
Bhima	HI
Ugra	YA
Kaladamshtra	YI
Jvaladanalamukha	YRI
Vayuvega	HII
Prachanda	YU
Raudrakshi	YLI
Sthulanasa	YAM

Table 5-18: Yoginis of the Eastern Lotus

Name	Direction	Colour	Seed	Emblem	Consort	Mount
Vaishnavi	South-East	Dark-Blue	KSHA	Wheel	Brahma	Garuda

Name	Seed
Shri	KSHI
Maya	YAA
Kirti	YII
Lakshmi	YRII
Suparamavijaya	KSHII
Shrijaya	YUU
Shrijayanti	YLII
Shrichakri	YAH

Table 5-19: Yoginis of the South-Eastern Lotus

Name	Direction	Colour	Seed	Emblem	Consort	Mount
Varahi	South	Red	HAH	Club	Rudra	Buffalo

Name	Seed
Kangkali	HRI
Kalaratri	RA
Prakupitavadana	RI
Kalajihva	RRI

Karali	HRII
Kali	RU
Ghora	RLI
Virupa	RAM

Table 5-20: Yoginis of the Southern Lotus

Name	Direction	Colour	Seed	Emblem	Consort	Mount
Kaumari	South-West	Red	KSHAH	Spear	Ganapati	Peacock

Name	Seed
Padma	KSHRI
Ananga	RAA
Kaumari	RI
Mrigapatigamana	RRII
Ratnamala	KSHRII
Sunetra	RUU
Lina	RLII
Subadra	RAH

Table 5-21: Yoginis of the South-Western Lotus

Name	Direction	Colour	Seed	Emblem	Consort	Mount
Raudri	North	White	HAM	Trident	Yama	Bull

Name	Seed
Gauri	HU
Ganga	VA
Nitya	VI
Paramatvarita	VRI
Totala	HUU
Lakshana	VU
Pingala	VLI
Krishna	VAM

Table 5-22: Yoginis of the Northern Lotus

Name	Direction	Colour	Seed	Emblem	Consort	Mount
Mahalakshmi	North-East	White	KSHAM	Lotus	Sangmukha	Lion

Name	Seed
Shrisveta	KSHU
Chandralekha	VAA
Sasadharavadana	VII
Hamsavarna	VRII
Dhriti	KSHUU
Padmesha	VUU
Taranetra	VLII
Vimalasasadhara	VAH

Table 5-23: Yoginis of the North-Eastern Lotus

Name	Direction	Colour	Seed	Emblem	Consort	Mount
Aindri	West	Yellow	HA	Vajra	Nairitya	Elephant

Name	Seed
Vajrabha	HLI
Vajragatra	LA
Varakanakavati	LI
Urvashi	LRI
Chitralekha	HLII
Rambha	LU
Ahalya	LLI
Sutara	LAM

Table 5-24: Yoginis of the Western Lotus

Name	Direction	Colour	Seed	Emblem	Consort	Mount
Brahmani	North-West	Yellow	KSHAA	Mace	Vishnu	Goose

Name	Seed
Savitri	KSHLI
Padmanetra	LAA
Jalajavati	LII
Buddhi	LRII

Vagisvari	KSHLII
Gayatri	LUU
Vidyut	LLII
Smirti	LAH

Table 5-25: Yoginis of the North-Western Lotus

The eight female deities and their consorts represent the sixteen intermediate channels of the navel chakra and the eight sessions of a day, equivalent to approximately four hours each. The sixty-four yoginis standing on the petals represent the sixty-four outer channels of the navel chakra.

The Thirty-Six Desire Goddesses

Standing on the plinth outside the walls are thirty-six Desire Goddesses whose number of faces and arms varies depending on the deity. These deities each represent the purification of the desire to engage in thirty-six activities. To simplify our study, we can divide them into two groups for each direction, the right and left of each gate, giving us eight groups in total.

Starting to the right of the eastern gateway there are five goddesses representing the desire (1) to divide; (2) for clothes; (3) to scratch; (4) to spit; and (5) to expel.

Name	Direction	Colour	Seed	Emblem
Vidveseccha	Right of East	Dark-Blue	CAH	Utpala
Amshukeccha	Right of East	Dark-Blue	CHAH	Clothing
Kanduyaneccha	Right of East	Dark-Blue	JAH	Curved Knife
Kaphotsarjaneccha	Right of East	Dark-Blue	JHAH	Wheel
Uccataneccha	Right of East	Dark-Blue	NYAH	Khatvanga

Table 5-26: Desire Goddesses to the right of east

To the left of this gateway there are four goddesses representing the desire (6) for torment; (7) for touch; (8) to shake limbs; and (9) to eat leftovers.

Name	Direction	Colour	Seed	Emblem
Samtapeccha	Left of East	Blue	HKAH	Curved Knife
Sparshaneccha	Left of East	Dark-Blue	SHAH	Sword
Sarvangakshodaneccha	Left of East	Dark-Blue	SAH	Curved Knife
Ucchistabhakteccha	Left of East	Dark-Blue	HPAH	Curved Knife

Table 5-27: Desire goddesses to the left of east

To the right of the southern gateway there are five goddesses representing the desire (10) to move; (11) to eat; (12) for bodily odour; (13) to dance; and (14) to be slim.

Name	Direction	Colour	Seed	Emblem
Stobhaneccha	Right of South	Red	TAH	Lotus
Bhojaneccha	Right of South	Red	THAH	Bowl of Food
Maleccha	Right of South	Red	DAH	Club
Nrityeccha	Right of South	Red	DHAH	Spear
Shosaneccha	Right of South	Red	NAH	Lotus

Table 5-28: Desire goddesses to the right of south

To the left of this gateway there are four goddesses representing the desire (15) to call; (16) to run; (17) to excrete; and (18) to fight.

Name	Direction	Colour	Seed	Emblem
Akristiccha	Left of South	Green	NGAH	Arrow
Dhavaneccha	Left of South	Red	GHAH	Axe
Mutravitsravaneccha	Left of South	Red	GAH	Curved Knife
Samgrameccha	Left of South	Red	KHAH	Curved Knife

Table 5-29: Desire goddesses to the left of south

To the right of the northern gateway there are five goddesses representing the desire (19) for increase; (20) for ornaments; (21) for a seat; (22) to reign; and (23) to speak.

Name	Direction	Colour	Seed	Emblem
Paustikeccha	Right of North	White	PAH	Utpala
Bhusaneccha	Right of North	White	PHAH	Mirror
Asaneccha	Right of North	White	BAH	Trident
Rajyeccha	Right of North	White	BHAH	Lotus
Mriduvacaneccha	Right of North	White	MAH	Utpala

Table 5-30: Desire goddesses to the right of north

To the left of this gateway there are four goddesses representing the desire (24) for music; (25) to bind; (26) to argue; and (27) for anger.

Name	Direction	Colour	Seed	Emblem
Vadyeccha	Left of North	Blue	HAH	Vinya
Bandhaneccha	Left of North	White	YAH	Hammer
Bahukalaheccha	Left of North	White	RAH	Curved Knife
Darakakroshaneccha	Left of North	White	VAH	Curved Knife

Table 5-31: Desire goddesses to the left of north

To the right of the western gateway there are five goddesses representing the desire (28) to stiffen; (29) for perfume; (30) to rest; (31) to swim; and (32) to bind.

Name	Direction	Colour	Seed	Emblem
Stambhaneccha	Right of West	Yellow	TAH	Wheel
Gandheccha	Right of West	Yellow	THAH	Conch of Perfume
Majjaneccha	Right of West	Yellow	DAH	Vajra
Plavaneccha	Right of West	Yellow	DHAH	Needle
Bandhaneccha	Right of West	Yellow	NAH	Wheel

Table 5-32: Desire goddesses to the right of west

To the left of this gateway there are four goddesses representing the desire (33) for sex; (34) to stab; (35) to deceive; and (36) to seize snakes.

Name	Direction	Colour	Seed	Emblem
Maithuneccha	Left of West	Green	KSHAH	Dharmodaya
Kilaneccha	Left of West	Yellow	SAH	Wheel
Vanyacaneccha	Left of West	Yellow	KAH	Curved Knife
Ahibandhaneccha	Left of West	Yellow	LAH	Curved Knife

Table 5-33: Desire goddesses to the left of west

The Deities of the Body Mandala

On the first floor of the enlightened mansion we find the deities of the Body Mandala. If we focus on the deities who abide in the mansion itself, we can speak of four groups: (1) the Twelve Male Deities of the Lunar Months; (2) the Six Wrathful Guardians; (3) the Ten Naga Kings and (4) the Thirty-Six Detachment Goddesses.

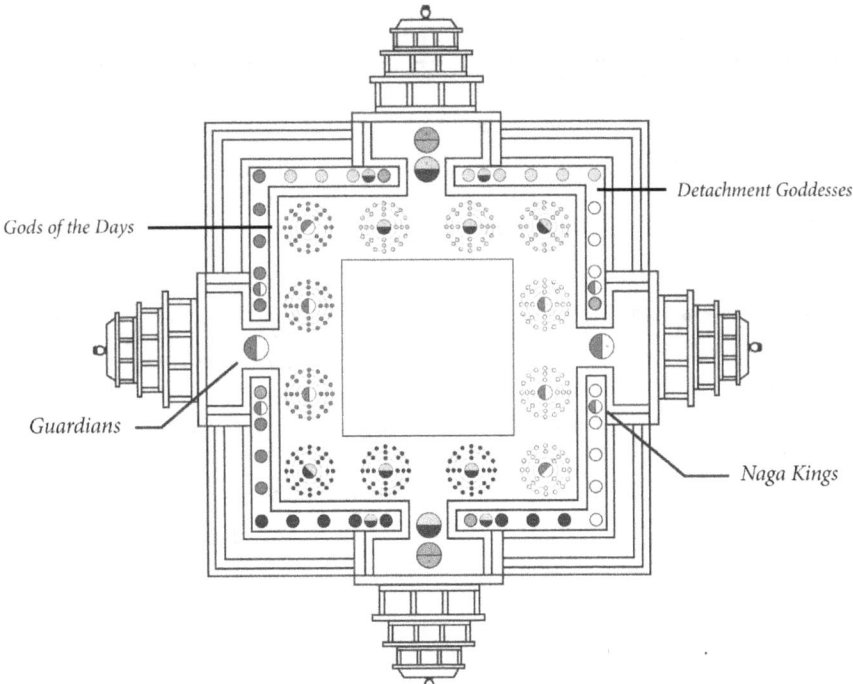

Gods of the Days

Detachment Goddesses

Guardians

Naga Kings

The Twelve Male Deities of the Lunar Months

Similar to the Speech Mandala, there are twelve Male Deities surrounded by twenty-eight yoginis. The central deity sits in union with his consort at the centre of a twenty-eight petalled lotus resting on top of an animal mount. The number of faces and arms varies for each of these deities.

The yoginis all stand atop a lotus petal in the dancing posture with one face and four arms. Their colour corresponds to the colour of the central deity that they surround. Each yogini is placed on the lotus starting from the direction facing the centre of the mandala and rotating in a clockwise direction. The lotus itself is divided into three sets of petals—inner, middle and outer. We start with the inner petals and work our way outward.

Name	Direction	Colour	Seed	Emblem	Consort	Mount
Rakshasa	Right of East	Dark-Blue	CAM	Sword	Rakshasi	Hungry Ghost

Group	Seed
Inner Petals	NYA, NYI, NRI, NYU
Middle Petals	NYLI, NYAM, JHA, JHI, JHRI, JHU, JHLI, JHAM
Outer Petals	JA, JI, JU, JLI, JAM, CHA, CHI, CHRI, CHU, CHLI, CHAM, CA, CI, CRI, CU, CLI

Table 5-34: Deities of the Month Caitra (Aries)

Name	Direction	Colour	Seed	Emblem	Consort	Mount
Vayu	South-East	Dark-Blue	NYAH	Wishing Tree	Prachanda	Deer

Group	Seed
Inner Petals	CAA, CII, CRII, CUU
Middle Petals	CLII, CAH, CHAA, CHII, CHRII, CHUU, CHLII, CHAH
Outer Petals	JAA, JII, JUU, JLII, JAH, JHAA, JHII, JHRII, JHUU, JHLII, JHAH, NYAA, NYII, NYRII, NYUU, NYLII

Table 5-35: Deities of the Month Vaishakha (Taurus)

Name	Direction	Colour	Seed	Emblem	Consort	Mount
Agni	Right of South	Red	TAM	Lance	Varuni	Sheep

Group	Seed
Inner Petals	NA, NI, NRI, NU
Middle Petals	NLI, NAM, DHA, DHI, DHRI, DHU, DHLI, DHAM
Outer Petals	DA, DI, DU, DLI, DAM, THA, THI, THRI, THU, THLI, TAM, TA, TI, TRI, TU, TLI

Table 5-36: Deities of the Month Jyaistha (Gemini)

Name	Direction	Colour	Seed	Emblem	Consort	Mount
Sanmukha	South-West	Red	NAH	Spear	Lakshmi	Peacock

Group	Seed
Inner Petals	TAA, TII, TRII, TUU
Middle Petals	TLII, TAH, THAA, THII, THRII, THUU, THLII, THAH
Outer Petals	DAA, DII, DUU, DLII, DAH, DHAA, DHII, DHRII, DHUU, DHLII, DHAH, NAA, NII, NRII, NUU, NLII

Table 5-37: Deities of the Month Asadha (Cancer)

Name	Direction	Colour	Seed	Emblem	Consort	Mount
Varuna	Right of North	White	PAM	Lasso	Varahi	Sea-Monster

Group	Seed
Inner Petals	MA, MI, MRI, MU
Middle Petals	MLI, MAM, BHA, BHI, BHRI, BHU, BHLI, BHAM
Outer Petals	BA, BI, BU, BLI, BAM, PHA, PHI, PHRI, PHU, PHLI, PHAM, PA, PI, PRI, PU, PLI

Table 5-38: Deities of the Month Shravana (Leo)

Name	Direction	Colour	Seed	Emblem	Consort	Mount
Ganapati	North-East	White	MAH	Axe	Kaumari	Lion

Group	Seed
Inner Petals	PAA, PII, PRII, PUU
Middle Petals	PLII, PAH, PHAA, PHII, PHRII, PHUU, PHLII, PHAH
Outer Petals	BAA, BII, BUU, BLII, BAH, BHAA, BHII, BHRII, BHUU, BHLII, BHAH, MAA, MII, MRII, MUU, MLII

Table 5-39: Deities of the Month Bhadrapada (Virgo)

Name	Direction	Colour	Seed	Emblem	Consort	Mount
Indra	Right of West	Yellow	TAM	Vajra	Vayavi	Elephant

Group	Seed
Inner Petals	NA, NI, NRI, NU
Middle Petals	NLI, NAM, DHA, DHI, DHRI, DHU, DHLI, DHAM
Outer Petals	DA, DI, DU, DLI, DAM, THA, THI, THRI, THU, THLI, THAM, TA, TI, TRI, TU, TLI

Table 5-40: Deities of the Month Ashvina (Libra)

Name	Direction	Colour	Seed	Emblem	Consort	Mount
Brahma	North-West	Yellow	NAH	Needle	Vidyut	Goose

Group	Seed
Inner Petals	TAA, TII, TRII, TUU
Middle Petals	TLII, TAH, THAA, THII, THRII, THUU, THLII, THAH
Outer Petals	DAA, DII, DUU, DLII, DAH, DHAA, DHII, DHRII, DHUU, DHLII, DHAH, NAA, NII, NRII, NUU, NLII

Table 5-41: Deities of the Month Kartikka (Scorpio)

Name	Direction	Colour	Seed	Emblem	Consort	Mount
Rudra	Left of North	White	SAM	Trident	Gauri	Bull

Group	Seed
Inner Petals	HKA, HKI, HKRI, HKU
Middle Petals	HKLI, HKAM, SHA, SHI, SHRI, SHU, SHLI, SHAM
Outer Petals	SA, SI, SU, SLI, SAM, HPA, HPI, HPRI, HPU, HPLI, HPAM, SA, SI, SRI, SU, SLI

Table 5-42: Deities of the Month Margashirsa (Sagittarius)

Name	Direction	Colour	Seed	Emblem	Consort	Mount
Kubera	Left of West	Yellow	HKAH	Mace	Dhanesha	Elephant

Group	Seed
Inner Petals	SAA, SII, SRII, SUU
Middle Petals	SLII, SAH, HPAA, HPII, HPRII, HPUU, HPLII, HPAH
Outer Petals	SAA, SII, SUU, SLII, SAH, SHAA, SHII, SHRII, SHUU, SHLII, SHAH, HKAA, HKII, HKRII, HKUU, HKLII

Table 5-43: Deities of the Month Pausa (Capricorn)

Name	Direction	Colour	Seed	Emblem	Consort	Mount
Vishnu	Left of East	Dark-Blue	KAM	Wheel	Shri	Garuda

Group	Seed
Inner Petals	NGA, NGI, NGRI, NGU
Middle Petals	NGLI, NGAM, GHA, GHI, GRI, GHU, GHLI, GHAM
Outer Petals	GA, GI, GU, GLI, GAM, KHA, KHI, KHRI, KHU, KHLI, KHAM, KA, KI, KRI, KU, KLI

Table 5-44: Deities of the Month Magha (Aquarius)

Name	Direction	Colour	Seed	Emblem	Consort	Mount
Yama	Left of South	Red	NGAH	Vajra-Club	Nairitya	Buffalo

Group	Seed
Inner Petals	KAA, KII, KRII, KUU
Middle Petals	KLII, KAH, KHAA, KHII, KHRII, KHUU, KHLII, KHAH
Outer Petals	GAA, GII, GUU, GLII, GAH, GHAA, GHII, GHRII, GHUU, GHLII, GHAH, NGAA, NGII, NGRII, NGUU, NGLII

Table 5-45: Deities of the Month Phalguna (Pisces)

The twelve central deities and their consorts combined with their retinue of yoginis make a total of three hundred and sixty deities representing the number of days in a lunar year. When divided into twelve groups of thirty, they correspond to the lunar months where the male deity represents the new moon and the female consort represents the full moon.

In accordance with the solar day, the twelve deities also represent the twelve houses of the zodiac that the sun passes through over the course of a single day. During each two hour period, the subtle winds circulate through five channels of the navel chakra giving us sixty channels. The winds pass through each channel for the duration of six "breaths" (approximately four seconds each). This gives us three-hundred and sixty breaths which correspond to the three-hundred and sixty deities.

The twelve deities also represent the twelve activity chakras located in the joints of the arms and the legs. The channels that branch out from these hubs correspond to the petals of the lotus seats in the mandala.

The Six Wrathful Guardians

The next set of deities is the Wrathful Guardians who are placed in the four gateways of the first floor standing on chariots drawn by different sets of animals. The four deities in the cardinal directions stand with one face, three bulging eyes and four arms. The remaining two deities have three faces and six arms and are usually visualised as being just outside the western and eastern gates, representing the directions of above and below.

Name	Direction	Colour	Seed	Emblem	Consort	Chariot
Niladanda	East	Dark-Blue	YA	Club	Marichi	Boars
Takkiraja	South	Red	RA	Arrow	Chunda	Horses
Achala	North	White	VA	Pestle	Bhrikuti	Lions
Mahabala	West	Yellow	LA	Mace	Shringkhala	Elephants
Ushnisha	Above	Green	HAM	Vajra	Atinila	Garudas
Sumbha	Below	Blue	HA	Trident	Raudrakshi	Eight-Legged Lions

Table 5-46: The Six Wrathful Guardians

When presented as six Wrathfuls, these deities represent the purification of the six faculties of mouth, arms and so forth, while their consorts represent the purification of the six actions of speaking, taking and so forth. In this case, both Ushnisha and Sumbha represent the supreme faculty while their consorts represent the two actions of urinating and emitting vital fluids respectively.

The Ten Naga Kings

The Naga Kings occupy the plinth outside the walls of the first floor mansion. They are placed on the mandala symbols of the elements located to the right and left of the four gateways. The two nagas which represent the elements of space and consciousness are located beyond the western and eastern gates. Each naga has one face with four arms and is embraced by one of the Very Wrathful deities as his consort. They can be distinguished from other deities by the hood of serpents that rises up from behind their heads.

Name	Direction	Colour	Seed	Emblem	Consort
Karkotaka	Left of East	Dark-Blue	HYA	Victory Banner	Jambukasya
Padma	Right of East	Dark-Blue	HYAA	Victory Banner	Garudasya
Vasuki	Left of South	Red	HRA	Svastika	Vyaghrasya
Shangkhapala	Right of South	Red	HRAA	Svastika	Ulukasya
Ananta	Left of North	White	HVA	Lotus	Shukarasya
Kulika	Right of North	White	HVAA	Lotus	Gridhrasya
Takshaka	Left of West	Yellow	HLA	Vajra	Shvanasya
Mahapadma	Right of West	Yellow	HLAA	Vajra	Kakasya
Jaya	Above	Green	HUM	Vase	Nila
Vijaya	Below	Blue	KSHUM	Vase	Vajrakshi

Table 5-47: The Ten Naga Kings

The Thirty-Six Detachment Goddesses

Sharing the outer plinth with the nagas are the thirty-six Detachment Goddesses whose appearance is the same as the Desire Goddesses of the Speech Mandala. In this case, the goddesses represent the purification of the absence of desire to engage in thirty-six activities. For completeness we can again use eight groups.

Starting to the right of the eastern gateway there are five goddesses representing the absence of desire (1) to divide; (2) for clothes; (3) to scratch; (4) to spit and (5) to expel.

Name	Direction	Colour	Seed	Emblem
Vidvesapraticcha	Right of East	Dark-Blue	CAM	Utpala
Amshukapraticcha	Right of East	Dark-Blue	CHAM	Clothing
Kanduyanapraticcha	Right of East	Dark-Blue	JAM	Curved Knife
Kaphotsarjanapraticcha	Right of East	Dark-Blue	JHAM	Wheel
Uccatanapraticcha	Right of East	Dark-Blue	NYAM	Khatvanga

Table 5-48: Detachment goddesses to the right of east

To the left of this gateway there are four goddesses representing the absence of desire (6) for torment; (7) for touch; (8) to shake limbs and (9) to eat leftovers.

Name	Direction	Colour	Seed	Emblem
Samtapapraticcha	Left of East	Blue	HKAM	Curved Knife
Sparshanapraticcha	Left of East	Dark-Blue	SHAM	Sword
Sarvangakshodanapraticcha	Left of East	Dark-Blue	SAM	Curved Knife
Ucchistabhaktapraticcha	Left of East	Dark-Blue	HPAM	Curved Knife

Table 5-49: Detachment goddesses to the left of east

To the right of the southern gateway there are five goddesses representing the absence of desire (10) to move; (11) to eat; (12) for bodily odour; (13) to dance and (14) to be slim.

Name	Direction	Colour	Seed	Emblem
Stobhanapraticcha	Right of South	Red	TAM	Lotus
Bhojanapraticcha	Right of South	Red	THAM	Bowl of Food
Malapraticcha	Right of South	Red	DAM	Club
Nrityapraticcha	Right of South	Red	DHAM	Spear
Shosanapraticcha	Right of South	Red	NAM	Lotus

Table 5-50: Detachment goddesses to the right of south

To the left of this gateway there are four goddesses representing the absence of desire (15) to call; (16) to run; (17) to excrete and (18) to fight.

Name	Direction	Colour	Seed	Emblem
Akristapraticcha	Left of South	Green	NGAM	Arrow
Dhavanapraticcha	Left of South	Red	GHAM	Axe
Mutravitsravanapraticcha	Left of South	Red	GAM	Curved Knife
Samgramapraticcha	Left of South	Red	KHAM	Curved Knife

Table 5-51: Detachment goddesses to the left of south

To the right of the northern gateway there are five goddesses representing the absence of desire (19) for increase; (20) for ornaments; (21) for a seat; (22) to reign and (23) to speak.

Name	Direction	Colour	Seed	Emblem
Paustikapraticcha	Right of North	White	PAM	Utpala
Bhusanapraticcha	Right of North	White	PHAM	Mirror
Asanapraticcha	Right of North	White	BAM	Trident
Rajyapraticcha	Right of North	White	BHAM	Lotus
Mriduvacanapraticcha	Right of North	White	MAM	Utpala

Table 5-52: Detachment goddesses to the right of north

To the left of this gateway there are four goddesses representing the absence of desire (24) for music; (25) to bind; (26) to argue and (27) for anger.

Name	Direction	Colour	Seed	Emblem
Vadyapraticcha	Left of North	Blue	HAM	Vinya
Bandhanapraticcha	Left of North	White	YAM	Hammer
Bahukalahapraticcha	Left of North	White	RAM	Curved Knife
Darakakroshanapraticcha	Left of North	White	VAM	Curved Knife

Table 5-53: Detachment goddesses to the left of north

To the right of the western gateway there are five goddesses representing the absence of desire (28) to stiffen; (29) for perfume; (30) to rest; (31) to swim and (32) to bind.

Name	Direction	Colour	Seed	Emblem
Stambhanapraticcha	Right of West	Yellow	TAM	Wheel
Gandhapraticcha	Right of West	Yellow	THAM	Conch of Perfume
Majjanapraticcha	Right of West	Yellow	DAM	Vajra
Plavanapraticcha	Right of West	Yellow	DHAM	Needle
Bandhanapraticcha	Right of West	Yellow	NAM	Wheel

Table 5-54: Detachment goddesses to the right of west

To the left of this gateway there are four goddesses representing the absence of desire (33) for sex; (34) to stab; (35) to deceive and (36) to seize snakes.

Name	Direction	Colour	Seed	Emblem
Maithunapraticcha	Left of West	Green	KSHAM	Dharmodaya
Kilanapraticcha	Left of West	Yellow	SAM	Wheel
Vanyacanapraticcha	Left of West	Yellow	KAM	Curved Knife
Ahibandhanapraticcha	Left of West	Yellow	LAM	Curved Knife

Table 5-55: Detachment goddesses to the left of west

The Deities of the Universe Mandala

The Universe Mandala is usually represented in the enlightened mandala by a series of concentric circles representing the elements of earth, water, fire, wind and space. Within this environment there are two groups of deities: (1) the Ten Very-Wrathful Deities and (2) the Thirty-Five Million Perimeter Deities. Of these, the first actually belongs to the Body Mandala and the second are too numerous to be included in the total deities.

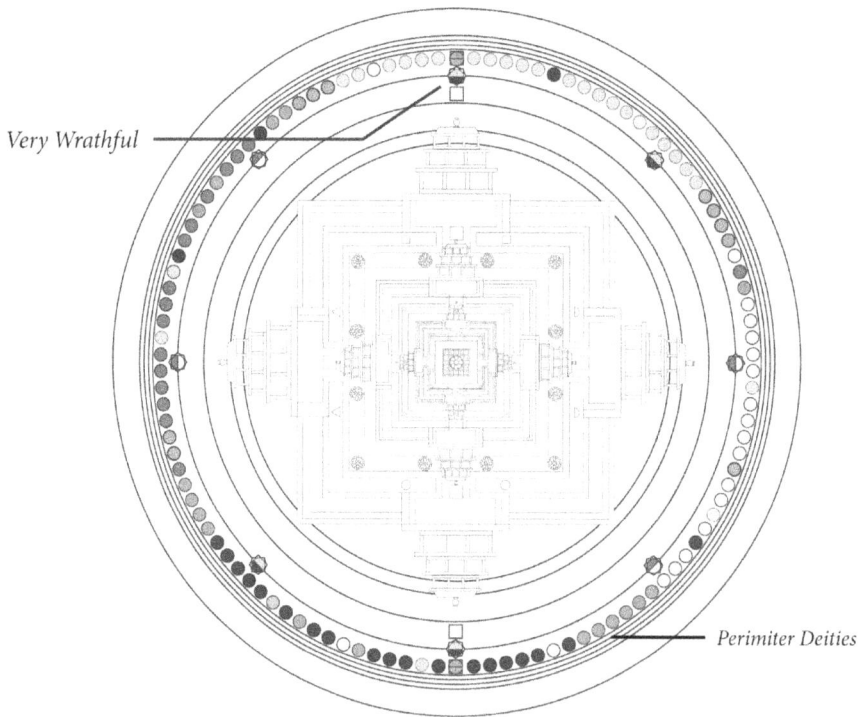

The Ten Very-Wrathful Deities

The Very-Wrathful Deities are placed in each of the ten cemeteries located on the boundaries of the fire and wind discs. They each have one face and two arms, with the head of an animal and the body of a human. They stand in union with the Naga Kings as consorts.

Name	Direction	Colour	Seed	Consort	Mount
Shvanasya	East	Dark-Blue	KA-KHA-GA-GHA-NGA	Takshaka	Rhinoceros
Kakasya	South-East	Dark-Blue	NYA-JHA-JA-CHA-CA	Mahapadma	Verundra Bird
Shukarasya	South	Red	KSHA-YA-RA-VA-LA	Ananta	Bear
Gridhrasya	South-West	Red	NA-DHA-DA-THA-TA	Kulika	Crane
Vyaghrasya	North	White	HA-YA-RA-VA-LA	Vasuki	Female Yak
Ulukasya	North-East	White	MA-BHA-BA-PHA-PA	Shangkhapala	Bat
Jambukasya	West	Yellow	HKA-SHA-SHA-HPA-SA	Karkotaka	Lion
Garudasya	North-West	Yellow	NA-DHA-DA-THA-TA	Padma	Nilika Bird
Vajrakshi	Above	Green	HA	Vijaya	Garuda
Nila	Below	Blue	HAH	Jaya	Eight-Legged Lion

Table 5-56: The Ten Very-Wrathful Deities

Not counting the directions of above and below, when the eight Very-Wrathfuls with consorts are combined with the eight Naga Kings (from the Body Mandala) with consorts, we arrive at thirty-two deities. These thirty-two represent the channels of the secret chakra. They also represent the activity chakras found in the joints of the feet and hands. The first thirty deities represent the thirty joints of the hands, while the last two Very-Wrathfuls represent the entire set of joints in the left and right feet respectively.

The Thirty-Five Million Perimeter Deities

The last set of deities represents the purification of the infinite manifestations that arise in ordinary experience. In the Jonang tradition, these deities are optional and can be included in the mandala based on personal preference. When included, they are normally placed in the outer half of the wind disc. The following is a list of some of the more common deities that are often depicted:

1. The ten planets
2. The twenty-eight lunar mansions
3. The twelve signs of the zodiac
4. The sixteen lunar phases
5. The worldly protectors of the ten directions
6. Various realm protectors
7. Celestial messengers
8. Human mahasiddhas

SADHANA PRACTICE IN THE JONANG TRADITION

Based on this preliminary presentation of the Kalachakra Mandala, we are now ready to begin the practices of the Kalachakra generation stage. This is done through the use of a *Sadhana* which is a sanskrit term that literally translates as "means to accomplishment". In this case, we use the sadhana to "accomplish" the deity, which is to generate the deity in our experience.

Practically speaking, we use the term to refer to a meditation manual used to work with different aspects of the mandala. These texts provide prayers, visualisations and mantras that guide us through the process in a step-by-step manner which facilitates practice.

Depending on which tradition you follow there are many sadhanas to develop different degrees of familiarity with the enlightened mandala. While some are very concise consisting of only a few pages, the more complex sadhanas can span many hundreds of pages. This variation in complexity means that some texts can be used for daily recitation whereas others are more suited for practice during retreat. This variation has given rise to three distinct approaches:

1. **Concise Approach:** This approach focuses on the principal deities of Kalachakra and Vishvamata in either the fully-manifest form of *Twenty-four Armed Kalachakra* or the essential form of *Innate Kalachakra*. Both sadhanas are suitable for daily recitation and provide an efficient means to establish the subtlety of mind needed for progressing along the path.

2. **Medium-Length Approach:** A slightly more complex variation is to focus on the nine deities of the *Essential Mandala*, providing the means for purifying the subtle channels and winds of the heart chakra. This practice can be extended to include the *Mind Mandala* by working with a total of seventy-two deities. The first can easily be performed as a daily practice, and the second is suited to the context of retreat.

3. **Extensive Approach:** Finally, we have the most extensive practice that incorporates the complete *Body, Speech and Mind Mandala* of six hundred and thirty-six deities. This sadhana practice can take many hours to complete and is therefore only suitable for those on full-time retreat. It includes extensive meditations on what are known as the *Four Branches of Approach and Accomplishment*: (1) The Supremely Victorious Mandala which establishes the clear appearance of the environment and deities; (2) The Supremely Victorious Activities which accumulate merit and create the causes for generating the form bodies of a Buddha; (3) The Yoga of the Drop which refines the mind and perfects the subtle generation stage; and (4) The Subtle Yoga which further concentrates the mind to prepare us for working with bliss in the completion stage.

In the Jonang Tradition, the generation stage practices are considered unique preliminaries for the completion stage practices of the Six Vajra Yogas. As such, most practitioners will concentrate first on the concise approach to purify their ordinary view and prepare their minds for non-conceptual meditation. Once they have gained some experience in the Six Vajra Yogas, the medium-length and extensive approaches are used as supplementary practices for refining the mind and accumulating merit.

REVIEW OF KEY POINTS

- In order to authentically practice Buddhist Tantra, you should gather four conditions: (1) establish a Buddhist view based on renunciation, Bodhicitta and a clear understanding of the teachings on emptiness and Buddha-nature; (2) develop a strong aspiration to practice Tantra; (3) receive the tantric vows and commitments from an authentic vajra master; and (4) receive permission to practice the generation stage through the Seven Empowerments of a Growing Child.

- The primary purpose of the generation stage is to abandon our ordinary sense of self and shift our identity to a pure conception of self. We do this through the practice of generating ourselves in the enlightened aspect of Kalachakra as our Yidam.

- Authentic practice of the generation stage requires five conditions: (1) the practice must come from an authentic source; (2) it must be transmitted through an authentic lineage; (3) our view must be rooted in emptiness; (4) the practice must be similar to the result and (5) we must have faith in its power.

- The generation stage creates the causes for manifesting the Rupakaya form bodies of a Buddha by training us in a way that purifies the process of birth, death and bardo.

- The Enlightened Mandala can be divided into two parts: (1) the enlightened environment that acts as a container; and (2) the deities who abide within that environment.

- With regards to the environment, there are two parts: (1) the universal mandala which provides the external support and (2) the enlightened mansion which provides the internal support.

- The enlightened mansion is divided into four levels representing the purification of the (1) body; (2) speech; (3) mind and (4) primordial wisdom.

- There are five mandalas of deities distributed throughout the mansion. Within the first three floors are located the mandalas of (1) body, (2) speech and (3) mind. The fourth floor contains the two mandalas of (4) great bliss and (5) essential nature.

- The Essential Mandala consists of three groups of deities: (1) the Principal Deity of Kalachakra Yab-Yum; (2) the Ten Shaktis and (3) the Four Emblems.

- The Great Bliss Mandala consists of two groups of deities: (1) the Twelve Buddhas and (2) the Ten Vases.

- The Mind Mandala consists of three groups of deities: (1) the Twelve Bodhisattvas; (2) the Five Wrathful Ones and (3) the Twelve Offering Goddesses.

- The Speech Mandala consists of two groups of deities: (1) the Eight Female Deities with Yoginis and (2) the Thirty-Six Desire Goddesses.

- The Body Mandala consists of four groups of deities: (1) the Twelve Male Deities of the Lunar Months; (2) the Six

Wrathful Guardians; (3) the Ten Naga Kings and (4) the Thirty-Six Detachment Goddesses.

- The Universe Mandala consists of two groups of deities: (1) the Ten Very-Wrathful Deities and (2) the Thirty-Five Million Perimeter Deities.

- In the Jonang Tradition most people practice the generation stage using a concise sadhana as a unique preliminary. Once experience in the completion stage practices has been developed, they will practice medium-length or extensive sadhanas as a supplement to their main practice.

CHAPTER SIX

Deity Yoga

The Concise Sadhana of Innate Kalachakra

Following our discussion of the general characteristics of the Kalachakra generation stage, we now move to the specific instructions for the essential practice of Deity Yoga. This profound technique provides a skilful means to cultivate the merit to view the enlightened nature of the inanimate universe and the animate beings who live there—effectively dissolving the ordinary appearances of the Outer and Inner Kalachakra to reveal the pure manifestations of the Enlightened Kalachakra.

At the root of this practice is the technique of visualising oneself in the aspect of the enlightened deity Kalachakra. Due to our strong grasping onto our ordinary sense of self, our visualisations can initially feel contrived, nothing more than a colourful fantasy we conjure up in our imagination. Unlike ordinary daydreams however, these visualisations are modelled on the ultimate nature of reality, and so they provide a path to discovering a deeper dimension of who we are. The more we work with them, the more layers we peel away and the more we learn about our nature. In time, we no longer think of ourselves in a limited way and our mind opens to the infinite capacity we all possess. What once felt so real to us takes on an illusory nature and the enlightened reality of Kalachakra feels like home.

This process is often referred to as *approach and accomplishment*. Through the formal practice of reciting a sadhana, we use visualisation to remind us of the qualities of the Yidam, then through mantra recitation we purify our winds and refine the subtlety of our mind.

This combination brings us closer to our ultimate nature and is known as "approaching the deity". The closer we come to the deity, the easier it becomes to experience a direct realisation of its nature which is known as "accomplishing the deity". With this achievement, we see the world from the deity's perspective and are ready to enter the next stage of the path.

THE THREE ELEMENTS OF DEITY YOGA

When practicing Deity Yoga, there are three elements we need to emphasise as without them, our practice will not become a cause for accomplishing the deity. They are: (1) clear appearance; (2) recollection of purity; and (3) divine pride. The first two elements are important, but the last is essential.

Clear Appearance

This element refers to the generation of a clear appearance of the deity in the mind. The term *visualisation* is often used in regard to this activity and although this is not incorrect, it doesn't fully express the nature of what a clear appearance should be. When we visualise something, the notion of real or unreal does not apply. You could just as easily visualise a flower in the sky or a rabbit with horns, neither of which exists in even a conventional sense. Another problem with this term is that it overly simplifies the process by emphasising only the visual aspect of the deity.

For these reasons, a more appropriate term is *generation*. When we speak of generating the deity, we refer to the act of bringing to mind the deity's qualities in our own experience. While this includes the visual component, it also incorporates the feeling of embodying these qualities. It is a lived experience that is multidimensional in nature and therefore carries with it greater strength than a mere visualisation.

Ultimately of course, there is nothing we need to generate as our nature already is Kalachakra. By practicing to "generate" ourselves in this way, we temporarily stop our deluded concept of self and allow our true nature to manifest. It is therefore more correct to say that we *unveil* our sacred truth.

Regardless of the terms we use, the practice remains the same. First we dissolve our ordinary appearance and consciously generate ourselves in the aspect of the deity. This process occurs in the mental consciousness, similar to the way a dream manifests when we are sleeping. Because it is mental in nature, do not expect the deity to arise as a visual form. The mind works in abstract concepts and generalisations, therefore it takes time for clarity to arise.

In the beginning the deity will appear in a fractured way as a collection of specific features. Your mind is likely to jump from detail to detail without an overall picture, as though you were look-ing through a stack of photographs. In one you may see an eye, in another a vajra ornament, and a syllable in yet another. Each detail takes effort to remember and you will constantly need to refresh your mindfulness.

After working for a time with individual details, you will generate clusters of features, for instance the entire face, crown or hands. You may even be able to attain an impression of the whole body. At this stage the appearance will still be vague and lack focus. Although you may have a sense for everything at once, the details are blurry, like an echo or something distant. Attempting to sharpen a detail causes you to lose the feeling of the whole.

As you develop stability in the practice, you will find it is possible to heighten your awareness of specific details while still maintaining the overall appearance, like adjusting the focus on a camera. By relaxing your mind into the meditation, the details will naturally become more vivid and clear. When the main details appear clearly, all at the same time, you have achieved an initial realisation of clear appearance.

Abiding continually in this realisation will eventually lead to mastery over the generation process itself. With the ability to instantly manifest the deity whenever you like and hold the appearance single-pointedly, this level is like the difference between standard and high definition television. The appearance can become so detailed that it looks and feels indistinguishable from anything you may experience through your senses.

Recollection of Purity

At a coarse level, recollecting purity means to develop mindfulness of the symbolic meaning of each detail of the deity. For instance, visualising Kalachakra's hands crossed behind the back of Vishvamata, holding a vajra and bell, we can remind ourselves that this represents the union of method and wisdom or immutable bliss and empty-form. By repeatedly connecting appearances with their definitive meaning, we strengthen our awareness of the ultimate and weaken our grasping onto the conventional. This element allows the conceptual appearance of a deity to function as a method for bringing us closer to our Buddha-nature.

On a more subtle level, the recollection of purity means to maintain an awareness of the empty-nature of the appearances arising in the mind. Rather than grasping onto the deity as something substantially existent, we should try to emphasise its illusory nature, considering it to be like a rainbow or hologram that appears vividly but lacks any real essence. Of the two levels, this second form of purity is much more important as it enables us to work with appearances without perpetuating our ignorance.

Furthermore, by recollecting the purity of the deity we remind ourselves of the provisional nature of the generation stage as a whole. Even though we may use concepts to shape our experience and cultivate virtue, we don't buy into the illusion. Like a lucid dreamer, we know that ultimately we need to wake up; to transcend the conceptual mind completely and experience the reality of the deity directly.

Divine Pride

The third and most important of the three elements is developing the stable conviction of being the deity. This is the thought "I am Kalachakra" and is known as holding *divine pride*. This mind is the direct antidote to our ordinary concept of self that identifies with the appearance of an inherently existent self. By familiarising ourselves with the qualities of an enlightened mind and identifying with those qualities, we shift our perspective and cut the root of our afflictive obscurations.

This mind is similar to the way we watch movies. The theatre lights go down and the projector comes on causing a steady stream of images to appear on the screen. Although we know the movie is not real, this fact doesn't stop us from being swept away by the experience. At some point, our mind suspends its disbelief and simply accepts the reality of the story. When this occurs, the movie can trigger feelings of happiness and suffering. However, if we remember the nature of the movie, its reality ceases to have power over us.

Similarly, even though there has never been nor ever will be an inherently existent self, we still believe it exists in the way that it appears. Because of this belief we perpetuate an endless stream of suffering and torment. When we stop believing in the reality of this self, it ceases to have any influence on our experience. As we think "I am Kalachakra", we affirm that the ordinary self is not who we "really" are. We remind ourselves of the illusion and choose to instead believe in our deeper and more profound nature. This is the actual essence of generation stage practice.

One area of this practice that can be particularly challenging is in relation to gender. For many practitioners a big part of their ordinary concept of self is based on their identify of being either male or female. As this quality of the self is often considered to be important, when it comes time to generate oneself as Kalachakra and Vishvamata, there is a tendency to project our present gender onto the visualisation. In these cases, female practitioners have problems visualising themselves as a male deity and male practitioners have problems visualising themselves as female. Both are indications of strong grasping and need to be dissolved in order to progress in the practice.

When dissolving our self into emptiness at the beginning of the practice, we should dissolve all aspects of our self, including our gender. This allows us to arise in the non-dual aspect of Kalachakra Yab-Yum who is neither exclusively male nor exclusively female. While it is traditional to refer to the deity by the male name, we must always remember that Kalachakra transcends all of these distinctions.

No matter how clearly the deity appears, you should always spend time cultivating the feeling of being Kalachakra, as it is this feeling that will bring the practice alive and make it a truly transformative experience. As with most qualities, divine pride manifests in stages. In the beginning, we focus on establishing a conceptual *belief* that we are Kalachakra. By reflecting on the nature of reality, we recognise the illusory nature of our ordinary experience and develop faith in a deeper level of existence. We may never have experienced this deeper level, but we still believe it to be more real than our present experience.

On the basis of our belief we establish an *attitude* that influences how we behave. Not only do we believe we are Kalachakra but we act in accordance with that belief. This means visualising ourselves engaging in activities in the same manner as a fully-enlightened being. Just like the Buddhas, we manifest countless emanations and bring limitless benefit to sentient beings. This is similar to identifying with our work, where our activities become part of our identity.

When you think you are Kalachakra and you visualise yourself acting like Kalachakra, it becomes possible to see yourself as Kalachakra. At this stage, your *pure perception* has become so strong, it is no longer a conceptual process and you actually adopt the perspective of the deity as your primary view, like an actor so fully embodied in their role, that they see the world through the eyes of their character. To ensure this level of perception is beneficial, we need to make sure we are not simply exchanging one delusion for another. This is why we must always contextualise our identity within a clear understanding of emptiness.

The last stage of an authentic divine pride is when we become so familiar with the experience of the deity, we *feel* like ourselves when we generate the mandala. This is similar to the feeling of returning home after an extended period abroad. There is a feeling of closeness you identify with and when it arises, the deity has become your default state of being. While you may manifest in order to perform worldly functions, you never lose the feeling of who you really are.

HOW TO PRACTICE THE CONCISE SADHANA OF INNATE KALACHAKRA

In the Jonang Tradition, meditation on the generation stage is seen as a unique preliminary to the practices of the Kalachakra Six Vajra Yogas. As such, emphasis is on establishing a subtle state of pure perception that focuses our attention on the definitive truth of our experience. This mind acts as a foundation for engaging in the non-conceptual meditation of the Three Isolations. The method for achieving this result is the recitation of the *Concise Sadhana of Innate Kalachakra* which highlights the non-dual wisdom of sublime emptiness as a basis for bringing ultimate benefit to others.

Dissolution of the Self

The practice begins by first reciting the following mantra:

OM SHUNYATA JÑANA VAJRA SVABHAVA ATMAKO HAM

As you say this mantra, visualise yourself and all phenomena dissolving into emptiness. This should not be a mere emptiness of

The Essential Nature of the Primordial Buddha—Innate Kalachakra

inherent existence, but a sublime emptiness that is endowed with infinite enlightened qualities. Recognise that the conventional truth of samsara does not truly exist; that it is nothing more than an illusory reality projected by the mind over the basis of our Buddha-nature. This is the emptiness as understood in the tradition of Zhentong Madhyamaka.

Remain in a non-conceptual state for a period, completely open and free of all thoughts. You should think with absolute confidence, "I am abiding in the primordial state of the fully-established nature, beyond all notions of subject and object". This experience of sublime emptiness is the actual appearance of Innate Kalachakra, a mind completely free of conventional phenomena and which is your true nature. When you recognise this, you become the enlightened deity.

Visualisation of the Innate Kalachakra Deity

From within this mind of Innate Kalachakra appears a vast wind mandala, followed by mandalas of fire, water and earth. From the centre of the earth mandala arises the multi-coloured Mount Meru with the five peaks at its summit. Resting on the central peak is a multi-coloured lotus. At its centre is a white moon disc, a red sun disc, a black rahu disc and a yellow kalagni disc, symbolising Bodhicitta, emptiness, immutable bliss and empty-form respectively.

Visualise yourself on top of this seat in the pure form of Innate Kalachakra. Your body is dark-blue in colour, symbolising the ultimate purity of the central channel. Your one face symbolises the ultimate truth of all phenomena, two arms symbolise method and wisdom or the inseparability of immutable bliss and empty-form and three eyes symbolise the direct perception of the past, present and future. You stand embracing your consort with your hands crossed and wrapped around her back, holding a vajra in your right hand and a bell in your left. This symbolises the inseparable union of the masculine and feminine aspects of enlightenment; the vajra represents indestructible masculine energy, method, compassion and immutable bliss while the bell symbolises feminine energy, wisdom and indestructible empty-form.

Your neck has three colours, the middle is black, the right side is red and the left side is white symbolising the elimination of rhythm (sattva), activity (rajas) and inertia (tamas). These terms have been appropriated from the Hindu Samkhya school to describe the qualities of substance (prakrti). In this context, they refer to the purification of the three poisons of ignorance, attachment and aversion respectively. This is a demonstration of how the Kalachakra teachings were skilfully designed to lead those holding such belief systems to a correct path.

Your two legs stand on top of two worldly gods, symbolising freedom from grasping onto samsara and nirvana. The left leg is white and slightly bent, crushing the chest of a white Rudra. He has one face and three eyes, wears a tiger skin and snake ornament and is lying face up, having fainted. This symbolises the purity of accomplishment, the transformation of the left channel (lalana) as well as the elimination of the four afflictions—grasping, hatred, ignorance and pride. The right leg is red and extended, crushing the chest of red Kamadeva. He has one peaceful face, two arms wearing jewelled ornaments and is lying face up, also having fainted. This symbolises the transformation of the right channel (rasana) and the elimination of the four maras of the aggregates, afflictions, death and pleasurable objects.

You have a topknot of thick hair plaited into locks which are so full, they hang loosely down your back. On top of this a precious wish-fulfilling jewel draped in silk, symbolising Vajrasattva who is the root of this mandala. In front of the top knot is a crossed vajra with four colours matching the colours of Mount Meru—dark-blue, red, white and yellow. These colours symbolise the four Buddha-activities which liberate beings—pacifying, increasing, magnetising and subjugating. Just above the crown of your head is a crescent moon symbolising the attainment of immutable bliss. You are adorned with numerous vajra ornaments made of indestructible vajras such as earrings, necklaces, armlets, belt, anklets and malas. Silk scarves also drape your body, symbolising the indestructible immutable bliss of the enlightened mind and you wear a lower garment of tiger skin, symbolising the elimination of pride and arrogance.

Your fingers are five different colours: yellow thumbs; white index fingers; red middle fingers; black ring fingers and green little fingers. These symbolise the purification of the five elements as well as the five qualities of the left channel and the attainment of the five wisdoms. Your finger joints are three different colours: the first (closest to the hand) is black; the middle joint is red and the third (nearest the tip of the finger) is white, symbolising the purity of the right channel and the attainment of the indestructible vajra body, speech and mind of a Buddha.

Five different colours radiate a body's length out from your body and are surrounded by a blazing ring of fire. Your teeth are slightly visible, revealing four semi-wrathful fangs. Your three eyes are rounded and slightly bloodshot and you have an expression that carries a mixture of wrath and ecstasy. These features symbolise non-conceptual compassion and immutable bliss.

Kalachakra embraces the consort Vishvamata. It is important to visualise them joined inseparably in union, forming the single deity of Kalachakra Yab-Yum. Vishvamata has a golden yellow body with one face, two arms and three eyes. Her right hand embraces Kalachakra and holds a curved-knife, while her left hand holds a skull cup with an offering of nectar. Her right leg is bent and her left leg is extended, standing with Kalachakra in sexual union. She is naked and adorned

The Kalachakra Ten-Fold Symbol of Power

with bone ornaments including a bone Dharma wheel on her crown and bone earrings, armlets, bracelets, anklets, belt and necklaces. Half her hair forms a crown and half flows down her back, symbolising the nature of all phenomena as empty-form.

Both deities are marked by the six syllables which represent the six elements and the six Buddhas. In the centre of the forehead chakra is the white syllable OM which represents the pure nature of the water element and Amitabha—the body of all the Buddhas. At the throat chakra is a red AH representing the pure nature of the fire element and Ratnasambhava—the speech of all the Buddhas. At the heart chakra is a black HUM representing the pure nature of the air element and Amoghasiddhi—the mind of all the Buddhas. At the navel chakra is a yellow HO symbolising the pure nature of the earth element and Vairochana—the indestructible primordial wisdom of all the Buddhas. At the secret chakra is a blue SVA representing the pure nature of the primordial mind element and Vajrasattva—the indestructible purity of the primordial mind. Finally, at the crown chakra is a green HA representing the pure nature of the space element and Akshobya—the activity of all the Buddhas.

The purpose of visualising the six syllables is not to bless or transform these locations on your body, but rather to understand that Kalachakra and Vishvamata are the pure embodiment of the six realms of samsaric existence and that their nature is no different from your own primordial nature.

Six colours of light emanate outwards from the six syllables, radiating throughout the entire universe so that the six realms become an inconceivably vast mansion representing the body, speech and mind of Kalachakra. The light then transforms all beings into the assembly of deities of the Kalachakra mandala. Although it is not necessary to include every detail of the mandala in your visualisation, you should feel as though you are standing on the central lotus of the

Essential Mandala and that all the deities are amassed around you.

With great confidence, remind yourself that you are Kalachakra and Vishvamata in union. Try to make the visualisation appear clear and translucent like the light of a rainbow, rather than a solid image or picture. Once you have built this visualisation, remain single-pointedly in this state.

Visualisation of the Kalachakra Symbol

At your heart, visualise a multi-coloured lotus with the four discs of moon, sun, rahu and kalagni. On top of these discs appears the *Kalachakra Ten-Fold Symbol of Power* (*namchu* in Tibetan). The unique form of this seed syllable represents the essence mantra of Kalachakra and consists of ten components: (1) Nada; (2) Bindu; (3) Visarga; (4) HA; (5) KSHA; (6) MA; (7) LA; (8) VA; (9) RA and (10) YA. The first three are portions of letters from Sanskrit grammar that modify pronunciation, while the remaining seven are actual syllables.

Depending on the tradition you follow, the symbol will be visualised slightly differently. In the Jonang Tradition, a specific design created by Jetsun Taranatha is used, which has four upright bars as opposed to the ten interwoven bars common in other traditions.

No single colour-scheme represents the definitive colour of this symbol as each of the ten components is coloured differently depending on the meaning being emphasised. In general, there are three levels of interpretation based on the three levels of reality: (1) outer; (2) inner and (3) enlightened other.

Symbolism Based on the Outer Kalachakra

The Outer Kalachakra is focused on the inanimate universe arising from the five elements of space, wind, fire, water and earth. This version of the symbol is useful for developing mindfulness of the general structure of the physical universal.

Component	Colour	Meaning
YA	Dark-Blue	The Wind Element Disc
RA	Red	The Fire Element Disc
VA	White	The Water Element Disc
LA	Yellow	The Earth Element Disc
MA	Multi-Coloured	Mount Meru and the rest of the Desire Realm
KSHA	Green	The Form Realm
HA	Blue	The Formless Realm
Visarga	Red	Sun
Bindu	White	Moon
Nada	Dark-Blue	Rahu and Kalagni

Table 6-1: The External Universe

Symbolism Based on the Inner Kalachakra

The Inner Kalachakra is concerned with the structure of the animate beings living in the physical universe. The two variations of this interpretation are based on: (1) the general structure of a human being and (2) the specific structure of the subtle body.

The Structure of a Human Being

This variation represents the structure of a human as a product of the six elements; the five physical elements plus consciousness. It provides a means for developing mindfulness of the correlations between the external and internal.

Component	Colour	Meaning
YA	Dark-Blue	Soles of the feet (wind)
RA	Red	Shins (fire)
VA	White	Knees (water)
LA	Yellow	Hips (earth)
MA	Multi-Coloured	Spine and Torso (all five elements)
KSHA	Blue	Throat and Forehead (consciousness)
HA	Green	Crown (space)
Visarga	Red	Right Channel and Red Essences
Bindu	White	Left Channel and White Essences
Nada	Dark-Blue	Central Channel and Subtle Winds

Table 6-2: The Coarse Body

The Structure of the Subtle Body

This variation relates to the structure of the subtle energetic system and is useful for developing mindfulness of the channel system used in advanced yogic techniques.

Component	Colour	Meaning
YA	White	Forehead Chakra
RA	Red	Throat Chakra
VA	Black	Heart Chakra
LA	Yellow	Navel Chakra
MA	Multi-Coloured	Activity Chakras (in the joints)
KSHA	Blue	Secret Chakra
HA	Green	Crown Chakra
Visarga	Red	Right Channel
Bindu	White	Left Channel
Nada	Dark-Blue	Central Channel

Table 6-3: The Subtle Body

Symbolism Based on the Enlightened Kalachakra

While the Outer and Inner Kalachakra are concerned with the conventional ground that requires purification, the Enlightened Kalachakra focuses on the path used to purify this ground and the result that manifests. In total, there are five variations at this level based on: (1) the generation of the enlightened universe; (2) the generation of the enlightened mansion; (3) the generation of the enlightened deities; (4) the practice of the Six Vajra Yogas; and (5) the resultant state of enlightenment.

The Generation of the Enlightened Universe

This variation represents the purity of the ultimate universe as presented in the enlightened universe mandala. Visualising the symbol in this way is useful for developing mindfulness of the support upon which the enlightened mansion is established.

Component	Colour	Meaning
YA	Dark-Blue	The purity of the wind element
RA	Red	The purity of the fire element
VA	White	The purity of the water element
LA	Yellow	The purity of the earth element
MA	Multi-Coloured	The purity of Mount Meru
KSHA	Green	The purity of birth manifesting as a lotus
HA	White	The purity of the moon as a disc
Visarga	Red	The purity of the sun as a disc
Bindu	Blue	The purity of the rahu and kalagni as discs
Nada	Green	The purity of the space element

Table 6-4: The Enlightened Universe

The Generation of the Enlightened Mansion

This variation represents the vajra ground that is represented in paintings of the enlightened mandala. It is useful for developing mindfulness of the various features of the enlightened mansion which is the environment of the enlightened deities.

Component	Colour	Meaning
YA	Dark-Blue	The perimeter of wind arising from the all-accomplishing wisdom.
RA	Red	The perimeter of fire arising from the wisdom of equality
VA	White	The perimeter of water arising from the wisdom of discrimination
LA	Yellow	The perimeter of earth arising from the wisdom of basic space
HA	Green	The perimeter of space arising from the mirror-like wisdom
MA	Multi-Coloured	The vajra ground and the five-fold walls of the enlightened mansion
KSHA	Blue	The lotus seats arising from Vajra-Wisdom
Bindu	White	The first floor of the mansion arising from Vajra-Body
Visarga	Red	The second floor of the mansion arising from Vajra-Speech
Nada	Dark-Blue	The third and fourth floors of the mansion arising from Vajra-Mind

Table 6-5: The Enlightened Mansion

The Generation of the Enlightened Deities

The last variation related to the Kalachakra generation stage focuses on the different deities that abide in the enlightened mansion. This is useful for developing mindfulness of the groups of deities which form the six hundred and thirty-six deities used in the Jonang Tradition.

Component	Colour	Meaning
YA	Dark-Blue	The 20 deities of the Universe Mandala
RA	Red	The 428 deities of the Body Mandala
VA	White	The 116 deities of the Speech Mandala
LA	Yellow	The 44 deities of the Mind Mandala
KSHA	Green	The 18 deities of the Great Bliss Mandala
HA	Blue	The 10 deities of the Essential Mandala
MA	Multi-Coloured	Kalachakra Yab-Yum, pervading all of the deities
Bindu	White	The Vajra-Body of Kalachakra
Visarga	Red	The Vajra-Speech of Kalachakra
Nada	Dark-Blue	The Vajra-Mind of Kalachakra

Table 6-6: The Enlightened Deities

The Practice of the Six Vajra Yogas

This variation focuses on the Kalachakra completion stage and is useful for developing mindfulness of the practices used in the Vajra Yoga path.

Component	Colour	Meaning
KSHA	Blue	Essence of Withdrawal Yoga
HA	Green	Essence of Stabilisation Yoga
YA	Dark-Blue	Essence of Life-Force Yoga
RA	Red	Essence of Retention Yoga
VA	White	Essence of Recollection Yoga
LA	Yellow	Essence of Absorption Yoga
MA	Multi-Coloured	Essence of the Five Primordial Wisdoms
Bindu	White	Essence of Vajra-Body—Empty-Form
Visarga	Red	Essence of Vajra-Speech—Immutable Bliss
Nada	Dark-Blue	Essence of Vajra-Mind—Union of Immutable Bliss and Empty-Form

Table 6-7: The Kalachakra Completion Stage

The Resultant State of Enlightenment

The final variation identifies the results of practicing the generation and completion stages. It is useful for developing mindfulness of the Six Buddha Families and the Four Bodies of Kalachakra.

Component	Colour	Meaning
YA	Dark-Blue	Purity of the Aggregate of Conceptions—Amoghasiddhi
RA	Red	Purity of the Aggregate of Feeling—Ratnasambhava
VA	White	Purity of the Aggregate of Perception—Amitabha
LA	Yellow	Purity of the Aggregate of Form—Vairochana
KSHA	Green	Purity of the Aggregate of Consciousness—Akshobhya
HA	Blue	Purity of the Aggregate of Awareness—Vajrasattva
MA	Multi-Coloured	Kalachakra—Pervasive Sovereign of All Families
Bindu	White	Emanation Body of Kalachakra—Nirmanakaya
Visarga	Red	Enjoyment Body of Kalachakra—Sambhogakaya

Table 6-8: The Results of the Path

It is worth being acquainted with each of these variations. When practicing in a retreat setting, they are particularly helpful for familiarising yourself with the different aspects of the path. If you find visualising the details difficult, Jetsun Taranatha recommends visualising the whole symbol as green as it pervades all colours, just as space pervades all phenomena.

Without abandoning the divine pride of Kalachakra Yab-Yum, focus your awareness on the symbol at your heart. Visualise it as no larger than a pea, radiating six colours of light out to the ten directions. The smaller you make the visualisation, the more concentrated your attention will become. Once you have attained a clear appearance of the symbol, you can move on to the next phase of the practice.

Mantra Recitation

While holding the visualisation, recite the Kalachakra mantra:

OM HA KSHA MA LA VA RA YANG SOHA

When the generation stage is your main practice, it is traditional to complete one million recitations of the mantra before being considered qualified to engage in the completion stage practices. The best practitioners can sustain a clear visualisation of Kalachakra Yab-Yum along with the deities of the mandala; however, in the Jonang Tradition it is not customary to practise the generation stage so extensively on its own. Practitioners are instead encouraged to combine their generation and completion stage practices as much as possible.

How to Recite the Mantra

The best grounding for reciting the mantra is for a practitioner to first receive initiation and to have knowledge of the different levels of meaning for each syllable, such as what is purified at each stage of practice and the result of the purification. When reciting the mantra try to engage in the generation stage practice with as much detail as possible, or at least generate some kind of visualisation. The mantra may be recited aloud or silently. Reciting with some audible sound is ideal, even if only a faint whisper, ensuring it is not too loud. Either way there must be a distinct sound for each syllable. Recitation should be performed until signs that the practice is accomplished appear, such as the ability to cure certain illnesses. It is traditional to include OM at the beginning of the mantra and SOHA at the end as it increases long life, merit and improves spiritual progress.

For the purpose of removing obstacles one can make the mantra more wrathful by changing SOHA for PHAT. If you would like to invoke the Buddhas and Bodhisattvas you can add HUNG after the main mantra. Likewise, to purify negativities one can add BEKATA;

to create a mind of peace NAMA can be added and to please the Yidam deities you can add WANATA.

The Benefits of Reciting the Mantra

The benefit of reciting this mantra are equal to the merit of reciting all the Buddha's teachings, as it is the essence of both the Sutras and Tantras. Reciting the mantra with the impure universe visualised as the pure Kalachakra mandala allows us to gradually unveil the pure state of Kalachakra Buddhahood. The following table provides some examples of the benefits that the mantra can have in relation to your physical body:

Syllable	Effect
YA	Removes all obstacles associated with the wind element, especially sickness relate imbalance of the inner wind.
RA	Removes all external obstacles associated with fire and sickness related to excess l
WA	Removes external obstacles associated with water and sickness related to the bloc
LA	Removes obstacles associated with the earth element and sickness of the musculoskeletal system.
MA	Removes external obstacles associated with all the elements, and any sickness cau by an imbalance of the elements.
KYA	Removes the obstacles to realising the true nature of desire as an aspect of pure primordial awareness.
HA	Removes any external or internal negative energies.
Visarga	Removes negativities associated with the feminine energy and attachment as well sickness related to an imbalance of the inner wind.
Bindu	Removes negativities of the masculine energy and anger as well as bile sickness.

Table 6-9: External effects of reciting the Kalachakra mantra

During the generation stage practice, recitation of this mantra brings us closer to Kalachakra as our Yidam and enables us to receive his blessings. After intensive practice, it is possible to have visions of the deity and receive prophecies from him. Good practitioners often gain the power to accomplish the four sublime activities of pacifying, increasing, magnetising and subjugating. Supernatural powers can thereby be attained so that the effects of natural disasters and negative forces can be overcome and more importantly, internal negative emotions or dysfunctional energies can be defeated. Gradually this will lead to attaining the state of Vajradhara.

Subsequent Visualisations

In order for the practice of Deity Yoga to successfully refine the mind, we need to constantly maintain mindfulness and vigilance. If we are not careful, our mind can easily become distracted, causing us to lose potential benefit. To help avoid this, we can use the following meditations to accumulate merit during the periods we are reciting mantras. While the mantra purifies our speech, the visualisations engage our mind and lay down the propensities for our future enlightenment.

During a single session you may choose to focus on one or more of these visualisations based on your preference. You can alternate between generating a visualisation and reciting the mantra or you can work with the visualisations and mantra simultaneously.

Mindfulness of the Kalachakra Mandala

From the Kalachakra mantra visualised at your heart, radiate infinite beams of light to the Sambhogakaya Buddha-realms and invoke all 636 Kalachakra deities and any other Yidam deities of the four classes of tantra. Kalachakra Yab-Yum absorbs all these deities so you become the embodiment of them. Keep your mind focused on this state and recite the mantra.

Mindfulness of the Root Guru

Continue visualising yourself as Kalachakra Yab-Yum and from the mantra at your heart, radiate light in all directions invoking your root guru in the space in front of you. After receiving the four empowerments from him, he dissolves into the jewel ornament at your crown, becoming inseparable from you. Keep your mind focused on this state and continue to recite the mantra.

Mindfulness of the Dharma Teachers

Continue to visualise yourself as Kalachakra in union with Vishvamata, and from the mantra at your heart, light radiates in every direction, invoking all the Dharma teachers with whom you have a connection. They all dissolve into your root guru, the embodiment of your spiritual teachers, who is inseparable from Vajrasattva on your crown. Keep your mind focused on this state while reciting the mantra.

Making Offerings to the Enlightened Beings

Visualising yourself as Kalachakra Yab-Yum, radiate infinite rays of light to all the Buddha-realms from the Kalachakra mantra at your heart. The rays transform into countless offerings made externally, internally and secretly, satisfying and pleasing the pure minds of the Buddhas. At the same time be certain that all beings accumulate oceans of merit. The rays of light then return, carrying the blessings of the body, speech and mind of the Buddhas in the form of images, mantras and symbols which dissolve into Kalachakra Yab-Yum. You receive the powers of the body, speech and mind of the Buddhas. Keep your mind focused on this state while reciting the mantra.

Purification of All Impure Realms

Continuing the visualisation of yourself as Kalachakra Yab-yum, infinite rays of light radiate from the mantra at your heart to all the impure universes. As the light touches each universe it instantly becomes a pure Buddha-realm filled with great palaces and the inhabitants become Kalachakra deities. The rays of light return and dissolve into Kalachakra Yab-Yum. This is known as purifying the impure universes and is equivalent to the Bodhisattva practice known as pure-land training. In this way all roots of virtue are transformed into a means for establishing a Buddha-realm where the state of enlightenment will be attained. For Mahayana sutra practitioners this practice is carried out over many aeons, yet a true Vajrayana practitioner could accomplish it in a very short time.

The Mantra Fire-Brand

As you visualise yourself as Kalachakra Yab-Yum with the Kalachakra symbol at your heart, remember that your true natural reality is empty of deceptive phenomena. All samsaric and enlightened phenomena are a manifestation of Kalachakra Yab-Yum. With great confidence see the syllables of the Kalachakra mantra—HA KSHA MA LA VA RA YA— radiate from his heart chakra travelling down the central channel to his secret vajra jewel and streaming forth with a great sound of bliss into Vishvamati's secret lotus. The stream of syllables then moves upwards through her central channel, flowing out of her mouth and into Kalachakra's mouth where it travels up to the crown chakra and back down to the heart. In this way, the mantra forms an unbroken chain of syllables circulating through the central channel of both Kalachakra and Vishvamata. Keep your mind focused on this state while reciting the mantra.

The Reverse Mantra Fire-Brand

Visualise yourself as Kalachakra Yab-Yum with the Kalachakra mantra at your heart as before. Recall that your true natural reality is empty of deceptive phenomena and that all samsaric and en- lightened phenomena are a manifestation of Kalachakra Yab-Yum. With great confidence, see the syllables of the Kalachakra mantra— HA KSHA MA LA VA RA YA—radiate from his heart and rise up the central channel curving forward at the crown chakra and exiting through Kalachakra's mouth and into Vishvamata's mouth. The mantra chain continues down her central channel through her secret lotus and streaming with a great sound of bliss into Kalachakra's secret vajra jewel. It then travels up through his central channel and dissolves into the Kalachakra symbol at his heart. The syllables continue to circulate in this fashion as you recite the mantra.

The Recitation that is Like the Buzzing of Bees

Continue to visualise yourself as Kalachakra Yab-Yum with the mantra at your heart. Think of the enlightened and sentient beings in the ten directions instantly manifesting in the form of Kalachakra. As they all recite the Kalachakra mantra with you, the only sound you hear is the sound of the mantra. Allow your mind to become totally immersed within this sound, keeping your mind focused while reciting the mantra single-pointedly.

The Four Extraordinary Activities

Again visualise yourself as Kalachakra in union with Vishvamata with the Kalachakra symbol at your heart. Rays of coloured light emanate from the symbol with a multitude of deities appearing on the tips of each ray, which extend to the farthest reaches of space to perform limitless activities for the benefit of sentient beings.

From your heart come rays of white light and the syllable AH, creating countless white deities who *pacify* conflict by dispelling sickness, afflictions and obstacles. Imagine that all sentient beings experience genuine peace and harmony in their lives.

From your heart come rays of yellow light and the syllable RI, creating countless yellow deities who *increase* the virtuous qualities of sentient beings by blessing their minds and guiding them in the Dharma. Imagine that all sentient beings experience an increase of longevity, merit, wealth and qualities.

From your heart come rays of red light and the syllable OO, creating countless red deities who *magnetise* sentient beings towards the Dharma by using their power and energy to influence their lives in a positive way, inspiring them to virtue. Imagine that through your influence, all sentient beings experience the bliss of the Dharma and create the causes to achieve full and complete enlightenment.

From your heart come rays of dark-blue light and the syllable LI, creating countless dark-blue deities who *subjugate* all powerful negative forces that act as obstacles for sentient beings to practice virtue. With a strong, wrathful energy, imagine that the deities defeat all maras and obstacles which impede the progress of sentient beings towards enlightenment. Imagine that sentient beings are firmly established in their practice and as a result are able to manifest limitless qualities.

The lights and deities return and dissolve back into you, eradicating your afflictions and obscurations to enlightenment. Your realisations are strengthened and you attain the ability to control your inner winds and subtle essences; all your ignorance and delusions are removed. Keep your mind focused on this state while reciting the mantra.

Dissolving the Visualisation

To conclude a practice session you should dissolve the visualisations you have created, including the environment and deities of the mandala. Begin from the outside and work your way inwards, dissolving each layer into yourself, allowing them to merge with your being just like water being poured into water. During this visualisation you should have a clear understanding that you abide in the nature of Kalachakra Yab-Yum. Vishvamata then dissolves into Kalachakra followed by Kalachakra dissolving from the edges into the mantra symbol at your heart.

The mantra symbol dissolves from the base upwards to the nada.

The nada at the top of the symbol then gradually disappears into emptiness like a strand of hair being consumed by fire. Remain in an open state of awareness for as long as you can.

Then, once again, instantly visualise yourself as Kalachakra Yab-Yum. Maintaining mindfulness of yourself as Kalachakra at all times is important and not exclusive to practice sessions, as each of the Six Vajra Yoga practices relies on a clear visualisation of these deities in union.

Dedicating the Merit

Upon finishing the dissolution you should dedicate the merit for the benefit of all beings so that they may uncover their natural enlightened state:

> Through this virtue may I quickly realise the state of Kalachakra and lead all beings without exception to complete enlightenment.

If the generation stage is your main practice, you may also like to recite this extensive aspiration prayer as a means to strengthen your awareness of the enlightened mandala:

> I pay homage to the foe destroyer, possessing all qualities of full enlightenment, the glorious Kalachakra, embodiment of the six Buddha-families.

> May I unveil the ground, the permanent, eternal and ultimate peace, immutable non-dual awareness, embracing all enlightened qualities and the 636 sublime deities.

> May I fully engage in the path, the pure inspired practice purifying all conventional phenomena with the great yoga of body and mind.

> May I engage in the indestructible path of the Six Yogas with the inner vajra body, the subtle channels, winds and essences, which are purified and liberated.

May I reach the result of elimination of afflictions, the all-pervasive enlightenment embodied by the six Buddha-families.

May I gain the state of outer Kalachakra, complete freedom from the aggregates and elements of the universe.May I be able to control all the aggregates and external elements. May I liberate and purify the internal channels, winds and drops.

May I gain the state of inner Kalachakra; complete freedom from the gross channels, winds and drops. May I attain the pure state of limitless empty form and enlightened activities.

May I attain the state of the enlightened other Kalachakra with realisation of the primordial state of Kalachakra Buddhahood.
May I pacify all sickness, obstacles and misfortune while following the path. May I increase my long life, health, prosperity and spiritual development.

May I control the goodness of the three realms of samsara and beyond samsara. May I subdue and eliminate all external obstructive forces and all internal obscurations to enlightenment.

May I gain the common siddhis of the five miraculous powers and the enlightened powers of the five paths and ten bhumis.
May I at least have the good fortune to enter the Golden Age of Shambhala.

May I attain immeasurable love and compassion and the incomparable mind of Bodhicitta. May I have genuine devotion, diligence, great concentration and wisdom. May I be the unsurpassed rescuer of all sentient beings from samsara.

May I reach Kalachakra Buddhahood in this very lifetime; the immutable state of enlightened empty-form.
May I abide eternally in the state of immutable great bliss.

ADVICE FOR PRACTICING DEITY YOGA

When done correctly, the benefits that come from practicing Deity Yoga can be truly extraordinary. Not only will it bring your mind closer to the Yidam, but it will also create the causes for all sentient beings to achieve enlightenment. To help actualise your potential, I would like to offer the following advice:

Building Your Visualisation

During the sadhana practice of Innate Kalachakra, you are asked to manifest yourself instantaneously in the aspect of Kalachakra Yab-Yum. To do this, you will first need to be familiar with Kalachakra's form. Initially it is worthwhile focusing the majority of your meditation on building up the details of this visualisation and then once you achieve a clear and stable appearance, time can be dedicated to reciting mantra and performing subsequent visualisations.

To establish your familiarisation, start by closely studying a suitable support such as a thangka painting or statue. As you sit in front of the support, examine each detail for a time, then close your eyes and try to reproduce the image in your mind. You could start with the face, moving to the head and body, then the arms and finally the legs. Once you feel you have a good impression of Kalachakra's features, repeat the sequence with Vishvamata.

Don't be discouraged if your visualisation lacks clarity or is unstable and constantly changes. With patience, gently focus your mind on a particular detail until it becomes clear, then move to the next detail. When you have developed familiarity with a cluster of details, try to view them as a whole. In time, you will be able to generate the appearance of the full deity with little difficulty. When this occurs you can shift your emphasis to the other stages of the practice.

Practice in the Dark

Visualisation practice is like painting a picture. If the canvas of your mind is already filled with ordinary appearances, it will be hard to paint a clear picture and immerse yourself in the feeling of the enlightened mandala you are manifesting. For this reason, it is recommended that you practice in a dark room with few external distractions. This can be achieved by practicing at night or simply closing your eyes.

Practicing in the dark requires you to memorise the sadhana which prevents you from being distracted by looking down at the pages. Committing the visualisations to memory also helps improve your recall of the details and establishes greater clarity. Fortunately, the concise sadhana of Innate Kalachakra is quite short and this should not be too difficult.

Maintaining Divine Pride

Generation stage practice is not limited to formal meditation sessions. From the moment you take the tantric commitments, you are pledging to do your best to maintain a constant awareness of your enlightened nature. This means that when you arise as Kalachakra at the end of your practice, you should try to maintain your divine pride without distraction or laziness.

To help develop this mindfulness, use the appearances you encounter in life as reminders of the enlightened mandala. For instance, think of the environment as being the universal mandala and view your body as the enlightened mansion. Consider all beings as deities, all sound as mantra and whatever thoughts arise in the mind, think of them as the primordial wisdom of Kalachakra and Vishvamata—the insepa-rable union of immutable bliss and empty-form. This is a way to focus on the pure nature of your experience at all times.

Transforming common activities such as eating, bathing and sleeping into opportunities to remind yourself of your true nature is another good way to strengthen your mindfulness of the enlightened mandala, while also generating vast stores of merit. When used skilfully, these simple visualisations create a continuity of practice that allows you to go considerably deeper in your formal sessions.

What to do When Eating

This first practice can be performed before eating a meal. If reciting prayers out loud causes others to feel uncomfortable, there is no problem saying them silently in your mind. Begin by reciting the following mantra three times:

OM AH HUM HO

When you recite OM, remember the innate purity of the food. As you say AH, imagine the food multiplying and becoming bountiful. When you recite HUM imagine the food takes on a perfect aspect of colour, taste, smell and nutritional essence and as you say HO, imagine the food transforms into pure enlightened nectar. Maintaining mindfulness of this purity, recite the following verses and offer the food to the deities of the enlightened mandala.

> To those who possess the four indestructible bodies,
> To the infinite examples of Dharma collections,
> To the noble assembly who demonstrate that Dharma,
> I make offerings to the Three Jewels—source of my refuge.

> To Kalachakra, Vajrasattva and Shakyamuni Buddha;
> To the Shaktis, the Ten Vases and the Four Vajras;
> To the Buddhas, the Bodhisattvas and the Wrathful-Ones;
> I make offerings to each of these and the goddesses.

To the Female Deities—central figures with surrounding yoginis;
To the Gods of the Days, the Nagas and the Goddesses of Detachment;
To the Very Wrathful, the Stars and the Planets, and the Guardians
of all Directions and Realms; I make offerings to the thirty-five
million manifestations.

To the Guru, the Yidam and the Assembly of Dakinis,
I make oceans of sublime offerings.
May all beings enjoy the great bliss
Of this ocean of wisdom-nectar.

Offer the enlightened nectar to the Three Jewels, while being aware that you are an enlightened being making an offering to other enlightened beings. As you eat, feel heat rising from your navel-centre as the nourishment melts, giving rise to blissful sensations. Offer this bliss to the 636 Kalachakra deities that reside in your body, pleasing them all.

Finally, purify and transform whatever food is left uneaten so it supplies the needs of all beings and dedicate the benefit of these remainders to those of the six realms, using the mantra:

OM SAMBHARA SAMBHARA BIMANA SARA MAHA JAVA HUM
OM SMARA SMARA BIMANA SKARA MAHA JAVA HUM

What to do While Bathing

Whenever you wash, shower or bathe, visualise yourself as Kalachakra with your root guru in the aspect of Vajradhara above your head. Imagine him pouring nectar on you from above, purifying your obscurations and bestowing on you the blessings of the four empowerments. As you visualise your body being filled with the nectar, strengthen the divine pride that you are Kalachakra Yab-Yum.

What to do When Falling Asleep

When going to sleep, maintain the recognition that you are Kalachakra Yab-Yum and vow to continue this awareness when you awaken. Falling asleep without losing this awareness enhances the possibility of becoming lucid in your dream and if this occurs, your dream can be used as an opportunity to practice the sadhana. Upon waking, instantly generate yourself as Kalachakra Yab-Yum and establish your divine pride.

REVIEW OF KEY POINTS

- Deity Yoga is a meditation practice in which a combination of visualisation and mantra recitation is used to generate the experience of a deity in our mind. This experience becomes the basis for a pure concept of self that accords with reality.

- There are three elements we should focus on when practicing Deity Yoga: (1) generating a clear appearance of the deity; (2) recollecting the purity of the deity's nature; and (3) establishing a divine pride that holds the deity as one's true self.

- When the generation stage is practiced as a preliminary to the Six Vajra Yogas, we focus on the Concise Sadhana of Innate Kalachakra. This sadhana is broken into five main parts: (1) dissolution of the self; (2) visualisation of the Innate Kalachakra Deity; (3) visualisation of the Kalachakra Symbol; (4) mantra recitation; (5) subsequent visualisations; (6) dissolving the visualisation and (7) dedicating the merit.

- The Kalachakra Ten-Fold Symbol of Power is made up of ten components: (1) Nada; (2) Bindu; (3) Visarga; (4) HA; (5) KSHA; (6) MA; (7) LA; (8) VA; (9) RA and (10) YA. Each

241

component is mapped to different meanings based on the aspect of the path you are focused on. The colours of each component also change based on the context.

- There are nine subsequent visualisations you can perform while reciting the mantra: (1) mindfulness of the enlightened mandala; (2) mindfulness of the root guru; (3) mindfulness of the Dharma teachers; (4) making offerings to the enlightened beings; (5) purification of all impure realms; (6) the mantra fire-brand; (7) the reverse mantra fire-brand; (8) the recitation that is like the buzzing of bees; and (9) the four extraordinary activities.

- When you are starting out with this practice, concentrate on generating a clear appearance of the deity. Use the support of a thangka or statue to familiarise yourself with the many details of Kalachakra's form. Focus on groups of details and try to recreate them in the mind.

- It is best to memorise the concise sadhana so you can practice in the dark, as this will help you to immerse yourself in the feeling of the visualisation.

- Maintain divine pride by seeing all forms as enlightened deities, all sound as enlightened mantra and all thoughts as primordial wisdom. You can also transform common activities such as eating, bathing or sleeping into opportunities to remind yourself of the enlightened reality of Kalachakra.

PART THREE

Actualising the State of Kalachakra

CHAPTER SEVEN

Pointing Out the Nature of the Mind

Following the Kalachakra Path may be paralleled to the life-cycle of a human being. Practicing the *Outer Preliminaries* resembles the period when a bardo being searches for its next rebirth. Filled with confusion, it takes on different forms until eventually it is drawn towards the womb of a new mother. Similarly, as we search for meaning in our lives we encounter alternative viewpoints and after much indecision and uncertainty, are eventually drawn towards a spiritual path like Buddhism where we take refuge in the Three Jewels.

Having entered the womb, the process of incubation and growth begins and slowly the body of the being takes shape, developing the faculties needed to experience the world as a human. Likewise, as we practice the *Inner Preliminaries*, we establish the foundations of the Buddha's teachings which ripen and mature our mind in preparation for entering the resultant path of Kalachakra Tantra.

As we receive the *Seven Empowerments of a Growing Child,* we are effectively born from the womb and are introduced to the world of the enlightened mandala. By practicing the *Kalachakra Generation Stage,* we purify our mindstream of ordinary perceptions and establish a view that sees the innate purity of who we truly are. This process can be likened to a child whose identity is shaped by the experiences they encounter as they grow up in the world.

In time the child matures into an adolescent and begins the transition into adulthood, characterised by the onset of puberty. Driven by the process of transformation occurring in their body, the teenager's view of the world drastically shifts as sexuality takes on an increasingly dominant role in their life. This focus propels them into their first sexual encounter, introducing them to a very different level of experience previously unknown to them.

Having tasted the range of potential states of experience that their human life has to offer, the child is now referred to as an adult. While they may still lack maturity, they at least have some points of reference for each of the four states of waking, dream, deep-sleep and blissful absorption. For the remainder of their adult lives their time will be spent familiarising themselves with these states, developing insight into their nature and hopefully gaining wisdom from their experiences.

On the Kalachakra Path our transition into spiritual adulthood is marked by our first direct experience with the nature of our mind. Just as with our first sexual encounter, this experience completely shifts our perspective, providing us with an initial glimpse into our deeper capacity. It is with this capacity that we practice through the gradual process of the *Kalachakra Completion Stage*.

Before this nature can manifest in our experience however, we need to change our approach. Up to this point, our use of conceptual methods has been instrumental in removing our many layers of misconception, but as they are embedded in the dualistic mind, these methods function as a subtle barrier to experiencing our definitive nature. For this reason, we need to abandon them in favour of a direct approach that works without conceptual fabrications.

We can achieve this transformation from conceptual to non-conceptual in two steps. Firstly we are introduced to the Kalachakra view by receiving the *Four Higher Empowerments*. Secondly, with the establishment of this view, we use the unique meditation technique of the *Three Isolations* to cut the proliferation of thoughts and abide in the nature of the mind. This chapter will examine the initial process of empowerment, while the following chapter looks at the foundations for the meditative practice.

THE NEED FOR POINTING-OUT INSTRUCTIONS

Of the different types of phenomena we can potentially encounter, there are those which are manifest and those which are hidden. A manifest phenomenon is something we can directly observe using one of our six senses, such as a table or car. Hidden phenomena are not immediately apparent to our senses and include subtle impermanence or the empty-nature of dependent phenomena. Due to this subtlety, unless we are shown what to look for, they will remain hidden and therefore we require the support of an external reference to draw our attention to them.

When it comes to the nature of the mind, we are faced with an additional problem. The mind is the medium through which we know all phenomena, therefore, in order for the mind to know the nature of the mind, it must be able to see itself. This is similar to using the eye to identify its own colour. Unless you rely on a mirror, this is an impossible task. Only by looking at a reflection of the eye is it possible to see the characteristics of that eye; a principle which holds true for our mind. To develop a direct awareness of the mind's nature, it is necessary to hold a mirror to the mind. This mirror comes in the form of our view.

So far we have used our philosophical view largely as a method for bringing meaning into our actions. For instance, in Book Two, we were introduced to the view of *Zhentong Madhyamaka* which provided us with a way of understanding how wisdom is developed on the Bodhisattva Path. We explored concepts such as the five dharmas, the three natures and the seven types of emptiness and by understanding these concepts, we were able to bring context to our Dharma practice.

The role of our view now takes on a very specific purpose where it is no longer enough to merely describe or understand how reality works. From this new context, our view is used as a basis for pointing-out the different aspects of our mind so we can actually experience its nature. This is not a conceptual process based on logic or reasoning, but instead a direct approach that clearly distinguishes where we should place our attention. Such a view is experiential, not conceptual.

The way we develop such a view in Kalachakra is through the empowerment ceremony of the *Four Higher Empowerments*. In this process the vajra master guides you through four distinct meditations, each designed to reveal a specific level of experience. By generating the visualisations and focusing on the experiences they produce, the non-conceptual nature of the mind can manifest more clearly. Our goal should be to familiarise ourselves as much as possible with this nature so it can be used as the basis for our practice.

TAKING BLISS AS THE PATH

One of the first things we may notice as we enter into the completion stage is the important role the experience of bliss plays. Within the empowerments themselves there is considerable sexual imagery that is used to arouse feelings of bliss as a support for developing realisations. As this type of imagery can be easily misunderstood in many cultures, it is necessary to discuss the reasoning for this approach.

When considering the four states of experience, the waking state, dream state and deep-sleep state all operate in one way or another with a conceptual mind. The state of blissful absorption is the only one where the conceptual mind becomes dormant and therefore has the least veils of obscuration. This state offers us the most direct opportunity to realise the ultimate nature of our mind.

With regards to how the experience of blissful absorption usually manifests, there is a rapid influx of energy into the central channel, followed by an explosive release of that energy. An example of this is when we sneeze. First there is an intake, then a moment in which the conceptual movement of the mind ceases, followed immediately by a powerful release. If the intake or release is particularly strong and fast, we may completely black out which occurs when we faint, fall asleep or during the process of death. The only other time where this type of mind manifests is during the moment of orgasm.

Due to the speed in which fainting and sneezing occur, it is very difficult to use these moments as supports for our practice. Sexual intercourse however provides the opportunity for a prolonged build-up of energy, allowing a skilled practitioner to approach the experience of non-conceptuality in a more controlled manner. Unfortunately, the experience of bliss that accompanies this activity is so intense, that it is difficult for all but the most advanced of yogis to transform.

Recognising that different practitioners possess different levels of spiritual maturity, the great mahasiddhas used a variety of supports to introduce their disciples to the state of blissful absorption.

1. **Past Training:** For practitioners who were extremely ripe, a skilled vajra master would often use unorthodox methods such as striking the student on the head, or startling them with a sudden or loud sound. Sometimes this was all that was needed to cause the student's energy to flow into the central channel and give rise to a non-conceptual awareness. This approach relied heavily on the student's past life training in the nature of the mind. Since these propensities were already well established, the master could use a variety of methods to skilfully re-awaken them. In the Jonang tradition, it is common to see participants of higher empowerments suddenly leap high into the air or

make spontaneous sounds. These phenomena are known as *paryo* and occur when a practitioner's mind spontaneously slips into a non-conceptual state.

2. **Physical Consort:** For those who lacked the karmic conditions for instantaneous empowerment, the Buddha designed an empowerment process that would allow the vajra master to gradually introduce the student to the nature of their mind. Originally, these higher empowerments were restricted to only those practitioners who had achieved mastery of the generation stage practices. This meant that the disciples had fully stabilised their pure perception and were able to abide in refined states of meditative concentration. Without the danger of grasping onto ordinary bliss, such practitioners would receive the empowerments in reliance on a physical consort. Due to the non-conceptual nature of this approach, it was possible to very quickly cut through their thoughts and establish a direct experience of non-conceptual awareness.

3. **Visualised Consort:** For those who had not stabilised their pure perception, working with a physical consort would only fuel their grasping and therefore this was not a suitable method for introducing the nature of the mind. In these situations the vajra master would bestow the empowerments on the basis of a visualised consort. The limitation of this approach is that it relies on the use of conceptual fabrications to generate an indirect experience of the state of blissful absorption. This indirectness reduces the strength of the empowerments and it is consequently more difficult for the disciple to achieve a truly non-conceptual mind.

Due to the degeneration of the Dharma, it is rare to find practitioners qualified to receive the empowerments of the first two approaches. The third approach is therefore generally the most common way to receive the empowerments in this present age. The ceremony still emphasises the sexual imagery of the text but at no point does anyone actually engage in sexual union. Even if you are unable to connect with the symbolism used, the process still lays down powerful propensities for you to realise your ultimate nature in the future. For this reason, if the opportunity to attend such a ceremony arises, you should do your best to take full advantage without feelings of apprehension or fear.

THE VIEW OF THE FOUR HIGHER EMPOWERMENTS

The purpose of the Four Higher Empowerments is to help you experience the feeling of your conceptual mind dissolving. Although this process is intended to be non-conceptual in nature, we can still benefit from developing conceptual clarity regarding the meaning behind the various stages of the ceremony.

Like the ceremony for the Seven Empowerments of a Growing Child, the Four Higher Empowerments are split into three main sections: (1) preliminaries; (2) the actual empowerments and (3) concluding activities. As the first and the last sections are virtually identical to the generation stage empowerments, here we will concentrate on the details of the actual empowerments.

To summarise, the four empowerments include: (1) the Vase Empowerment; (2) the Secret Empowerment; (3) the Wisdom Empowerment and (4) the Word Empowerment. Of these four, the first three are considered worldly empowerments as they describe ultimate truth from the perspective of conventional reality. The fourth empowerment is the only one considered transcendental in that it provides an opportunity to experience the ultimate truth. The first three are therefore provisional empowerments to prepare your mind for experiencing the fourth and definitive empowerment.

Each empowerment focuses on a specific aspect of ultimate truth. By familiarising ourselves with these aspects, we gain insight into the specific approach used by the *Six Vajra Yogas* in order to produce the state of enlightenment. In this way, the four empowerments can be seen as an essential blueprint for the structure of the Kalachakra completion stage. The following table summarises some of the important correlations to keep in mind during this discussion:

Truth	Empowerment	Focus	Basis	Purifies
Conventional	Vase	Empty-Form	Body	Waking
	Secret	Immutable Bliss	Bhaga	Dream
	Wisdom	Inseparable Union	Relative Bodhicitta	Deep-sleep
Ultimate	Word	Non-Dual Awareness	Ultimate Bodhicitta	Blissful Absorption

Table 7-1: The Four Higher Empowerments

The Vase Empowerment

The first empowerment is the *Vase Empowerment* and is specifically designed to introduce us to the empty-nature of appearances. Due to our intense grasping, our mind projects a level of reality onto appearances that they do not possess. By superimposing imputations, we limit reality to being simply this or that. When we investigate the ultimate nature of these appearances however, we find they are completely empty of these superimpositions. While the ultimate is empty, it is also simultaneously filled with infinite qualities and therefore is known as the *Sublime Emptiness that is Endowed with All Aspects*. This is the *wisdom aspect* of our Buddha-nature. It is associated with the feminine energy of Vishvamata and is often referred to as the mother as it is the basis for all experiences to arise.

When we consider the types of appearances we encounter, we can identify two categories:

1. **Karmic Appearances:** These appearances manifest as a result of the subtle winds circulating in the left and right channels and are directly conditioned by the habitual propensities of our karma. Since karma is based on the ignorance of self-grasping, these appearances are dualistic in nature and are therefore considered conventional truths.

2. **Empty-Forms:** When the subtle winds enter the central channel, the conceptual mind supported by those winds becomes dormant, creating the opportunity for the natural qualities of Buddha-nature to manifest. These pure appearances are non-physical in nature and are not dependent on the conditioning of physical energy. As empty-forms are the spontaneous display of our Buddha-nature, they are considered ultimate truths.

To understand how empty-forms manifest, it can be helpful to use our sunlight example. Buddha-nature is the sun that constantly shines brightly and the clouds are the karmic appearances produced by the conceptual movements of the dualistic mind. When this mind begins to dissolve, it is as though a gap opens up in the clouds, allowing rays of sunlight to stream through, which corresponds to the experience of empty-forms. As we continue to dissolve our concepts more gaps appear, allowing more rays of light to break through. From our perspective, the empty-forms seem to proliferate when in actuality, we are simply expanding our capacity to experience the fullness of what was already present in our Buddha-nature.

As we progress along the path, we experience various types of empty-forms and although each is equal in nature, they are experienced differently based on the degree of ignorance which remains to be dissolved.

1. **Objective Empty-Forms:** These empty-forms appear separately from the awareness that experiences them. While there is no grasping onto them as existing inherently from their own side, they still appear to the mind as objective in nature.

2. **Subjective Empty-Forms:** When we experience objective empty-forms as inseparable from our own subjective awareness, they cease to be seen as objective and are instead identified as being the spontaneous manifestation of our fully-established nature.

3. **Great Consort of Empty-Form:** Through incorporating all empty-forms into our awareness, even the most subtle forms of conceptual grasping can be dissolved. When the last afflicted obscuration is removed, we experience a sublime emptiness endowed with all aspects. This fully-established form of emptiness is completely free from conventional fabrications and is known as the *Great Consort of Empty-Form*.

In this way, the sublime emptiness is not realised in a single moment, but is revealed gradually by working with the great diversity of empty-form aspects experienced in a non-conceptual mind. This realisation is like the waxing moon which begins as a sliver and slowly expands into a full moon over time.

Truth	Type	Mind	Appears
Conventional	Karmic Appearances	Conceptual	Dualistic
Ultimate	Objective Empty-Forms	Non-Conceptual	
	Subjective Empty-Forms		
	Great Consort of Empty-Form		Non-Dualistic

Table 7-2: Types of Empty-Forms

During the ceremony we are asked to visualise ourselves engaging in sexual foreplay with a consort. The consort's body represents the object of our perception and the acts of caressing and fondling are the conditions for bliss to arise. As the mind becomes aroused, we use the appearance of bliss as the basis for reflecting on its empty-nature. We try to see the bliss as a natural manifestation of our Buddha-nature— an empty-form completely free from any conventional existence.

Through the Vase Empowerment, we purify the sensory appearances of the waking state, while establishing the propensities to experience the bliss of joy and to ultimately attain the Vajra-Body of Kalachakra. As this empowerment uses the body of the consort as its basis, it is known as the *Empowerment of the Body Mandala*.

The Secret Empowerment

The second empowerment is the *Secret Empowerment* and is designed to focus our attention on the blissful nature of our awareness, which is the ultimate form of compassion. On the conventional level, the aim of compassion is that sentient beings be free from suffering. Ultimately, the taste of this freedom is experienced as bliss. As each obscuration is removed, this experience of bliss grows stronger and more pervasive, revealing that bliss is a fundamental aspect of our ultimate nature. When bliss is perfected, all of the causes for suffering have been eliminated. This is the *method aspect* of our Buddha-nature. It is associated with the masculine energy of Kalachakra and is often referred to as the father.

If we look at the way bliss manifests, we find it is closely linked to the degree of grasping present in the mind. When grasping is reduced, bliss arises and when it is strong, bliss is repressed. This leads to three levels of bliss we can experience while practicing the path:

1. **Ordinary Pleasure:** When the mind is dominated by self-grasping it sees the world through the lens of desire and seeks to fulfil those desires through the manipulation of conditions. When a desire is temporarily satisfied, we experience

pleasurable sensations which are the temporary cessation of our manifest suffering. There are many degrees of pleasure we can feel based on the degree of separation between our current state and the state we desire. For instance, if we are currently suffering from intense cold, any warmth is experienced as pleasurable and this feeling becomes more intense as we approach our desired temperature. Once we reach the peak of our desire however, any additional warmth can quickly turn into suffering. This is the nature of ordinary pleasure as there is always a limit to how much we can take.

2. **Mutable Bliss:** Actual bliss arises when conceptual grasping is dissolved. It is experienced by a mind absorbed in deep states of samadhi and is the subjective aspect of our Buddha-nature. As the mind withdraws from the desire realm, it temporarily releases its grasping onto gross phenomena and abides in a state of blissful serenity. The more subtle the mind becomes, the more intense the feeling of bliss. However, regardless of the subtlety, as long as we operate from the perspective of a dualistic mind, the bliss we experience will be limited to periods of meditative absorption. As the root of samsara is not severed completely, the bliss is unstable and is still conditioned by karma.

3. **Immutable Bliss:** Ultimately, Buddha-nature is always blissful. It is the complete absence of any form of suffering, permanently manifesting in every moment and pervading all experience. It is only due to our grasping that we do not constantly experience this nature. By perfecting our realisation of empty-forms, we can sever the root cause for even the most subtle forms of grasping and thereby permanently remove all obscurations that limit our experience of bliss. When the mind abides in such a state completely free from grasping, it is known as *Immutable Bliss.*

As actual bliss only manifests when the conceptual mind is dormant, we can only work with it through non-conceptual methods. It is for this reason that the completion stage emphasises practising with the subtle energetic system of channels, winds and drops. Based on the interdependence between the dualistic mind and the subtle body, it is possible to achieve increasingly more refined states of absorption, allowing for more intense forms of bliss to be experienced. By continually dissolving the grasping that arises in relation to that bliss, we remove the most subtle layers of obscuration.

This process is like approaching a fire. From a distance you can feel its warmth on your skin and as you move closer to the flames, its light becomes brighter and its heat becomes stronger. If you were to abide within those flames, the fire would consume everything, burning all impurities and leaving only the nature of the fire itself. In a similar way, our Buddha-nature is like the fire and the feeling of bliss is like its warmth. When we refine our experience of bliss through working with the subtle body, we come closer to our ultimate nature. If we can abide within that nature, all our karmic conditioning is effectively burnt away, leaving only the bliss of the enlightened mind.

Truth	Type	Mind	Appears
Conventional	Ordinary Pleasure	Conceptual	Dualistic
Ultimate	Mutable Bliss	Non-Conceptual	
	Immutable Bliss		Non-Dualistic

Table 7-3: Types of Bliss

During the empowerment, you will be asked to visualise your vajra master in the aspect of Kalachakra, entering into sexual union with a visualised consort in the aspect of Vishvamata. This Kalachakra Yab-Yum emanates light and draws in countless enlightened beings who dissolve into the guru's crown. They transform into subtle essences which travel down the guru's central channel and gather at its lower opening. Holding the essences there, the guru experiences immutable bliss. This mind manifests in the form of a single drop of subtle fluid which is offered to you to taste.

This visualisation purposefully challenges our ordinary view in order to strengthen our pure perception. In this scenario, Kalachakra and Vishvamata represent the union of immutable bliss and empty-form, which is the primary method used to achieve enlightenment. The merging of the subtle essences with enlightened beings indicates those essences to be the support on which we must rely. Through sexual union, the essences are made to melt, providing the support for generating increasingly more subtle levels of bliss. When the essences gather at the lower opening of the central channel, they produce the experience of immutable bliss.

It is this potential realisation of immutable bliss that is offered to us by the vajra master in the form of the subtle fluid. When we take the liquid onto our tongue, we recognise that we too are endowed with the necessary channels, winds and subtle essences, and therefore we also have the capacity to generate the mind of immutable bliss and achieve enlightenment. This recognition is the most secret form of refuge for a tantric practitioner.

Usually substances like semen and blood are perceived as ordinary and often disgusting. Tantrayana challenges us to see beyond this mind of aversion and recognise the extraordinary nature of these appearances. With faith in this underlying purity, we visualise ourselves tasting the subtle fluid and allow the experience to trigger a strong feeling of bliss in the mind. This bliss is then used as a basis for recognising the empty-nature of the drop. During the actual ceremony, we are usually given a taste of alcohol to symbolise the subtle fluid.

Through the Secret Empowerment, we purify the conceptual appearances of the dream state, while establishing the propensities to experience the bliss of supreme joy and to ultimately attain the Vajra-Speech of Kalachakra. As immutable bliss can only be established on the basis of empty-forms, it is said to arise from the source of bliss—the *bhaga*. This sanskrit term is used as a symbol to represent the wisdom aspect of Buddha-nature that is associated with feminine energy. It is for this reason that the empowerment is known as the *Empowerment of the Bhaga Mandala*.

The Wisdom Empowerment

The third empowerment is the *Union of Great Bliss and Wisdom Empowerment* or simply the Wisdom Empowerment. Through the first two empowerments we are introduced to the aspects of empty-form and bliss in isolation. This helps us to clearly distinguish their characteristics so we can identify them within our experience. In the wisdom empowerment, our focus shifts to the dynamic relationship between these two aspects. Our aim is to recognise that bliss and emptiness are co-emergent, meaning that wherever there is one, there is also the other. This is the *inseparable aspect of method and wisdom* which is represented by Kalachakra and Vishvamata in sexual union.

To understand the inseparable quality of Buddha-nature, we need to consider the dualistic nature of conventional reality. The reason for our suffering is rooted in a fundamental misconception. Due to our ignorance of sublime emptiness, we confuse its pure manifestations to be an objective reality that exists independently from ourselves and at the same time, we grasp onto our blissful awareness as being a subjective reality. We thereby create a dualism of subject and object; a separation that is completely illusory and has no existence whatsoever. It is merely a conceptual fabrication that is projected onto Buddha-nature by emphasising one aspect more than another.

Making matters worse, the concepts of subject and object are not the only concepts we generate. Once we are trapped in a dualistic perspective, our mind continues to separate the different phenomena that appear to us. We divide our experience into layer upon layer of abstraction, creating a completely fractured mind, consisting of countless pieces. If we are to realise the inseparable nature of our mind, we must gather together all these illusory pieces and re-integrate them into a cohesive whole.

This process of unification is produced by working progressively with four types of phenomena to reverse the various layers of separation we have created. We begin with the most coarse level of experience and unify it with increasingly more subtle levels until eventually everything becomes of one flavour.

1. **Appearances:** The first layer of separation is based on the belief that the objective appearances we perceive through our senses are separate from our Buddha-nature. This step emphasises realising the empty-nature of sensory appearances. We start by establishing all sights as empty-forms and extend this realisation to encompass all other types of perception. The result of this process is *The Union of Emptiness and Appearances.*

2. **Awareness:** The next layer of separation is based on the belief that the mind is something "other" than these perceptions. We can dissolve this feeling by recognising the presence of pristine awareness in every moment that empty-forms manifest. When we recognise that there is never a time when the two are not present together, they begin to mix like water into water. The result of this process is *The Union of Emptiness and Awareness.*

3. **Mutable Bliss:** Emptiness and awareness represent the objective and subjective aspects of our Buddha-nature and when they are first united, the experience is mutable bliss. This type of bliss is still affected by the very subtle grasping that maintains the interdependent relationship between the subtle energetic body and the mind. As long as the winds are moving, they will create a pattern of fluctuation in which we experience states of bliss with greater or lesser intensity. To overcome this separation,

we must establish a state of meditative absorption where the movement of the winds is completely dissolved. The result of this process is *The Union of Emptiness and Great Bliss.*

4. **Immutable Bliss:** As long as the energy stored in the subtle essences is distributed throughout the body, then a very subtle conception of self will remain and dualistic appearances will continue to arise. Through the process of melting and gathering the essences at the tip of the central channel, the most subtle of level of grasping can be removed, thereby actualising an unwavering experience of immutable bliss. The result of this process is known as *The Supreme Union of Immutable Bliss and Empty-Form.*

Although all of these realisations of union are established within the context of ultimate truth, the first three are considered to be partial realisations that act to remove obscurations. Only the fourth brings together a complete realisation of empty-form with a complete realisation of immutable bliss. Therefore, only this realisation can be considered a fully-established experience of ultimate truth free from dualistic grasping.

Truth	Union	Basis	Appears
Ultimate	Emptiness and Appearances	Perceptions	Dualistic
	Emptiness and Awareness	Awareness	
	Emptiness and Great Bliss	Winds	
	Immutable Bliss and Empty-Form	Subtle Essences	Non-Dualistic

Table 7-4: Types of Union

During the empowerment, you will be asked to visualise yourself in the aspect of Kalachakra and your consort in the aspect of Vishvamata. At the centre of the six main chakras of both figures, you will visualise six seed syllables representing the six Buddha Families who are the essence of your Buddha-nature. These syllables are to remind you that the immutable bliss of Kalachakra is ultimately of the same nature as the empty-form of Vishvamata.

Having visualised the father and mother respectively, you then specifically visualise their sexual organs as a vajra and lotus, both marked by seed syllables. The purpose of this step is to recognise that the division of empty-form and immutable bliss into two separate aspects is a mere imputation. Empty-form has the nature of immutable bliss and immutable bliss has the nature of empty-form. When the two aspects of vajra and lotus are brought together in union, the resulting bliss is used as the basis for realising their indestructible nature.

Through the Wisdom Empowerment, we reduce the feeling of separation between subject and object and thereby purify our grasping onto the dualistic appearances of the deep-sleep state. This process establishes propensities for us to experience the bliss of special joy and to ultimately attain the Vajra-Mind of Kalachakra. We call this empowerment the *Empowerment of Relative Bodhicitta* in reference to the subtle essences used as a basis for refining our experience of bliss and for developing our realisation of the inseparable aspect of Buddha-nature.

The Word Empowerment

The fourth empowerment is known by some as the *Word Empowerment* as it uses words to reveal the ultimate nature of reality through direct experience. The focus of this empowerment is to distinguish between the dualistic appearances of conceptual understanding and the non-dual experience of pristine awareness. Rather than a matter of *what* we need to know, it is a matter of *how* we need to know it.

Up to this point, we have worked to develop a view that incorporates the concepts of empty-form, immutable bliss and their inseparable nature. Just as a clear reflection of the moon in a still pool of water can be used to indirectly know the nature of the moon, so too can these concepts be used as a skilful means for developing familiarity with our Buddha-nature. While these imputations may be true, they are still deceptive in nature and therefore we need to transcend them in order to experience reality as it is. Rather than merely looking at its reflection, we need to look at the moon itself.

The key to this achievement is to clearly distinguish between the *final natures* of conventional and ultimate truths. Here the term "final" is used to refer to the way that reality is experienced from the perspective of primordial wisdom. When such a wisdom is brought to bear on a conventional truth, that truth is found to be completely empty of any essence, like an illusion or a dream. However, when the same wisdom abides in ultimate truth, the final nature is found to be filled with infinite enlightened qualities. This is the dividing line between the two truths.

Understanding this, we can identify three types of mind that are each capable of knowing a different level of reality:

1. **Conceptual Consciousness:** This is a coarse dualistic mind which experiences reality through layers of imputed projections. It is dominated by the obscurations of ignorance and therefore is unable to experience the ultimate truth directly. It must use concepts as a means to indirectly reveal the nature of hidden phenomena.

2. **Non-Conceptual Awareness:** In this mind, coarse concepts have become dormant as a result of meditative absorption. Without the intermediate layer of imputations, this mind can directly experience the ultimate truth. However, due to the presence of subtle grasping onto the accumulated aggregates, this experience is still conditioned by karma and therefore

appears in a dualistic way. By practising with non-conceptual yogic methods, this grasping can be gradually dissolved so the dependent nature of reality is seen to have never existed.

3. **Pristine Awareness:** This is a non-dualistic mind in which all conventional truths have completely dissolved. As it is no longer influenced by the conditioning of karmic obscurations it is able to experience all enlightened qualities of ultimate truth simultaneously and without distortion. Such a mind transcends the *eight extremes of conceptual fabrication*: (1) arising and (2) ceasing; (3) existence and (4) non-existence; (5) coming and (6) going; and (7) singular and (8) plural. Only this mind is able to abide permanently in the fully-established nature of suchness.

Although we may have experienced moments of non-conceptuality during our practice of the path, the completion stage practices require a mind that abides in non-conceptuality. This is why the practice of the *Three Isolations,* which will be introduced in the next chapter, is still considered to be a preliminary. It is the primary method used to cut the movement of conceptual fabrications and to stabilise the experience of non-conceptual awareness. This mind is refined through the practice of the *Six Vajra Yogas*, to eventually give rise to the pristine awareness that unifies empty-form with immutable bliss. Once the initial realisation of pristine awareness is established, it is perfected, resulting in the enlightened mind of a Buddha.

Truth	Mind	Nature	Appears
Conventional	Conceptual Consciousness	Imputed	Dualistic
Ultimate	Non-Conceptual Awareness	Dependent	
	Pristine Awareness	Fully-Established	Non-Dual

Table 7-5: Levels of Mind

For this empowerment, no visualisation needs to be generated. Instead, you are asked to adopt the seven-point meditation posture of

Vairochana and with eyes wide open gazing into the space in front of you, allow your mind to become spacious and still. Rest your awareness without any form of grasping or conceptual activity. As the vajra master speaks, simply experience the empty nature of the words without thinking about them in any way. Let both your body and mind become completely free from any sort of movement.

Through the Word Empowerment, we temporarily stop the proliferation of our thoughts, and experience an undistorted taste of our Buddha-nature which purifies the state of blissful absorption. This process establishes our propensities to experience the bliss of innate joy and to achieve the Vajra-Wisdom of Kalachakra. As this empowerment relies on a direct experience of ultimate truth, it is known as the *Empowerment of Ultimate Bodhicitta*. Here, the term "Bodhicitta" literally refers to the mind of enlightenment experienced by a fully realised Buddha.

ADVICE FOR RECEIVING THE HIGHER EMPOWERMENTS

Receiving the Four Higher Empowerments from a qualified vajra master is like being handed the keys to a wondrous kingdom. Within this process you are introduced to everything you need in order to achieve Buddhahood within a single lifetime. There is no greater kindness and no greater expression of compassion. The following points of advice are worth keeping in mind to maximise the transformative impact of this profound experience.

Seeing the Extraordinary in the Ordinary

For practitioners of the Vajrayana, we must do everything we can to avoid falling into our habitual patterns of ordinary perception. When we fail to cultivate pure perception, we stop taking appearances seriously and we see them as being normal and uninspiring. Rather than looking for good qualities, all we see are faults and imperfections. The result of this judgemental attitude is that we close ourselves off to the blessings we could potentially receive from the ceremony.

Filling our mind with false expectations based on what we hope to experience is one of the primary causes for such an attitude to arise. We enter the ceremony thinking something extraordinary should happen, such as visions of coloured lights or levitating off the ground. Even without a clear idea in mind, we still often expect to achieve some sort of obvious altered state of reality.

The result of thinking in this way is that we spend the entire ceremony waiting for our expectations to be fulfilled. Instead of actually experiencing anything, we lock ourselves into a judgemental loop that makes a constant comparison to our fantasy. The more exaggerated the fantasy, the more "ordinary" our actual experience appears.

In order to avoid this trap, we need to learn to see the extraordinary *in* the ordinary; there is no where else we need to look. Every ordinary moment and every ordinary appearance is an opportunity to discover a deeper truth about the nature of reality. Recognising this, we keep our focus on the present moment. It doesn't matter what shape that moment takes, we can always use our present reality as a reminder of our innate purity and as such, everything is seen as important and nothing is seen as useless or trivial.

Prior to the empowerment ceremony, we should familiarise ourselves with the essential nature of the process. This provides you with the clarity needed to settle into the present moment and keep your mind from veering off into uncertainty and doubt. As you listen to the words of the vajra master and generate the various visualisations, allow each experience to remind you of the corresponding aspect of Buddha-nature you are concentrating on. Let this essence pervade your experience like a perfumed scent pervades the air.

Resting the Mind in its Natural State

Even though we use visualisations as a support for the first three empowerments, we must not forget they are provisional in nature. The foundation of the completion stage is a *non-conceptual awareness* and it is this state of mind that the ceremony is designed to produce. For this reason, allowing your mind to become distracted by an endless stream of conceptual thoughts will only act as an obstacle to receiving the empowerments.

One way to cut the proliferation of thoughts is to focus on establishing an undistracted mind that is free from grasping. Sit in a relaxed posture with eyes wide open, gently resting your gaze in the space in front of you. Allow the movements of the ceremony to fade into the background and bring your awareness into the sphere of the mind. With one part of your mind, listen to the instructions given to you by the guru and with the other part, observe whatever arises in the space of the mind.

If you meditate in this way during the first three empowerments, as you arrive at the fourth, your mind should be settled. This will make it easier to follow the pointing-out instructions of the guru and to rest your awareness in the stillness of a non-conceptual awareness.

REVIEW OF KEY POINTS

- The Kalachakra Completion Stage uses non-conceptual methods to reveal the ultimate nature of our mind. In order to authentically practice these methods, we must first establish a non-conceptual view. This is done in two steps: (1) establish the view based on the Four Higher Empowerments and (2) stabilise that view through meditation on the Three Isolations.

- The only way to know the very subtle nature of the mind is through using the mind itself. We rely on the pointing-out instructions of the guru so we can develop a first-hand experience of this nature which can then be expanded on through meditation.

- Of the four states of experience, the fourth of blissful absorption is the only state in which the conceptual mind becomes dormant. It is within this state that the completion stage practices are performed.

- Sexuality is used in the completion stage because it is one of the few activities in life that produces the state of blissful absorption. By learning how to bring sexuality into the path, we gain access to extremely powerful methods for realising the ultimate nature of reality.

- There are three supports vajra masters use to introduce their students to the non-conceptual state of blissful absorption: (1) extremely ripe students can be introduced on the basis of their past training in meditation; (2) very pure students rely on a physical consort; and (3) impure students must rely on symbolic visualisations.

- The general structure of the ceremony for the Four Higher Empowerments is similar to the Seven Empowerments of a Growing Child. It consists of three sections: (1) preliminaries; (2) the actual empowerments and (3) concluding practices.

- The Four Higher Empowerments are: (1) the Vase Empowerment; (2) the Secret Empowerment; (3) the Wisdom Empowerment and (4) the Word Empowerment. The first three are provisional and the fourth is definitive.

- The essence of the Vase Empowerment is to introduce the empty-nature of appearances. This empowerment helps us distinguish between (1) karmic appearances produced by ignorance and (2) empty-forms which are the natural manifestation of Buddha-nature.

- Empty-forms can be divided into three types: (1) objective empty-forms which appear as separate from awareness; (2) subjective empty-forms which appear as inseparable from awareness and (3) the Great Consort of Empty-Form which is the actual experience of a sublime emptiness endowed with all aspects.

- The essence of the Secret Empowerment is to introduce the blissful nature of awareness. This empowerment helps us to distinguish between (1) ordinary pleasure that is based on the temporary cessation of manifest suffering; (2) mutable bliss which arises during states of meditative absorption; and (3) immutable bliss which arises when the mind is completely free from all forms of coarse and subtle grasping.

- The essence of the Wisdom Empowerment is to introduce the inseparable nature of emptiness and bliss. In order to realise this inseparability, we focus on establishing four types of union in our experience: (1) The Union of Emptiness and Appearances based on recognising that all appearances have an empty-nature; (2) The Union of Emptiness and Awareness based on recognising that all empty-appearances arise in the mind and are co-emergent with awareness; (3) The Union of Emptiness and Great Bliss produced by dissolving the winds into the subtle essences; and (4) The Supreme Union of Immutable Bliss and Empty-Form produced by gathering the subtle essences at the lower opening of the central channel.

- The essence of the Word Empowerment is to introduce the ultimate nature of reality through direct experience. The empowerment helps us to distinguish between (1) conceptual consciousness which experiences the imputed nature of reality;

(2) non-conceptual awareness which experiences its dependent nature; and (3) pristine awareness which experiences the fully-established nature.

- When receiving the Four Empowerments, try to clear your mind of any expectations. Focus your attention on the experiences arising in the present moment as much as possible. Avoid any sort of judgemental attitude that will damage your pure perception.

- Use the first three empowerments as a means to gradually settle the mind into its natural state. Then when it comes time to receive the fourth empowerment, it will be easier to rest in a non-conceptual awareness.

CHAPTER EIGHT

The Three Isolations

Using the Subtle Body to Achieve Shamatha

We can liken the experience of the Four Higher Empowerments to a zoologist guiding us through the bush and pointing out the presence of a wondrous creature hidden amongst the trees. By directing our gaze in the right direction and describing the creature's characteristics, they inform us what to look for. Then, through careful observation, we are able to clearly distinguish its shape from the background and in that moment, the creature that was previously concealed to us, becomes visible.

Similarly, in accordance with the words of our precious master, we are encouraged to look inwards to the mind, to where our sacred truth is hidden. We are then introduced to aspects of our Buddha-nature so we can establish an understanding of how it manifests. Finally, by resting our mind as naturally as possible, we are given the opportunity to experience this nature for ourselves. If we are fortunate, the veils of our obscurations may have weakened enough, enabling us to glimpse ultimate reality.

Initially such a glimpse may be fleeting, lasting only for the duration of the empowerment and as our habitual patterns come rushing back, our profound experience of the nature of the mind can feel like a distant memory. For this reason, before we can move forward on the swift path of the Kalachakra Completion Stage, we need to learn to stabilise our mind within its own nature. This is achieved through the single-pointed concentration of Shamatha.

While there are many ways to establish the mind of Shamatha, the technique presented in the pith instructions of the Kalachakra Path are particularly efficient. What makes this form of meditation distinct from other methods is the way it incorporates a profound understanding of the interdependence between body and mind; knowledge which comes from the Kalachakra teachings on the subtle energetic system of channels, winds and drops. As this theory forms the foundation of all completion stage practices, we will explore this system in detail before moving to a general presentation of the techniques themselves.

THE SUBTLE BODY ACCORDING TO KALACHAKRA

The *subtle energetic body* is formed by the patterns of energy that arise from the movements of a dualistic mind. Through subtle shifts in energy, the mind can effect change on coarse levels of phenomena, such as the physical body. Likewise, changes in the coarse body can condition the functions of the subtle body, influencing the experiences which arise in the mind. In this way, the two are thoroughly enmeshed.

In order to effectively practice the yogic techniques of the completion stage, we need to develop a working understanding of how this subtle body functions. Although it is not necessary to achieve the level of familiarity a professional doctor has attained, we should be comfortable enough with this system to identify its three main components: (1) channels and chakras; (2) inner winds and (3) subtle essences. We will now examine each in greater detail.

Channels and Chakras

A *channel* is a pathway through which energy flows. Two-dimensional drawings tend to depict channels as veins or tubes, but we need to be careful of considering them in such a coarse manner. They are actually more comparable to the optical-illusion of a circle created by a whirling firebrand or the patterns of light formed by traffic moving in the night. Although our mind experiences them as patterns of energy flowing through specific areas of the body, the channels themselves do not have any substantial structure.

With this in mind, there are approximately 72,000 channels in a fully matured human body, forming a complex network of pathways similar in shape to the central nervous system. To help simplify the complexity of this system, we can focus our attention on the particular features used in the completion stage practices, giving us three groups to consider: (1) the three channels; (2) the primary chakras and (3) the secondary chakras.

The Three Channels

The easiest way to think of the channel system is in the form of three groups of channels—those on the left of the body, those on the right and those in the middle. Regardless of the number of branch channels belonging to each group, they are all rooted in the three primary channels that form the trunk of the system:

1. **The Central Channel (Skt. avadhuti, Tib. uma):** This channel runs from the point between the eyebrows back to the crown of the head, straight down the spinal column and from the perineum to the tip of the genitals. Above the navel, this channel is known as the Rahu channel, and below the navel it is known as the Kalagni channel.

2. **The Left Channel (Skt. lalana, Tib. kyangma):** This channel begins in the left nostril and runs parallel to the central channel down to the anus. Above the navel this channel is known

as the moon channel and below the navel it is known as the excrement channel.

3. **The Right Channel (Skt. rasana, Tib. roma):** This channel starts in the right nostril and also runs parallel to the central channel, terminating at the tip of the genitals. Above the navel this channel is known as the sun channel and below the navel it is known as the urine channel.

Location	Channel	Name	Colour
Above Navel	Central	Avadhuti	Green
	Left	Lalana	White
	Right	Rasana	Red
Below Navel	Right	Mesa	Dark-Blue
	Left	Pingala	Yellow
	Central	Shankini	Blue

Table 8-1: The Three Primary Channels

The Primary Chakras

There are six points where the left and right channels coil around the central channel, forming energy centres known as *chakras*. These centres are like knots that redirect the energy flowing through the left and right channels and are the main cause for the creation of the various branch channels. You can think of them as being like the junction points on a highway.

As all the energy circulating in the body must pass through these chakras, they are very important for our practice. Familiarising ourselves with the structure of each chakra enables us to manipulate the movement of our energy in very precise ways. The six primary chakras are described in the Kalachakra teachings as follows:

1. **The Secret Chakra:** This chakra is located at the base of the perineum where three layers of channels branch out. The

innermost layer has six channels, four of which split into two, creating a middle layer of ten channels. Of these ten, six split into two making an outer layer of sixteen channels. When the three layers are combined we have a total of thirty-two channels which are considered "empty-channels", as the coarse winds do not flow through them.

2. **The Navel Chakra:** This chakra is located four finger widths below the navel and consists of four layers of channels. The innermost layer has four channels branching out from the centre, four of which split into two to create the first intermediate layer of eight. These eight split into two to create a second intermediate layer of sixteen. Of these sixteen, four are considered empty-channels, leaving twelve channels through which the coarse winds circulate. These twelve each split into five channels, making a total of sixty-four channels in the outer layer.

3. **The Heart Chakra:** This chakra is located twelve and a half finger widths above the navel chakra and has eight channels branching out from its centre: (1) *rohini* in the east; (2) *hastijihva* in the south-east; (3) *pingala* in the south; (4) *pushya* in the south-west; (5) *jaya* in the west; (6) *alambusa* in the north-west; (7) *mesa* in the north; and (8) *kuha* in the north-east.

4. **The Throat Chakra:** This chakra is located twelve and half finger widths above the heart chakra. Of its three layers, the innermost layer has eight channels branching out from the centre. These eight then branch into two forming sixteen and these sixteen branch into two forming thirty-two. Four of these are considered empty-channels.

5. **The Forehead Chakra:** This chakra is located twelve and half finger widths above the throat chakra in the centre of brain and has two layers of channels. The innermost layer has eight channels, which split into two to form an outer layer of sixteen. Two of these channels are considered empty-channels.

6. **The Crown Chakra:** This chakra is located at the crown of the head and consists of four channels branching out from its centre.

Location	Colour	Branches	Layers			
Crown	Green	4	4			
Forehead	White	16	8	16		
Throat	Red	32	8	16	32	
Heart	Dark-Blue	8	8			
Navel	Yellow	64	4	8	16	64
Secret	Blue	32	6	10	16	

Table 8-2: The Six Primary Chakras

The Secondary Chakras

In relation to the six primary chakras, there are a total of 156 channels identified. From the perspective of our yogic practice, these are all the channels that are needed, but we should be aware that there are other chakras found in the body. There are many points where branch channels converge to form the secondary chakras and of these, two groups are worth mentioning:

1. **The Jewel Chakra:** This chakra is found at the very tip of the sexual organ and the lower opening of the central channel. This is a very important point in the completion stage as this is where all the subtle essences are gathered in order to produce the experience of immutable bliss.

2. **The Activity Chakras:** The scriptures identify three hundred and sixty joints distributed throughout the body and at each of these joints is a chakra. These chakras are known as activity chakras because they allow us to move our limbs and therefore engage in different activities. The main activity chakras are found in the twelve joints of the arms and legs as well as the sixty joints in the hands and feet.

Inner Winds

The inner winds refer to the way the subtle body changes over time. To understand how they work, we can consider them to be like the currents in the ocean. Due to the force of gravity exerted by the earth and moon, the water in the ocean is pushed and pulled in different directions creating a variety of currents which cause the water level to rise in some areas and to fall in others. As the water accumulates in one place, it swells into a wave. The higher a wave rises, the more violently it crashes down, thereby returning its energy back into the ocean. In this way, the shape of the ocean is constantly transformed by the presence of the different currents.

Similarly, the subtle body is like an ocean of energy. Due to the influence of the mind, the energy is pushed and pulled in different directions, accumulating in some parts and dispersing in others. The system of channels and chakras described above forms the general shape of the energy resulting from the conceptual patterns of the mind. Changing the state of our mind also changes the shape of the energy it is connected to. Just like the waves, when too much energy builds up in one area, it must eventually be released back into the system; a process which can occur gradually or can happen explosively depending on the conditions.

When the energy moves, the mind moves with it, just as a rider moves with a mount. While thoughts can catalyse the energy to move, the movement of energy also has the capacity to generate thoughts in the mind. This mutual interdependence means that the two function to perpetuate movement in both the body and mind.

Understanding this, we should not regard the inner winds as being like air passing through tubes. As the channels and winds are not coarse phenomena, it is more accurate to think of them as different aspects of subtle energy. The channels are the present shape of the energy, and the winds are the patterns of change responsible for producing its shape. We call these patterns "movements" in the sense that they transform the energy from one state into another. When the winds are active, the system is in flux and when they are dormant, the system is stable.

With respect to our path, there are ten winds we need to be familiar with: (1) the five primary winds and (2) the five secondary winds. These winds represent ten distinct patterns for the way the conceptual mind influences our subtle energy. They are not mutually exclusive and therefore it is possible to have multiple winds of different strengths active within the same moment. No matter how strong or weak a wind may be, if it is not completely dissolved, it will always have an effect on the subtle body.

The Primary Winds

There are five winds considered primary as they provide the basic mechanism through which the mind sustains and manipulates the body. Without these winds we would not be able to perform any bodily functions and the connection between body and mind would dissolve.

1. **The Life-Supporting Wind:** This wind pervades all channels and is related to the pattern of *contraction* in which energy is drawn in or concentrated, such as in the act of inhalation or swallowing. It corresponds to the element of space and is connected to the Buddha Akshobhya.

2. **The Downward-Clearing Wind:** This wind also pervades all channels and is related to the pattern of *expansion* in which energy is pushed out or expelled, as in the act of exhalation, excretion or urination. It corresponds to the element of consciousness and is connected to the Buddha Vajrasattva.

3. **The Fire-Accompanying Wind:** This wind originates in the eastern petal of the heart chakra. It is related to the pattern of

accumulation in which energy is gathered in order to fuel the various processes of transformation in the body, such as the digestion of food. It corresponds to the element of wind and is connected to the Buddha Amoghasiddhi.

4. **The Upward-Moving Wind:** This wind originates in the southern petal of the heart chakra and is related to the pattern of *direction* in which energy is distributed from one part of the body to another. This movement is closely tied to our intentions and is used to perform actions like speaking, recalling memories or exerting effort. It corresponds to the element of fire and is connected to the Buddha Ratnasambhava.

5. **The All-Pervading Wind:** This wind originates in the northern petal of the heart chakra and is related to the pattern of *connection*, resulting from energy pervading every cell of our body. Through this wind we can manipulate our body with the mind to perform motor activities such as walking or moving our arms. It corresponds to the element of water and is connected to the Buddha Amitabha.

Name	Element	Pattern	Functions
Life-Supporting	Space	Contraction	swallowing, inhalation and concentration
Downward-Clearing	Consciousness	Expansion	excretion of faeces, urine, vital fluids
Fire-Accompanying	Wind	Accumulation	digestion and metabolism
Upward Moving	Fire	Direction	speech, memory and diligence
All-Pervading	Water	Connection	motor activities

Table 8-3: The Five Primary Winds

The Secondary Winds

Whereas the primary winds emphasise the mind's influence over the body, the secondary winds emphasise the body's influence over the mind. Specifically, these five winds provide the mechanism through which our sensory organs generate the different sensory appearances we experience.

1. **The Naga Wind:** This wind originates in the western petal of the heart chakra and provides the basis for our sense of sight. When this wind is active, we experience the pattern of *visual forms.* It corresponds to the element of earth and is connected to the Buddha Vairochana.

2. **The Tortoise Wind:** This wind originates in the south-eastern petal of the heart chakra and provides the basis for our sense of hearing. When this wind is active, we experience the pattern of *sounds.* It corresponds to the element of wind and is connected to the Buddha Amoghasiddhi.

3. **The Lizard Wind:** This wind originates in the south-western petal of the heart chakra and provides the basis for our sense of smell. When this wind is active, we experience the pattern of *fragrances.* It corresponds to the element of fire and is connected to the Buddha Ratnasambhava.

4. **The Devadatta Wind:** This wind originates in the north-eastern petal of the heart chakra and provides the basis for our sense of taste. When this wind is active, we experience the pattern of *flavours.* It corresponds to the element of water and is connected to the Buddha Amitabha.

5. **The Dhanamjaya Wind:** This wind originates in the north-western petal of the heart chakra and provides the basis for our sense of touch. When this wind is active, we experience the pattern of *tactile sensations.* It corresponds to the element of earth and is connected to the Buddha Vairochana.

Name	Element	Pattern	Functions
Naga	Earth	Forms	Sense of Sight
Tortoise	Wind	Sounds	Sense of Hearing
Lizard	Fire	Fragrances	Sense of Smell
Devadatta	Water	Flavours	Sense of Taste
Dhanamjaya	Earth	Sensations	Sense of Touch

Table 8-4: The Five Secondary Winds

It is important to distinguish that each of these winds represents a specific correlation between a mixture of mental and physical phenomena. For instance, in the case of the naga wind, it represents the correlation between the electrical impulses generated by the eye, the pattern of impulses triggered in the brain and the visual forms that are experienced by the mind. Likewise, the upward-moving wind represents the correlation between our desire to do something, the awareness of the body part needed to do it and a pattern of electrical impulses sent to that part to fulfil the desire. As all of these relationships are held together by grasping, when the grasping is dissolved, the wind is also dissolved and the connection between the components is broken.

Subtle Essences

Every configuration of energy has a qualitative aspect to it—a feeling that distinguishes one state from another. When our winds are dominated by states of mind rooted in ignorance, they give rise to a dysfunctional channel system which is plagued by energy imbalances. These imbalances manifest as a wide variety of ailments that we experience as suffering. However, when our winds operate on the basis of wisdom, they give rise to a functional and balanced channel system that results in the experience of bliss.

This relationship between energy and experience is encapsulated within the abstract concept of a *subtle essence*. We can think of an essence as a single point in which the mind and body are fused together by the strength of the mind's grasping. When this occurs, the two become bound to space and time; where *space* is the physical position of energy and *time* is the momentary experience of that energy in the mind.

When the mind perceives a distinction in a quality of an appearance, it effectively splits into two aspects. Due to the interdependence between body and mind, when the mind splits, so too does the energy, resulting in one essence becoming two, which becomes four, which becomes eight and so on. As the proliferation of thoughts expand, the energy branches outwards, forming a complex network of channels and distributing the essences throughout the body. This leads to a fractured mind dominated by dualistic appearances.

From this perspective, our collection of essences can be thought of as being like a physical manifestation of our dualistic self that functions as an energetic basis for our feeling of "me". As this self is dependent on our energy being spread across the body, we can overcome this concept by gathering our energy into a single point and holding it there. This is the non-conceptual way of unifying the mind and dissolving our dualistic experience.

To understand how these essences are used on the path, we need to understand two subjects: (1) The Red and White Drops and (2) The Four Drops. The first represents the means through which the essences are gathered, and the second represents the process by which these essences are refined.

The Red and White Drops

Even though subtle essences arise from the same source, we should not make the mistake of thinking they are all equal. As each essence is the result of a unique manifestation of mind joined with a unique particle of energy, they manifest in different ways. In general, however, we can divide subtle essences into two broad categories:

1. **Red Drops:** These subtle essences have a dominance of feminine energy. They are produced when the wisdom aspect of Buddha-nature is more dominant in the mind component of the essence. Red drops provide a basis for realising the empty-nature of the mind and are mostly located in the lower half of the body.

2. **White Drops:** These subtle essences have a dominance of masculine energy. They are produced from the method aspect of Buddha-nature and provide the basis to realise the blissful-nature of the mind. These drops are mostly located in the upper half of the body.

The word "dominant" is of particular importance here. Although a drop may manifest more of one aspect over another, each is complete in that it has a balance of both feminine and masculine energy. Similarly, while the majority of the red drops are located below the heart and the white drops above, it is possible to find both distributed throughout the body. As we will see in the following chapter, by joining the red and white drops, we can manifest the ultimate nature of the mind to clear away our very subtle grasping.

Drop	Location	Energy	Aspect	Nature
Red	Below	Feminine	Wisdom	Emptiness
White	Above	Masculine	Method	Bliss

Table 8-5: The Red and White Drops

To work with these drops effectively, we need to understand both their subtle and coarse manifestations. Depending on the scope of grasping involved, we can speak of four types of drops:

1. **Subtle Essence:** This is the most subtle level of drop and refers to the combination of subtle *energy and consciousness*. It is the most essential form of drop created by the root ignorance that grasps onto a subject and object. This drop can be either red or white, based on the balance of feminine and masculine energy.

2. **Subtle Drop:** When a subtle essence of energy and mind is combined with the genetic material of a mother and father at the moment of conception, it gives rise to a subtle drop that will eventually form the *nucleus* to a cell. At this level, the subtle essence exerts a direct influence on the way the DNA is

expressed and is how the mind shapes and regulates the way the body will develop.

3. **Coarse Drop:** Through the interaction of the four components of a subtle drop, the genetic material in the nucleus begins to produce various biological components, forming a coarse drop that we call a *cell*. The type of cell produced is based on the cell's interactions with external stimuli as well as the internal reactions of the cell's components. Red and white drops are each responsible for generating different types of cells to form the substances that make up the body. Once a cell is formed, the mind has considerably less control over how the components interact.

4. **Very-Coarse Drop:** As similar types of cells are produced by similar minds, they share a karmic connection that manifests as a cohesive force. This force is one of the reasons similar cells cluster into groups. When this force is strong, the cells are packed very tightly together making them solid and less flexible as in bone and hair. When the force is weaker, the cells are more liquid in nature as seen in blood and other vital fluids. The more compact cells become, the less capacity the mind has to influence them, making them harder to manipulate. This means that within the context of our path, a very-coarse drop generally refers to a single drop of *liquid*.

Type	Form	Components
Subtle Essence	Dualistic Mindstream	Consciousness and energy
Subtle Drop	Cell Nucleus	Dualistic mindstream and genetic material
Coarse Drop	Cell	Cell nucleus and biological components
Very-Coarse Drop	Liquid	Collection of similar cells

Table 8-6: Types of Drops

When considering the nature of the drops, remember that the mind is a non-physical phenomenon and so while we may describe a subtle essence as being located in the nucleus of a cell, there is nothing physical keeping it bound there. There is only the connection created when the mind grasps onto the cell as the self. If the mind releases this grasping, it is free to move as needed. This means that with the right methods it is possible to extract the essence from each cell, like butter being extracted from milk.

The Four Drops

Due to the interaction between the winds and drops, appearances arise within the mind. The nature of these appearances changes depending on the area of the body in which they are active. The drops can be divided based on the types of appearances they support, producing four groups which support the four states of experience. Each group is in the nature of awareness and therefore does not exist as physical energy apart from the winds and drops present in the subtle body.

1. **The Body Drop:** This drop is located in the region surrounding the brain. It encompasses the interaction of winds and drops in the head where the majority of the sense sources are located. It is responsible for the coarse sensory appearances of the waking state.

2. **The Speech Drop:** This drop is located in the region of the throat where the vocal chords are formed and through which the breath flows in and out of the body. It is from this drop that the subtle mental appearances of the dream state arise.

3. **The Mind Drop:** This drop is located in the region around the heart and encompasses all the vital organs of the upper torso. These drops sustain the physical manifestation of the self and give rise to the very-subtle subjective appearances of the deep-sleep state.

4. **The Wisdom Drop:** This drop is located around the region of the navel and encompasses the organs found in the lower

torso. These include the digestive organs responsible for break-ing down matter, as well as those used for the expulsion of waste or fluids. From these drops are produced the non-conceptual appearances of the state of blissful absorption.

For a mind dominated by ignorance, our energy is primarily gathered in the upper half of the body. During the day it collects around the head, giving rise to our waking state appearances. As we fall into sleep, the energy passes through the throat area and settles at the heart. During the night, our energy circulates between the throat and heart, giving rise to the alternating experience of dreams and deep dreamless sleep. Upon waking, the energy returns back to the head from the heart. This is not to say that when energy gathers in one part of the body, everything else stops working, it is simply an indication of where the mind is actively focused.

In order to gather the energy in the lower half of the body, special conditions need to be created. We can manipulate the energy either by way of the body or by way of the mind. An example of the former is when we use sexual intercourse to draw energy down to the tip of the genitals. An example of the latter is when we enter into states of deep meditative absorption.

When the mind abides in the non-conceptual awareness of the state of blissful absorption, the coarse conceptual mind becomes dormant. This suppresses the ignorance of dualistic appearances and allows the pure appearances of wisdom to arise. When this happens, a second set of four drops located in the lower regions of the torso can be distinguished. These drops can be used to refine our awareness and realise our sacred truth.

1. **The Ultimate Body Drop:** This drop is located in the navel and is co-emergent with the conventional wisdom drop. This means that the navel area can manifest differently depending on the presence of either ignorance or wisdom. When wisdom

is active, this drop gives rise to the pure appearances of empty-forms which are the basis for the countless emanation bodies of a Buddha.

2. **The Ultimate Speech Drop:** This drop is located around the secret chakra and is a source for the pure appearances of great bliss. It is the basis for manifesting the complete enjoyment body of a Buddha.

3. **The Ultimate Mind Drop:** This drop is located in the centre of the genitals where the winds and drops converge to give rise to a union of method and wisdom. This is the basis for realising the wisdom-truth body of a Buddha.

4. **The Ultimate Wisdom Drop:** This last drop is located at the very tip of the genitals and is the point at which all winds and drops are held, giving rise to the ultimate truth of immutable bliss. It is this drop that is the basis for generating the blissful nature body of a Buddha.

Drop	State	Conventional	Ultimate
Body	Waking	Forehead	Navel
Speech	Dream	Throat	Secret
Mind	Deep-Sleep	Heart	Centre of Genitals
Wisdom	Blissful Absorption	Navel	Tip of Genitals

Table 8-7: The Four Drops

HOW THE SUBTLE BODY DEVELOPS

With a theoretical understanding of the different components that comprise the subtle energetic system, we can use this knowledge to gain insight into the nature of our suffering. In the following section we will explore the general life-cycle of a human as a way of identifying how the subtle body contributes to the perpetuation of cyclic existence.

Throughout the Kalachakra Tantra, various terms were appropriated from the vedic culture of ancient India as a means of skilfully guiding practitioners. An example of this is the names for the *Ten Avatars of Vishnu* which explain the stages of development in a human life. This is a case where a name familiar to the audience of the time is given a new meaning. The following table summarises how the ten avatars are mapped to the different stages of life:

Stage	Symbol	Period
Pregnancy	Fish	First two months
	Turtle	Third and fourth months
	Wild Pig	Fifth month until birth
Childhood	Man-Lion	Birth
	Midget	Birth until first set of teeth
	Rama	Baby teeth to second set of teeth
	Ramana	Permanent teeth until end of puberty
Adulthood	Krishna	End of puberty until the onset of grey hair
	Buddha	Growth of grey hair until death
	Kalki	Death

Table 8-8: Stages of a Human Life

The entire process begins with *conception* when a bardo being enters the womb of a human mother who is engaged in sexual intercourse. At this stage, the bardo being consists of a single subtle essence of subtle energy and a dualistic consciousness which combines with the semen and egg to form a subtle drop.

After conception, we enter the stage of pregnancy during which the form of a child is established. The first period spans two months and is called the *Fish* as the subtle drop resembles a red Rohita fish. During the first month, there is little more than a mixture of blood and semen, as the cells begin to divide and the foundations of a body begin to form. In the second month, the heart chakra and the upper and lower central channels are produced, giving rise to the ten winds, and fuelling the growth process. From this movement the navel chakra is formed.

The next period spans the third and fourth months of the pregnancy and is called the *Turtle* as the protrusions of the developing limbs make the foetus look similar to a turtle. By the end of the fourth month, the foetus has a near complete set of hands, feet, face, throat and so forth. At this point, the secret, throat, forehead and crown chakras have formed as well as all of the joint chakras.

The final phase of the pregnancy extends from the fifth month until birth but the actual length of this period varies depending on the baby's karma. It is known as the *Wild Pig* because the baby's consciousness begins to manifest again and the experience of the womb is similar to a pig sitting in filth. During the seventh month the mind begins to stir, giving rise to the subtle winds. Until birth, the winds remain in the central channel resulting in dream-like experiences drawn from the memories of the being's previous life. As the foetus dreams, its bones solidify, along with its flesh, skin and hair.

The beginning of childhood is marked by birth and this phase is called the *Man-Lion* in reference to the avatar of Vishnu who defeated his enemy by ripping out its stomach. In a similar way, the baby bursts forth from the womb amidst much pain, a process generally so traumatic for the baby that all memory of its past life is lost.

The next phase of childhood spans from birth until the baby's full set of teeth have grown and for most children this usually occurs by the third year. It is known as the *Midget* as the child looks like a small adult. By the end of its first month, the child will have completed a process that began in the second month of pregnancy where roughly 200 channels were formed each day, giving a total of 72,000 branch channels. Once the channels are complete, the subtle essences begin to multiply, establishing a period of growth in the child's body. It also marks a process of ageing in which the child starts to lose two channels each day for the remainder of its life. When all of the channels are gone, the connection between mind and body is severed. This means that most humans have a maximum lifespan of approximately 100 years, based on the 360 days of a lunar year. This number however is only an estimate derived from the rate of decaying channels, the actual lifespan of an individual is determined by their karmic propensities.

To understand how this ageing process occurs, we need to consider the role our breath plays in circulating the winds throughout our body. Every day we take about 21,600 breaths where each breath includes a full cycle of one exhalation and one inhalation. The flow of breath predominantly through the right or left nostril, indicates that the winds are circulating predominantly through the right or left channels respectively. When the breath is balanced equally across both nostrils this is an indication that the winds are circulating through the central channel.

Over a single day, we experience twelve shifts of breath, each lasting approximately 1,800 breaths. For each shift, the winds predominantly flow in either the left or right channel for 1,743.75 karmic breaths, then at the end of a shift, the winds flow through the central channel for 56.25 wisdom breaths. Therefore, for 675 breaths each day, the conceptual mind of ignorance is dormant causing two branch channels to dissolve. In our childhood, the effect of ageing is minimal as with so many channels, we barely notice the loss of a few. It is not until midlife that the overall system begins to break down and our bodies no longer function as optimally as they once did.

The next phase in our childhood development extends from the completion of our baby teeth to when they are replaced by a permanent set. During this period, the structure of our subtle body does not change significantly beyond the progressive decay of ageing. However, due to the increase of the red and white drops the child experiences significant growth in the size and shape of their physical body. This phase is known as *Rama*.

The period from the development of permanent teeth until the end of puberty is *Ramana*. It is during this time that the red and white drops complete their process of increase and the child's body becomes fully matured. The end of childhood is signified by menstruation or when semen is ejaculated.

From the perspective of Kalachakra, the first phase of adulthood begins when the subtle body is fully matured and the being becomes sexually active. Lasting from the end of puberty until the onset of grey hair, it is called *Krishna*. It is during this time we first gain a truly precious human rebirth as not only do we have a fully functional system of channels, winds and drops, we also potentially have sufficient wisdom to see the advantages of dedicating ourselves to the Vajra Yoga Path.

Following this phase is the period spanning the onset of grey hair to death and is known as *Buddha* in acknowledgment of the Buddha's peaceful mind and stable behaviour. Likewise, an adult during this phase demonstrates a similar mind and behaviour as they are much less sexually active. This phase also marks a steady decline in vitality as close to half the branch channels have been dissolved. As each day passes, the channel system continues to decay, increasing the frequency of energy imbalances.

The final phase of our adult life is entry into the process of death. The actual time of death is not fixed in accordance with the channels. The decay of the channels merely weakens the bond between body and mind, making it easier for sickness to break them apart permanently. This period is known as *Kalki* which means to "make of one caste"; a reference to death being the great equaliser as there is no one born in samsara who will not die. At this point the mind withdraws from the coarse and subtle body, returning to the original subtle essence located at the heart. This essence then separates from the body and is propelled by the compulsion of karma into its next rebirth.

THE ENERGETIC CAUSES FOR CYCLIC EXISTENCE

From within this process of birth and death, we can identify two energetic patterns that drive the formation and disintegration of cyclic existence: (1) the formation of the subtle body created by the emission of vital fluids and (2) the formation of thoughts created by the circulation of winds. By preventing these patterns from arising, we can cut the cycle of pain and suffering that they produce.

Emission of Vital Fluids

As long as the mind operates under a dualistic perspective of ignorance, it will remain intermingled with energy. This connection forms when the mind makes contact with energy and grasps onto it as existing in the way it appears. Once a connection is made, the mind exerts influence over that energy in proportion to the degree of grasping present. This is like a drop of perfume soaking into a piece of paper. The quantity and quality of the perfume will determine how much fragrance the paper takes on.

When a mind grasps onto the accumulation of energy as being a self, a body is formed. It becomes a home where the mind "resides", allowing the mind to develop a close bond with each and every cell that comprises it. Over the course of a life, the energy we identify with changes significantly as we constantly take in new energy and replace the old.

A good example of this is the way our breath works. When we breathe in, we draw in oxygen which is a specific pattern of energy that when entering the body, gives rise to a particular feeling we desire. Through this process, the shape of the energy transforms and a new pattern arises which we call carbon-dioxide. This type of energy gives rise to feelings we do not desire and therefore we expel it from our bodies by breathing out.

When we release our energy into the environment, we are also releasing a portion of our grasping. While we may no longer grasp onto the energy as a self, we still grasp onto it in other ways. This residual grasping forms a persistent connection between our mind and the energy and is the energetic basis for understanding collective karma.

Consider the number of human beings living on this planet that each day take 21,600 breaths. For each breath, we draw in energy from our immediate environment and expel energy from our bodies. The energy you breath in carries with it the connections of all the minds that it came into contact with before you. Likewise the energy you breath out carries with it a connection to your mind. Through this simple process repeated countless times over the span of a lifetime, we are all actively contributing to a vast network of low-level karmic connections that bind the beings of this planet together.

As the length of a normal breath is quite short, the strength of grasping involved in breathing is not particularly intense. The exception to this is in situations where we are deprived of oxygen. Out of fear of death, we strongly grasp onto each breath in the hope of removing the suffering we are experiencing.

Another example is the consumption of food. In today's world this process carries an enormous degree of attachment as we exert considerable effort to shape our food to maximise the pleasure we feel when we eat. In the end however, food is simply energy and is broken down in the same way regardless of the sensory experience. When the food has been stripped of everything we need, the waste is expelled through our lower orifices. Eventually all the waste we release into the environment breaks down to mix with the rest of the energy, which then forms the basis for more food to be consumed by others. Considering our opposing reactions to appealing food and our excrement, we can see how the entire process is fuelled by either attachment or aversion and these are the states of minds we connect with the energy.

A more intense experience of grasping arises during sexual intimacy. When two people come together, very strong attachment is generally involved which forms a close bond between the energy of the partners. Impelled by their mutual desire for the body of the other, they grasp onto the pleasurable feelings which arise and this grasping increases in intensity until the moment of orgasm when the vital fluids are emitted. This process creates a strong karmic connection between the mind and the energy stored within the fluid and it is this connection which draws our attention to a particular womb during the transitionary period after death.

Based on the connections formed between our minds and energy, the entire physical universe is given shape. On a cosmic scale, the combined influence of countless minds forms an endless array of stars and planets. We are then drawn to the world where we have the strongest energetic bond. Our bodies are formed from the energy produced during sexual union and our experience is shaped by the people and things made from the energy we once consumed.

In this way, the act of emitting one's vital fluids while absorbed in intense desire is a direct cause for taking rebirth in an endless stream of samsaric joys and sufferings. If we do not form these types of bonds with energy, we will not be drawn to them at a later time. This is the primary reason why the Kalachakra teachings encourage the guarding of our vital fluids. This does not mean we should be worried about the literal loss of our fluids as they are little more than configurations of energy, but rather the guarding of these liquids avoids the creation of intense karmic connections with energy based on desire and grasping.

Circulation of Winds

In order to stop samsara from arising, we must dissolve the connection between our mind and energy. As the root of this connection is grasping, we need to therefore reflect on how grasping arises in the first place. The answer to this question lies in understanding the relationship between the inner winds and the drops.

As we previously discussed, the winds are patterns of the mind that condition or alter our experience of the subtle body. In essence, they are the movements of energy driven by our habitual propensities. When we say that the winds are circulating in the left and right channels, this means our energy is distributed unevenly throughout the body. This imbalanced energy gives rise to different types of dualistic appearances, which then trigger reactions of grasping in the mind. This grasping causes the energy to move which generates more appearances, which generates more grasping and on it goes.

From this context we can then say that the cause of grasping is the movement of energy. If the energy is still, the dualistic appearances will not arise and the mind will not have anything to react to. Instead of becoming involved with a reality that is illusory in nature, the mind can abide in its own pristine awareness, completely free from all forms of suffering. To achieve this sublime state, we need to bring the winds into the central channel by balancing our energy so it is evenly distributed across the body. When we no longer experience a difference between left and right, our awareness can abide in the middle. This perfect balance is the result of the yogic practices of the completion stage.

THE PRELIMINARY PRACTICE OF THE THREE ISOLATIONS

To summarise the purpose of the completion stage, we can say that all the practices are designed to purify grasping so we can achieve an unchanging pristine awareness of the sublime nature of reality. This process involves a steady refinement of mind that progresses from the most coarse forms of grasping to the most subtle.

Using the discussion of the *Four Drops* as a structure for our practice, there are eight stages of refinement. The first four focus on the conventional drops in order to achieve the non-conceptual awareness of Shamatha and are accomplished by practicing the *Three Isolations*. The last four focus on the ultimate drops in order to achieve the non-dual pristine awareness of immutable bliss and are accomplished through the practice of the *Six Vajra Yogas*. To authentically practice the Vajra Yogas, we first need to familiarise ourselves with three subjects: (1) the Four Disregards; (2) the Three Isolations; and (3) the Four Absorptions.

The Four Disregards

Before we begin our practice of the Three Isolations, we should establish a conducive attitude for our meditation. This attitude is made up of four conducts known as the *Four Disregards*:

1. **Disregard for Physical Enjoyment:** In this conduct, we recognise that we are constantly engaging in physical activities in order to reduce our discomfort and achieve some degree of physical enjoyment. Therefore, we develop the attitude that disregards pain as a problem and desires to abide in stillness. This is the foundation for purifying the body-drop and achieving the first and second vajra yogas.

2. **Disregard for Vocal Enjoyment:** Here, we recognise the distracted mind that is constantly engaged in various forms of afflicted speech in order to relieve the boredom of inactivity. With a mind that disregards the pleasures of such speech, we develop the desire to abide in silence. This is the foundation for purifying the speech-drop and achieving the third and fourth vajra yogas.

3. **Disregard for Mental Enjoyment:** This is the recognition of our compulsion to constantly project qualities onto things as a way of avoiding the confusion of our lived experience. We counteract this compulsion by developing a disregard for the pleasures of conceptual understanding and instead develop a desire to stop thinking. This is the foundation for purifying the mind-drop and achieving the fifth vajra yoga.

4. **Disregard for the Enjoyment of Emission:** Finally, we recognise the many activities of body, speech and mind that we perform in order to experience the state of blissful absorption and temporarily escape the suffering nature of our lives. While it definitely feels pleasant when it arises, it doesn't last and therefore perpetuates our dissatisfaction. With a mind that disregards the ordinary bliss of orgasm, we develop a desire for the immutable bliss of non-emission. This is the foundation for purifying the wisdom-drop and achieving the sixth vajra yoga.

The Three Isolations

Of the four conventional drops, the first three of body, speech and mind are considered forms of *conceptual consciousness* as they are linked to experiences of reality through a layer of dualistic imputations. Only the fourth drop is free from these projections and therefore it is referred to as a *non-conceptual awareness.* Our aim with the Three Isolations is to achieve a single-pointed concentration that abides in non-conceptual awareness. To do this, we need to isolate our awareness from our consciousness which is another way of saying we make consciousness dormant so awareness can manifest.

Isolation of the Body

Across our lives, due to the power of afflicted states of mind, the channels in the subtle body curve in different ways forming knots that block the natural flow of energy. These blockages force the energy to flow in distorted ways, leading to corresponding distortions in the mind. As long as the channels remain in this tangled mess, our mind will be anchored in the gross sensory appearances of the waking state.

To overcome this form of grasping we can train with a specific yogic posture designed to channel energy downwards towards the navel. As the energy moves, it encounters knots giving rise to involuntary movements and experiences of pain or discomfort. If we can hold our body still without reacting to these appearances, the blockages clear and the channels eventually heal.

As a result of purifying the body drop in this way, we are able to sit without discomfort for as long as we desire. While we may still feel fatigue at times, our bodies will generally feel light and flexible. This physical pliancy is a direct result of the winds moving freely through our channels and ensures that we have no problem with sitting in any of the completion stage postures. With the body no longer distracting the mind, we can fully withdraw from sensory appearances and rest the mind in a purely mental experience.

Isolation of the Speech

Regular breathing is fuelled by a form of grasping that forces the winds into a rhythm of expansion and contraction. When the subtle channels remain fragmented and tangled, the constant movement of the breath in and out causes the inner winds to be dispersed into different parts of the body. This imbalance of the winds create ripples in the mind and leads to the proliferation of thoughts which are the appearances of the dream state.

To purify these appearances, we need to let go of the desire to moderate or control the breath in any way. Instead, we learn to simply rest the awareness while the body breathes by itself. When the mind disengages from this process, the breath naturally settles, becoming increasingly more subtle until it is no longer perceptible to the mind.

As a result of purifying the speech drop, we are able to rest in complete silence for as long as we wish, without experiencing any form of hardship or boredom. The winds remain still and our mind is totally at ease. Without the constant distraction of thoughts, the mind will withdraw deeper into the subtle subjective experience of the foundational consciousness.

Isolation of the Mind

When the winds become still, the subjective qualities of the mind's nature begin to manifest more clearly. By projecting existence onto these appearances, we actively reinforce a very subtle layer of concepts that limit our capacity to experience our nature. This is like a light that is barely noticeable because the dimmer has been turned all the way down.

To dissolve these limitations and reveal the brilliance of the mind's nature, we must work to counteract our habit of grasping onto whatever arises. We do this by resting the mind in a vivid awareness without projecting any sort of reality onto the experience. This is a training in non-action as we are not *trying* to do anything in particular.

As a result of purifying the mind drop, we completely subdue our mind and are able to abide single-pointedly in a non-conceptual awareness of our dependent nature. This state is characterised by being blissful, intensely vivid and completely free of thoughts. Such a mind can easily be directed towards any object, which makes it ideal for realising our Buddha-nature.

The Four Absorptions

During our practice of the Three Isolations, four qualities known as the *Four Absorptions* will begin to manifest. At first these qualities will arise sporadically in dependence on our individual karma. Over time however, they will become more stable and strong. The four qualities are:

1. **Single-Pointedness:** This is the quality of a mind that abides in single-pointed focus without distraction. Through this quality we develop increasingly profound levels of absorption.

2. **Non-Conceptuality:** This is the quality of a mind free from imputed projections. When perfected, the mind is able to establish a direct experience of whatever phenomena it is focused on.

3. **Non-Grasping:** This is the quality of a mind which is able to abide in equanimity regardless of what is appearing to it. The mind is completely still, without preferences or desires.

4. **Effortlessness:** This is the quality of a mind that is able to rest at ease in its own nature. Such a mind does not meditate, or engage in any form of action. It just is.

The Progressive Stages of Correct Meditation

In order to develop these qualities, we will need to go through several different stages or processes before being able to rest single-pointedly in the non-conceptual state. In total there are five progressive stages:

1. **Movement:** When beginning to meditate our mind is like a waterfall and we are easily distracted, unable to remain with any kind of single-pointed focus. It seems that we have many more thoughts than usual. This is actually a good sign because it

means we have gained a slight ability to meditate. Normally we have streams of thoughts arising continuously yet our mind is always focused outside so we do not recognise them. This time our mind is partially "inside" and we begin to recognise this stream of thoughts for the first time. We therefore gain recognition of movement during this stage.

2. **Perceiving:** If we continually apply the antidotes to agitation and dullness the mind will gradually settle. At this stage the mind has greater awareness yet it cannot remain single-pointed for very long. At times it will become still without effort and thoughts will appear like the sound of flowing water in a deep valley. At this time the mind is beginning to abide naturally, and this is known as the stage of perceiving.

3. **Habituation:** The mind then goes through a stage where it becomes still. Thoughts arise again as previously experienced, yet this time the mind stays single-pointed more often like a frog leaping into the air then stopping, again and again. As thoughts arise they spontaneously vanish and we are able to remain single-pointed without effort. This is known as the stage of habituation.

4. **Stabilisation:** By continuing to practise in this way, eventually the thoughts will hardly arise at all; our mind will not be disturbed and we will not lose concentration. Thoughts now arise like ripples on a pond; they arise and then gently pass away. This is known as mental stabilisation and is the result of practising the previous two stages.

5. **Perfection:** Continually practising mental stabilisation, our mind will stay single-pointed and never become agitated or

distracted, just like a still lake. The mind becomes so skilled we can choose whether to have a still mind which is spontaneously single-pointed, or to focus without distraction on a topic of analysis. This is known as perfection of mental stabilisation. This perfect mind of mental stabilisation is the only mind that can remain single-pointed. It can investigate any topic with perfect single-pointed focus; however, it is not the same as the stabilisation of the primordial natural mind. This will only become perfected when we reach Buddhahood.

When we have perfected the ability to stay single-pointed and can remain perfectly focused on any object, we will have achieved the mind of Shamatha. The mind of Shamatha is a prerequisite for vipashyana meditation, which leads to insight into the true nature of reality. From the viewpoint of this tradition of Vipashyana, only those who have attained Shamatha are able to discover things with greater penetration using the mind of Vipashyana.

The Need to Receive Pith Instructions

The actual instructions for how to practice the Three Isolations are restricted to those who have received the Four Higher Empowerments and as such, they are not included in this book. If you have already completed the preliminaries and would like to begin practice of the completion stage, you should seek out a qualified master who can bestow both the empowerments and pith instructions. Practicing in this way ensures the preservation of the blessings of these teachings and makes certain that you are properly supported by a master who can guide you on this very subtle path. Without the teacher's guidance, there is no way to attain authentic realisations.

REVIEW OF KEY POINTS

- Before practicing the Vajra Yogas, we need to establish the single-pointed concentration of Shamatha in order to stabilise our experience of the non-conceptual awareness introduced to us in the Four Higher Empowerments.

- In the Kalachakra Path, Shamatha is achieved through the practice of the Three Isolations. This incredibly efficient method of meditation takes advantage of the subtle energetic system to produce a profound state of meditative absorption in a short period of time.

- The subtle energetic body is formed by the patterns of energy that arise due to the movements of a dualistic mind. It consists of three main components: (1) channels and chakras; (2) inner winds and (3) subtle essences.

- A channel is a pathway through which energy flows. Of the 72,000 channels in a fully matured human body, there are three primary channels: (1) the central channel known as avadhuti; (2) the left channel known as lalana; and (3) the right channel known as rasana.

- There are six chakras formed at the points where the left and right channels coil around the central channel: (1) the crown chakra with four branches; (2) the forehead chakra with sixteen branches; (3) the throat chakra with thirty-two branches; (4) the heart chakra with eight branches; (5) the navel chakra with sixty-four branches; and (6) the secret chakra with thirty-two branches.

- The inner winds refer to the way the subtle body changes over time due to the movements of the mind or energy. There are ten winds in total, with five primary and five secondary.

- The primary winds are: (1) the life-supporting wind; (2) the downward-moving wind; (3) the fire-accompanying wind; (4) the upward-moving wind and (5) the all-pervading wind.

- The secondary winds are: (1) the naga wind; (2) the tortoise wind; (3) the lizard wind; (4) the devadatta wind and (5) the dhanamjaya wind.

- A subtle essence is the combination of subtle energy and mind fused together by grasping. The body is filled with two types of subtle essences: (1) red drops which have a predominance of feminine energy and (2) white drops which have a predominance of masculine energy. The red drops are mostly located in the lower half of the body, while the white drops are mostly in the upper half.

- There are four levels of subtlety in which the red and white drops are found: (1) a subtle essence is the combination of energy and mind; (2) a subtle drop is the union of a subtle essence with genetic material; (3) a coarse drop is the union of a subtle drop with biological components making up a cell; and (4) a very-coarse drop is the union of multiple coarse drops in a cluster.

- The Four Drops represent the types of appearances that are produced in the mind as a result of the interaction between the winds and drops of different regions in the body. These are: (1) the body drop surrounding the brain; (2) the speech drop in the throat region; (3) the mind drop in the heart region; and (4) the wisdom drop in the navel region.

- When the mind is absorbed in meditative concentration, the Ultimate Four Drops become manifest: (1) the ultimate body drop at the navel; (2) the ultimate speech drop at the secret chakra; (3) the ultimate mind drop at the centre of the genitals; and (4) the ultimate wisdom drop at the tip of the genitals.

- A human being passes through ten phases of development from the moment of conception to the moment of death: (1) Fish; (2) Turtle; (3) Wild-Pig; (4) Man-Lion; (5) Midget; (6) Rama; (7) Ramana; (8) Vishnu; (9) Buddha; and (10) Kalki;

- The two energetic patterns that drive the formation and disintegration of cyclic existence are: (1) the formation of the subtle body created by the emission of vital fluids and (2) the formation of thoughts created by the circulation of winds.

- The completion stage is designed to dissolve grasping so that we can achieve an unchanging pristine awareness of the sublime nature of reality. The practice of the Three Isolations is used to achieve the non-conceptual awareness of Shamatha, while the Six Vajra Yogas unveil the non-dual pristine awareness.

- The Four Disregards are attitudes that provide the foundation for achieving a non-conceptual awareness: (1) disregard for physical enjoyment; (2) disregard for verbal enjoyment; (3) disregard for mental enjoyment and (4) disregard for the enjoyment of emission.

- The Three Isolations achieves single-pointed concentration by isolating the body, speech and mind which causes the conceptual consciousness to go dormant and allows the non-conceptual awareness to manifest.

- The Four Absorptions are qualities that will arise as a result of practicing the Three Isolations. They are (1) single-pointedness;

(2) non-conceptuality; (3) non-grasping and (4) effortlessness.

- The qualities of the four absorptions are developed over five stages: (1) movement; (2) perceiving; (3) habituation; (4) stabilisation and (5) perfection.

- The Three Isolations should only be practiced by those who have received the Four Higher Empowerments and the corresponding pith instructions from a qualified vajra master.

CHAPTER NINE

The Six Vajra Yogas of the Kalachakra Completion Stage

Upon completion of the two outer, the five inner and the two unique preliminary practices of the Kalachakra Path, we are ready to enter the indestructible and profound path of the Six Vajra Yogas. These advanced yogic techniques are like a wish-fulfilling jewel with the capacity to grant us everything our hearts desire in the blink of an eye. For a diligent practitioner whose mind is sufficiently pure, enlightenment can be achieved within only a few short human years. Even mastery of a single yoga is enough to ensure one is never again reborn into the suffering cycle of death and rebirth.

It is an extraordinary blessing to simply hear the names of the Six Vajra Yogas and therefore it is difficult to comprehend how exceedingly rare and precious it is to encounter the teachings that describe them or to have the incredible fortune to actually practice them. It is for this reason, as we continue forward, we should embrace a sense of immense appreciation for just how special these teachings really are. Such an attitude makes certain that we form a strong karmic connection, creating the causes to encounter these teachings again in the future and to ultimately actualise their definitive meaning.

Recognising the potential power of these practices, the sublime lineage masters of the Vajra Yoga Path protected and preserved the teachings for over two thousand years, guaranteeing that even today we have access to the unbroken stream of their blessings. Although written commentaries exist which enable us to familiarise ourselves with the general structure of the practices, this tradition relies heavily on the profound pith instructions that only a qualified vajra master can impart.

The pith instructions are generally only bestowed on a student when the vajra master observes that the necessary foundations have been gathered through the preliminary practices. While it is not essential to achieve mastery of each practice, our commitment to achieving enlightenment for the benefit of all beings needs to have been demonstrated. Lacking stability in our determination will not only damage our relationship with the vajra master, but also create a cause for the teachings to degenerate. Therefore, to be a sincere and authentic practitioner, we must do all we can to properly prepare ourselves.

Once we are accepted by the vajra master, the pith instructions are given in a gradual manner: first we receive a set of instructions, we put the teachings into practice and then we report our experiences to the master at regular intervals. This constant monitoring forms an important part of our training as it allows the master to make any necessary adjustments and ensures we do not get caught in the many pitfalls related to the subtlety of the practices.

When the master establishes our firm grasp of the practices, the next set of instructions are bestowed and in this way, the Vajra Yogas are revealed in an experiential manner, allowing us to cultivate considerable confidence in our practice. After repeated cycles of instruction, practice and report, the foundation of realisations that is developed can be refined in order to gain mastery over each phase of the practice.

Keeping this process in mind, we will now explore a general presentation of the Vajra Yoga Path to help develop clarity regarding its phases and how they relate to each other. The purpose of this chapter is to generate faith in the techniques and to strengthen our aspiration to practice them. It is my hope that, on this basis, you will be inspired to seek a qualified master to guide you on this most profound of paths.

THE STRUCTURE OF THE VAJRA YOGA PATH

The Vajra Yoga Path consists of six branches of practice designed to establish and stabilise the realisation of the inseparable union of immutable bliss and sublime emptiness endowed with all enlightened qualities. These branches are as follows:

1. **The Yoga of Withdrawal (Skt. Pratyahara, Tib. sordut):** The essence of Withdrawal Yoga is to manifest empty-forms by stopping the movement of the coarse winds which support the conceptual mind.

2. **The Yoga of Stabilisation (Skt. Dhyana, Tib. samten):** The essence of Stabilisation Yoga is to extend our realisation of empty-forms so that all perceptions arise as awareness.

3. **The Yoga of the Life-Force (Skt. Pranayama, Tib. sogtsol):** The essence of Life-Force Yoga is to subdue the subtle karmic winds so they are balanced in the central channel.

4. **The Yoga of Retention (Skt. Dharana, Tib. zinpa):** The essence of Retention Yoga is to completely subdue the subtle karmic winds so their movement ceases and they merge with the subtle essences distributed throughout the body.

5. **The Yoga of Recollection (Skt. Anusmirti, Tib. jeeten):** The essence of Recollection Yoga is to refine our experience of great bliss through the practice of *Inner Fire* (Tib. tummo).

6. **The Yoga of Absorption (Skt. Samadhi, Tib. ting nge dzin):** The essence of Absorption Yoga is to abide in the Union of Immutable Bliss and Empty-Form.

Each of these yogas provides the prerequisite capacities needed to progress to the next yoga. The degree of realisation achieved at any given stage will depend on the level of mastery accomplished in the previous stages. As we do not know how long our present karmic conditions will remain, it is beneficial to develop an initial familiarity with these practices within the context of a three year retreat. By doing this, even if we are unable to master them before we die, we are still creating the necessary propensities to propel our mind into the Vajrayana Pure Realm of Shambhala, where we are guaranteed to complete the path within a single lifetime.

Divisions of the Six Yogas

Over the centuries, the Vajra Yoga Path has been presented in different ways as a means of highlighting different aspects of its structure. While these categories are merely imputed labels, as you may encounter them in your studies they are worth considering:

1. **The Two-Fold Division of Empty-Form and Immutable Bliss:** This division is based on the aspect most emphasised by each yoga. In general, we can say the first four branches are primarily focused on establishing a direct realisation of sublime emptiness which is considered the *Great Consort of Empty-Form* (Mahamudra). The remaining two yogas emphasise utilising this realisation as the basis for establishing and then perfecting our experience of *Immutable Bliss*. Ultimately the aim is to unify both aspects into a pristine non-dual awareness.

2. **The Three-Fold Division of the Three Purities:** This division is based on the effect the six yogas have on the subtle energetic system. It highlights the purification of the energetic basis of cyclic existence to then actualise enlightenment in a non-conceptual way. The first two yogas are referred to as the Purity of Virtue in the Beginning, purifying the channels and chakras. The third and fourth yogas are the Purity of Virtue in the Middle, purifying the inner winds, and the final two yogas are the Purity of Virtue in the End, purifying the subtle essences.

3. **The Four-Fold Division of Approach and Accomplishment:** This division is based on the purification of the four drops. In the stage of Approach, the first two yogas purify the Body Drop, giving rise to the realisation of Vajra-Body. This is followed by the stage of Near Accomplishment in which the third and fourth yogas purify the Speech Drop, giving rise to the realisation of Vajra-Speech. In the stage of Accomplishment the fifth yoga purifies the Mind Drop, giving rise to the realisation of Vajra-Mind. Finally, in the stage of Great Accomplishment, the sixth yoga removes the last obscurations from the Wisdom Drop, giving rise to the supreme realisation of Vajra-Wisdom.

Aspect	Purity	Purifies	Stage	Drop	Yoga
Empty-Form	Beginning	Channels	Approach	Body	Withdrawal
					Stabilisation
	Middle	Winds	Near Accomplishment	Speech	Life-Force
					Retention
Immutable Bliss	End	Drops	Accomplishment	Mind	Recollection
			Great Accomplishment	Wisdom	Absorption

Table 9-1: Divisions of the Six Vajra Yogas

How the Six Yogas Accomplish the Five Paths

Referencing the Five Paths of Attainment can be helpful for understanding the overall progression of a practitioner through a path structure. As we saw in Book One of this series, each of the five paths can be linked to the different practices and realisations according to the level of the vehicle being practiced. The following is a short summary of how the five paths are experienced in relation to the uncommon teachings of the Kalachakra Tantra:

1. **The Path of Accumulation:** The essence of this path is to gather the conditions needed to realise the sublime emptiness endowed with all aspects. It is divided into three stages with the

first two corresponding to the practices of the *Kalachakra Generation Stage*, whereby we generate ourselves as the Kalachakra Yidam and then engage in countless enlightened activities, accumulating vast quantities of merit and wisdom. Then, in the third stage, the practices of the *Three Isolations* and the *Yoga of Withdrawal* are used to perfect the meditative absorptions of Shamatha and Vipashyana, establishing a direct experience of empty-form. While these appearances are merely aspects of our sublime emptiness, they provide a valid working basis for progressing on the path.

2. **The Path of Preparation:** Building on our initial realisation of emptiness, the essence of this path is to remove all subtle forms of grasping so we can experience the complete manifestation of sublime emptiness. This is done in three stages. In the first stage, the *Yoga of Stabilisation* is used to purify the objective appearance of empty-forms and in the second, the *Yoga of the Life-Force* subdues the subtle mental activity caused by the movement of the winds. In the third, the *Yoga of Retention* completely dissolves the subtle winds into the subtle essences, preventing the dualistic mind from manifesting.

3. **The Path of Insight:** When dualistic appearances no longer manifest, all that remains is the experience of the Great Consort of Empty-Form. This is the first instance when a fully manifest form of sublime emptiness is realised. Through the practice of the *Yoga of Recollection*, this realisation is further refined so the Union of Immutable Bliss and Empty-Form can be achieved.

4. **The Path of Habituation:** Once a realisation of immutable bliss has arisen, it can then be used to clear the most subtle karmic traces preventing the enlightened mind of a Buddha from manifesting. Through the *Yoga of Absorption*, the conventional

experience of white and red drops is completely dissolved into a single immutable drop, which is the final experience of perfect ultimate truth. As this process unfolds, it is akin to rapidly traversing all the Bodhisattva grounds.

5. **The Path of No More Learning:** With no obscurations left to anchor the mind to cyclic existence, the enlightened mind of Vajradhara is perfected and spontaneously manifests an infinite array of form-bodies for the benefit of sentient beings. At this stage, training is complete and there is nothing left to be done.

Path	Practice	Realisation
Accumulation	Generation Stage	Accumulation of wisdom
		Accumulation of merit
	Three Isolations	Abide single-pointedly in foundational consciousness
	Withdrawal	Direct experience of empty-forms as appearances
Preparation	Stabilisation	Dissolve appearances into awareness
	Life-Force	Dissolve awareness into winds
	Retention	Dissolve winds into subtle essences
Insight	Recollection	Direct experience of immutable bliss
Habituation	Absorption	Burn away residual karmic traces
No More Learning	--	Attain the enlightened mind of Vajradhara

Table 9-2: The Vajra Yoga Path to Enlightenment

The Qualities Developed on the Vajra Yoga Path

Taken as a whole, the six yogas represent a progression of refinement in which three aspects of Buddha-nature are gradually perfected:

1. **The Appearance of Empty-Forms:** Initially, empty-forms are experienced objectively as images, to then be experienced as mere appearances, inseparable from awareness. When this

awareness is focused on the movements of subtle energy, they arise as winds and when these winds are subdued, they arise as subtle drops. Through the practice of inner fire, they are then experienced as the essence of blazing and melting. As a result of this process, the melted drops converge into an inseparable and immutable drop in which all enlightened qualities are simultaneously manifest.

2. **The Experience of Bliss:** Due to training in the meditative concentration of Vipashyana, bliss arises in the form of subtle mental pliancy. The refinement of this state of concentration becomes a pure form of joyful bliss. As the winds are balanced in the central channel, bliss from the merging winds arises, followed by the great bliss from the joining of the winds and the coarse drops. This great bliss is intensified through the melting of the subtle drops, until it eventually gives rise to immutable bliss.

3. **The Abandonment of Duality:** The first layer of duality is abandoned by realising the empty-nature of appearances with a non-conceptual awareness. Then by realising that all appearances are of the same nature as this awareness, objective and subjective appearances adopt the same flavour. When the winds cease to flow in the left and right channels and are made to dissolve in the central channel, coarse and subtle dualistic appearances stop arising altogether. As the experience of bliss is further refined, each moment becomes indistinguishable. Finally, by abiding in this state of bliss, all conventional truths of subject and object are seen to be uncreated and the duality of conventional and ultimate is dissolved in the immutable nature of suchness.

The following table illustrates how each of these aspects evolves in parallel:

Yoga	Empty-Form	Bliss	Non-Duality
Withdrawal	Image	Subtle Mental Bliss	Empty Nature
Stabilisation	Mere Appearance	Pure Joyful Bliss	One-Taste
Life-Force	Winds	Bliss of Merging Winds	Balance
Retention	Subtle Essences	Bliss of Merging with Drops	Non-Movement
Recollection	Melting Essences	Great Bliss of Melting Drops	Blissful Nature
Absorption	Immutable Drop	Immutable Bliss	Immutable Nature

Table 9-3: The qualities developed on the Vajra Yoga Path

AN OVERVIEW OF THE SIX VAJRA YOGAS

We will now proceed to a general presentation of each Vajra Yoga in order to introduce the structure of their individual practices and provide enough information to clearly distinguish each branch. For an in-depth presentation of these practices, the written commentaries of the great lineage masters such as Kunkhyen Dolpopa and Jetsun Taranatha will need to be referred to.

For each yoga we will follow a six-fold structure: (1) the meaning of the name; (2) the time for meditation; (3) the branches of practice; (4) the signs of attainment; (5) the basis of purification; and (6) the results obtained.

The Yoga of Withdrawal

The first yoga is *Withdrawal* and refers to the process of meditation used to direct the inner winds into the central channel. Under normal conditions, the winds circulate unevenly through the left and the right channels resulting in the coarse appearances of the four states of experience. As long as the winds flow in this way, we are unable to experience the sublime emptiness directly. For this reason, we must withdraw our awareness away from the external world so everything we perceive becomes a pure manifestation of our pristine nature.

Meaning of the Name

The sanskrit name for this yoga is *Pratyahara*, and consists of two parts, *pratya* meaning "individual" and *ahara* meaning "withdrawal". The literal translation is therefore "individual withdrawal". The name indicates that through this yoga we individually sever our connection to external sensory objects by withdrawing our winds into the central channel.

Time for Meditation

To practice this yoga, we need to have developed a stable experience of the four absorptions: single-pointedness, non-conceptuality, non-grasping and effortlessness, which is done through the Three Isolations. The best time for engaging in this practice is when the winds transition from the left nostril to the right, as during this time the earth element is particularly weak, making it easier to dissolve impure appearances into the experience of space. That being said, if Withdrawal is your main practice, you should practice at any time you are not sleeping.

Branches of Practice

The posture and instruction for this practice are similar to those used for the Three Isolations, with the distinguishing feature being a matter of where emphasis is placed. While the Three Isolations concentrate on developing single-pointed concentration (shamatha), Withdrawal Yoga is more concerned with establishing special insight (vipashyana). The dividing line between the practices is the appearance of empty-forms which occurs when the winds begin to enter the central channel.

In total, ten types of empty-forms will arise which correspond to the dissolution of each of the ten winds. They are identified by ten unique signs: (1) smoke; (2) mirage; (3) clouds; (4) fire-flies; (5) blazing; (6) moonlight; (7) sunlight; (8) eclipse; (9) lightning and (10) drop.

These signs should not be taken as literal manifestations of smoke and so forth. Think of them more as general indications of the nature of how empty-forms manifest. For instance, the sign of smoke indicates a wispy aspect to the appearances, whereas the sign of mirage implies a shimmering aspect.

Some of these signs may arise sporadically during the practice of the Three Isolations as the winds temporarily pass through the central channel. For a sign to be considered an authentic sign of the Withdrawal Yoga, it should arise consistently in the above order. This sequence is connected to the way our elements and aggregates dissolve from coarse to subtle during the process of dissolution at the time of death. True withdrawal occurs when the inner winds are drawn into and dissolve in the crown chakra.

With regards to practice, the Yoga of Withdrawal consists of two phases:

1. **The Night-Time Practice:** In this phase our focus is to withdraw the winds associated with our gross sensory consciousnesses. To aid this process we need to be isolated from sensory phenomena as much as possible, therefore the practice is performed in complete darkness. Through this practice, we experience the first four signs as an indication of the secondary winds entering the central channel.

2. **The Day-Time Practice:** As a result of the night-time practice, our mind becomes open and spacious, like the clear blue sky. To emphasise this quality of space, this phase of practice is traditionally performed outside during the day, focusing on an empty sky free from clouds. This method connects us with our primordial nature, which just like the sky, has no centre or circumference, no distinct colours, and extends across a limitless spatial expanse. If the sky is covered by clouds, we continue to practice in the dark room as before. Through this practice, we experience the remaining six signs.

Practice	Sign	Wind	Element	Aggregate
Night-Time	Smoke	Naga	Earth	Form
	Mirage	Tortoise	Water	
	Clouds	Lizard	Fire	
	Fire-Flies	Devadatta	Wind	
Day-Time	Blazing	Dhanamjaya	Space	
	Moonlight	All-Pervading	Consciousness	Perception
	Sunlight	Upward-Moving		Feelings
	Eclipse	Fire-Accompanying		Conceptions
	Lightning	Downward-Clearing		Consciousness
	Drop	Life-Supporting		Awareness

Table 9-4: Signs arising during the Yoga of Withdrawal

Signs of Attainment

As we familiarise ourselves with these practices, the signs will become stronger, clearer and more stable, forming an "inner world" of empty-forms, isolated from our experience of external objects. Even though their empty-nature will be obvious to us, they still appear to exist as separate from the mind, like illusions or dreams. These empty-forms are experienced in reliance on a direct valid cognition of the eye sense power, meaning that we see them as visions.

Basis of Purification

Generally speaking, the basis of purification for all six yogas is the sublime ground of Buddha-nature. However, for each yoga there is a set of six constituents which is the ground that is specifically purified by the practices. In the case of Withdrawal Yoga, the impure basis of purification is the six constituents of consciousness: (1) the aggregate of pristine awareness; (2) the element of consciousness; (3) the mental sense power; (4) sound; (5) the lower central channel and (6) the emission of urine.

The means by which these constituents are purified is through the withdrawal of the ten winds, giving rise to ten levels of increasingly more subtle awareness.

Results Obtained

With diligence in the practice of Withdrawal, we eventually gain mastery over the process of dissolution itself. As we become more familiar with each of the winds, we can trigger the signs at will and in any order we wish. This capacity allows us to enter the death process with awareness and therefore we no longer have to take an uncontrolled rebirth. Ultimately, the result of mastering this yoga is that the six constituents of consciousness arise as an infinite array of deities belonging to the Vajrasattva Family.

The Yoga of Stabilisation

The second yoga is the Yoga of Stabilisation and is the practice through which the perception of empty-forms attained in the previous yoga is indivisibly unified with the awareness of an inner perceiver. Whereas the first yoga allows us to perceive the empty-forms of the ten signs as objects of the mind, the second yoga enables the practitioner to spontaneously "mix" or integrate these signs with the mind's nature. In other words, the dualistic appearance of a separate subject and object are merged together.

Meaning of the Name

The sanskrit name for this yoga is *Dhyana*, which literally means "single-pointed concentration". It also denotes taking hold of the object of focus in the sense that we take hold of our realisation of empty-form so we can control it more effectively.

Time for Meditation

Ideally we should practice Stabilisation Yoga after achieving mastery of Withdrawal Yoga. As we are able to generate the ten signs of empty-form at will, we then have a stable basis for analysis. However, even without mastery of generating empty-forms, the minimum we need is for empty-forms to arise long enough to observe them closely.

Branches of Practice

Prior to this stage, we mainly practice with the eye sense power and visual forms. We now extend our practice to include the other forms of sense consciousness such as sound, smell, taste and touch. When we develop proficiency in this yoga, a dark room is no longer necessary as the internal objects merge with the mind, and external objects no longer affect our experience.

Through this meditation, any form of normal perception can be experienced as empty-forms, inseparable from the mind. For example, if we meditate near a waterfall, the sound would arise as empty-sound perceived by the wisdom ear of yogic perception. Likewise, all taste, smell and tactile sensations are integrated into our pure experience and in this way, objects of the mind are eventually experienced as inseparable from the nature of the mind.

The process used to achieve this merging is divided into five aspects:

1. **Understanding:** The first step is to simply observe the different types of empty-forms arising. In this phase we come to understand how sense objects manifest to non-conceptual awareness.

2. **Appreciation:** When we develop greater familiarity with the range of empty-forms arising, we recognise them as inseparable from our own mind. In this moment, the distinction between subject and object begins to dissolve.

3. **Analysis:** By continually observing the nature of the way these empty-forms manifest, we gain confidence and certainty that they are nothing other than the mind. This confidence allows the mind to release coarse grasping and rest in stillness even when empty-forms actively manifest.

4. **Joy:** As the mind learns to abide single-pointedly without grasping onto empty-forms, an experience of bliss arises in the body and mind. When this bliss pervades all appearances, they take on a similar "taste" meaning that subjectively, they are experienced with the same blissful aspect.

5. **Unwavering Bliss:** Eventually when all distinctions between subject and object are dissolved, we develop a meditative concentration in which all appearances arise as empty-forms and all empty-forms are experienced as blissful awareness.

First there is only understanding, then with it comes the simultaneous arising of appreciation. In this way, each subsequent aspect is integrated with the previous realisation so that when unwavering bliss arises, all five aspects are present.

Signs of Attainment

When the mind achieves meditative stabilisation, the ten signs from the previous yoga arise simultaneously and continuously. Initially our yogic perception lacks clarity, but eventually it becomes clear and then very clear. With practice, the perception of these signs also becomes increasingly subtle and this process is described in five stages: (1) first they appear more subtle, and then (2) they occur with light, (3) with luminous light, (4) with moving luminous light and finally (5) with indestructible light. At this point, it is very important to have the guidance of a qualified master as it is easy to become lost in the subtlety and thereby fall into a wrong path.

Although this yoga leads to the merging of mind and sensory objects, one's perception still depends on the sense consciousnesses rather than being completely dependent on the mind consciousness alone. While there is no distinct subject and object, the sense organ consciousnesses continue to be involved, perceiving things in a way that is free from words, pictures and conceptual ideas.

Basis of Purification

The impure basis of purification for the Stabilisation Yoga is the six constituents of space: (1) the consciousness aggregate; (2) the space element; (3) the organ of hearing; (4) the element of mental phenomena; (5) the sexual organs; and (6) the control of vital fluids.

These constituents are purified by achieving meditative stability on the five subjective aspects of understanding and so forth in relation to the five types of empty-forms corresponding to the five sense objects.

Results Obtained

The temporary result of the Yoga of Stabilisation is the achievement of the five types of clairvoyance including wisdom-eye, wisdom-ear, wisdom-nose, wisdom-tongue, and wisdom-body consciousness. Ultimately, mastery of this yoga results in the six constituents of space arising as an infinite array of deities belonging to the Akshobhya Family.

The Yoga of the Life-Force

During the practice of the Life-Force Yoga, the power of the winds are harnessed to help integrate our non-dual perception of empty-forms with the movement of the inner winds. Through this process the five primary and five secondary winds are unified by causing them to enter and to abide within the central channel. By mastering this process, we gain full control of our channels and winds, enabling us to survive solely on the subtle energy in our bodies, thereby we are no longer dependant on coarse foods for nourishment.

Meaning of the Name

The sanskrit name for this yoga is *Pranayama*, where *prana* means "vital energy" or "life-force", and *ayama* means "to control", so that pranayama means to control the vital energy. The energy being controlled refers to the inner winds which are directed into the central channel.

Time for Meditation

The actual Life-Force Yoga can only be authentically practiced after attaining mastery of the five stages of meditative stabilisation in the previous yoga. However, as beginners can still benefit from purifying their channels and working with their winds to stabilise them, we are encouraged to start practicing this yoga after gaining some degree of experience in either the Withdrawal or Stabilisation yogas.

Branches of Practice

The practice of this yoga works primarily by subduing the karmic winds that circulate through the sixty branch channels of the navel chakra. This is done through two types of yogic meditation:

1. **Vajra Recitation:** In this practice we connect the three phases of each breath—inhalation, holding, and exhalation—to specific mantra syllables visualised at key points in the navel chakra. Through continual meditation in this way, each of the twelve shifts of breath are integrated and balanced so the winds are made to abide constantly within the central channel. When this practice is accomplished, we can experience the colours of the chakras and winds arising as empty-forms.

2. **Vase Breathing:** With all ten winds flowing evenly in the central channel, the life-supporting and downward-clearing winds need to be unified at the navel chakra. This is done

through the use of specific visualisations combined with forceful breathing patterns to draw the life-supporting wind down and the downward-clearing wind up, allowing them to meet at the navel. When this is achieved, the process of normal breathing ceases and the karmic winds are stabilised.

Signs of Attainment

There are unique signs indicating accomplishment of the third yoga. In the earlier yogas, with effort we could melt the subtle essences, generating bliss from above, whereas now this can be achieved spontaneously. We can also generate this bliss from below with a consort by controlling and directing our vital fluids into the central channel. At this stage however, this requires enormous effort and is not spontaneous.

Prior to this stage we are not qualified to practice with a physical consort but must rely instead on visualisations, dreams or visions. After mastery of the third yoga, however, we have developed the ability to practice with a physical consort in order to further our progress. Whether or not we need to engage in such practice is determined by our vajra master.

Basis of Purification

The impure basis of purification for the Life-Force Yoga is the six constituents of wind: (1) the aggregate of conceptions; (2) the wind element; (3) the nose; (4) touch; (5) the anus; and (6) the expulsion of excrement.

These constituents are purified through the ten winds of the left and right channels that are subsequently unified in the central channel.

Results Obtained

As we can now make the inner winds remain in the central channel, innumerable experiences arise such as visions of the pure lands and the six samsaric realms. In addition, our knowledge and wisdom increase spontaneously and we experience empty-forms directly without the conceptual mind. Clairvoyance is developed and we start to perceive appearances of the winds as though we were inside the central channel. Ultimately, mastering this yoga results in the six constituents of wind arising as an infinite array of deities belonging to the Amoghasiddhi Family.

The Yoga of Retention

Mastery of the Life-Force Yoga gives rise to a powerful and highly concentrated blissful awareness known as inner fire. Now, through the Yoga of Retention, we take this experience and intensify it by working in a similar way with the remaining five chakras. This process enables us to completely stop the movement of the winds in the central channel, thereby unifying them with the subtle essences.

Meaning of the Name

The sanskrit name for this yoga is *Dharana* which refers to "retaining" or to "the object that is retained". In this context it means to stop the winds so they dissolve into the subtle essences.

Time for Meditation

To practice this yoga, all ten subtle winds must abide in the central channel and the life-supporting wind and the downward-clearing wind need to be united. Only with this stability can we work with the chakras in a manner precise enough to completely stop the winds. However, as with the Life-Force Yoga, there is benefit from familiarising oneself with these meditations beforehand as this will help clear the central channel and facilitate deeper states of absorption.

Branches of Practice

Through the power of our meditative concentration, energy is first gathered at the navel, then moved upwards to the heart, followed by the throat, forehead and finally the crown chakra. At each point the winds are held so they can absorb into the surrounding essences. The energy is then brought downwards in reverse order, from the crown to the navel chakra. This process is repeated up and down the central channel until all the winds are experienced as inseparable from the essences. At this stage, the subtle essences themselves arise as empty-forms.

As some of the very subtle winds are difficult to work with, some practitioners may be encouraged to work with a physical consort to enhance their practice. This is a powerful method to stabilise the winds and dissolve them into the essences, especially the all-pervasive wind which is linked to the movement of the body.

Signs of Attainment

The Yoga of Retention is accomplished when the integrated life-supporting wind and downward-clearing wind are made to abide, stabilise and dissolve into the essences of the six chakras, representing the six elements. As a result numerous signs appear, including the ability to see innumerable visions such as the ten signs previously described, pure realms, samsaric realms and enlightened beings within a tiny circle the size of a black mustard seed. This is often regarded as an "eleventh sign", with our body appearing as the Kalachakra Yab-Yum in a Sambhogakaya-like form. This realisation is the first fully qualified appearance of an empty-form consort and is the basis for moving to the next yoga.

Basis of Purification

The impure basis of purification for the Yoga of Retention is the six constituents of fire: (1) the aggregate of feeling; (2) the fire element; (3) the eye; (4) taste; (5) the faculty of the arms; and (6) the activity of going.

These constituents are purified through the entry and exit of energy at the navel, heart, throat, forehead and crown. This creates ten levels of realisation resulting in the vital essences gathering at the upper opening of the central channel.

Results Obtained

The result of accomplishing the Yoga of Retention is the dissolution of the ten winds into the essences. This provides us with full control over the essences so that our body, speech and mind possess high degrees of vitality. Imbalances such as sickness and ageing can then be averted and we have some control over death. Having also freed ourselves from internal conflict and negative external influences caused by the circulation of karmic winds in the left and right channels, we are no longer influenced by negative emotions.

Furthermore, we have a level of control over the four maras—the aggregates, afflictions, death and pleasurable objects. The body meanwhile has increased energy and clarity, and because the tummo fire has been ignited, whenever we eat, waste does not need to be excreted. There is also the attainment of pliancy of the body, ensuring a healthy and long life. The Great Kalachakra Mahasiddha Manjuvajra stated that at this stage one can be without food yet never be hungry, and with no downward-clearing wind one is always comfortable. This is known as a vajra stomach.

Ultimately, the result of mastering this yoga is that the six constituents of fire arise as an infinite array of deities belonging to the Ratnasambhava Family.

The Yoga of Recollection

The fifth yoga is known as Recollection and stabilises what has already been achieved momentarily in the fourth yoga. Recollecting the experience of great bliss attained in the previous stage, with the dissolving of the inner winds into the essences and the igniting of the inner fire, the experience of union with the empty-form consort deepens. One thus learns to practice the union of the great bliss of the enlightened nature and the great consort of empty-form.

Meaning of the Name

The sanskrit name of this yoga is *Anusmirti,* consisting of two words; *anu* meaning "subsequent" and *smirti* meaning "recollection". Literally translated, it is called "subsequent recollection". In this context, the *anu* refers to being "superior" and entails repeatedly recollecting the superior mind of Mahamudra previously established.

Time for Meditation

To engage in the practice of Recollection, we must first master the Yoga of Retention. Only then have we thoroughly blended the channels, winds and subtle essences to such a degree, that the great bliss of inner heat arises as an enlightened array of the sublime emptiness endowed with all aspects.

Branches of Practice

As the aim of Recollection Yoga is to give rise to immutable bliss, we must refine our experience so we can abide in union with an empty-form consort without movement. We do this by continuing our practice with four types of consort:

1. **The Physical Consort:** Ordinary practitioners without refined control of their winds, channels and essences need to practice with a physical consort. This process intensifies the experience of bliss, making it easier to achieve deeper states of absorption.

2. **The Manifested Consort:** Through the bliss produced during sexual activity, the subtle essences move and we experience ourselves as the enlightened form of Kalachakra Yab-Yum. When we achieve a sufficient level of stability with this type of consort, we no longer need to rely on a physical support and are able to generate the experience at will.

3. **The Consort of Inner Fire:** By abiding in union with a manifested consort, our inner fire is ignited and the essences melt. This process causes the fire to blaze more intensely, causing more essences to melt. In this way the inner fire grows stronger, producing the progressive experience of the four joys: (1) joy; (2) supreme joy; (3) special joy; and (4) innate joy. As the essences melt, we experience these joys descending from the top of the body, moving downwards and collecting at the tip of the lower opening of the central channel. By holding the energy there, we experience an even more subtle and intense set of joys emanating from the lower opening up to the top of the crown chakra.

4. **The Great Consort of Empty-Form:** Through the practice of inner fire, we refine our experience of bliss to such a degree that all subtle forms of grasping completely dissolve. This gives rise to an actual Great Consort of Empty-Form which is a fully-established, non-dual awareness of the sublime emptiness, endowed with all enlightened qualities.

When we become proficient with the process of refining the subtle essences, generation of the manifested consort is no longer needed as we are able to directly practice with the empty-form consort. At this stage, while the blissful experience of inner fire is still present, it is not identified as the consort of inner fire, as sexual activity is no longer required to produce the four joys. Instead the bliss occurs spontaneously with the generation of the empty-form consort.

There are many instructions concerning the selection of a qualified consort, but as this is only relevant for those with mastery of the third yoga, it is not appropriate to discuss them at this time. Until our vajra master gives us permission to practice with this type of consort, we should focus our energy on simulating these experiences through visualisation.

Signs of Attainment

The Yoga of Recollection is accomplished when immutable bliss is attained for the first time by practicing in union with the Great Consort of Empty-Form. This occurs when the four joys are experienced from above, melting downwards (known as melting from above) and when the four joys are then prevented from leaving the physical body, to instead resonate up through the four chakras (known as stabilising from below).

A sign of this attainment is that we experience everything as empty-form in a continual state of meditative absorption, so that all six senses are blissful. Along with this experience of joy, the physical body is perceived as an enlightened form of radiating rainbow light.

At this point, our yogic direct perception is also perfected and we experience visions of innumerable worlds of pure and impure realms. Inside the 72,000 channels the essences warm and melt, and we thereby attain the first of twelve stages of immutable bliss. According to the Kalachakra Tantra, this is the *Union of Immutable Bliss and Empty-Form*.

Basis of Purification

The impure basis of purification for the Yoga of Recollection is the six constituents of water: (1) the aggregate of perception; (2) the water element; (3) the tongue; (4) visible forms; (5) the faculty of the legs; and (6) the activity of taking.

These constituents are purified through the arising of ten stages of bliss known as: (1) thought; (2) desire; (3) physical plague; (4) a mouth with dry lips; (5) aversion to food; (6) trembling; (7) insanity; (8) idiocy; (9) a befuddled mind and (10) a deep swoon.

Results Obtained

The temporary result of practicing the Yoga of Recollection is filling the 72,000 channels with subtle essences radiating from the inside out. The practitioner experiences their body as an indestructible empty-form even though the physical body has not yet transformed into an enlightened body. There is a constant blissful experience as clairvoyance and the ability to perform miracles develops enormously. Ultimately, the result of mastering this yoga is the arising of the six constituents of water as an infinite array of deities belonging to the Amitabha Family.

The Yoga of Absorption

The sixth yoga is the Yoga of Absorption and leads to the immutable blissful experience of empty-form as the gross essences completely dissolve and the subtle essences are refined to perfection. The experience of bliss established in the practice of the previous five yogas is not immutable as the subtle essences are not yet fully refined. At this stage however we become completely absorbed in the immutable bliss of empty-form. The distinguishing feature of this practice is the practitioner's ability to stack the white drops from the lower opening of the central channel with the red drops from the crown.

Meaning of the Name

The sanskrit name for this yoga is *Samadhi*, literally translated as "meditative absorption". In this context it carries the connotation of abiding in complete equipoise within the sublime emptiness that is free of all forms of dualistic appearances. This is the immutable state of the fully-established nature of suchness.

Time for Meditation

The time to practice the Yoga of Absorption is from the moment the union of immutable bliss and empty-form is first generated.

Branches of Practice

The sixth yoga emphasises the inseparability of immutable bliss and empty-form and its purpose is to dissolve the impure aggregates so a non-dual body of pristine awareness can be manifested. This is done through abiding for 21,600 moments in a supreme state of absorption.

When the melting bliss of the four joys is held immovably at the lower tip of the central channel, it becomes the cause for the stopping of one karmic wind, the dissolving of 1/21,600 of the three channels into the ultimate central channel, the stacking of one red drop manifesting as the pristine wisdom of emptiness at the crown and the stacking of one white drop manifesting as immutable bliss at the bottom of the central channel.

At each of the chakras there are 3,600 white essences, corresponding to 3,600 moments of immutable bliss, 3,600 material components of the body and 3,600 winds. As these white essences build or draw together at the secret chakra, 3,600 moments of immutable bliss arise and the first and second Bodhisattva grounds are attained. Meanwhile the corresponding material components of the body and inner winds disappear. The following table illustrates how each ground is achieved:

Chakra	Drops	Stage
Secret	1,800	Supreme Joy
	3,600	Stainless
Navel	5,400	Illumination
	7,200	Radiant
Heart	9,000	Difficult to Overcome
	10,800	The Approaching
Throat	12,600	Far Gone
	14,400	The Immovable
Forehead	16,200	Good Intelligence
	18,000	The Mere Path
Crown	19,800	The Special Path
	21,600	The Uninterrupted Path

Table 9-5: The stages of dissolution arising in the Yoga of Absorption

As the white essences successively build at each of the centres, there is a corresponding movement of red essences downwards from the crown of the head. As the material components of the body are exhausted in this manner, one attains a *Great Transference Rainbow Body*. We can think of this as pure energy and awareness arising in the form of Kalachakra and Vishvamata in an enlightened embrace.

Signs of Attainment

As this process unfolds we gain the ability to perceive and explore various realms that were previously inaccessible to us. In the first of the twelve stages we can access 2,000 realms and this figure increases until we experience 24,000 realms simultaneously. The final stage is known as the initial union of the indestructible body, or initial enlightenment, which is the state of a Dharma King of Shambhala. From this point on, the karmic body, speech and mind are extinguished and we spontaneously complete our two accumulations so that we can quickly meet with the full enlightenment of Buddhahood.

Basis of Purification

The basis of purification for the Yoga of Absorption is the six constituents of earth: (1) the aggregate of form; (2) the earth element; (3) the organ of the body; (4) smells; (5) the genitalia; and (6) the activity of speaking.

These constituents are purified by twelve stages of immutable great bliss based on the six chakras divided into two equal halves. Each half becomes filled with immutable bliss and this eradicates one of the twelve links of dependent origination, leading to the actualisation of the twelve aspects of enlightenment and the inseparability of spontaneous compassion and wisdom.

Results Obtained

Unification with the co-emergent body, speech and mind of Kalachakra is therefore achieved with the union of divine masculine and feminine energies. This is the Kalachakra deity which has always resided within our own mental continuum, to be fully realised and experienced as a continuous stream of bliss.

Ultimately, mastery of this yoga results in the six constituents of earth arising as an infinite array of deities belonging to the Vairochana Family. In this way, each of the six yogas purifies the six constituents revealing thirty-six deities belonging to the six Buddha Families.

Yoga	Family	Aggregate	Element	Source	Object	Faculty	Action
Withdrawal	Vajrasattva	Awareness	Consciousness	Mind	Sound	Shankini	Urine
Stabilisation	Akshobhya	Consciousness	Space	Ears	Phenomena	Genitals	Emitting
Life-Force	Amoghasiddhi	Conceptions	Wind	Nose	Touch	Anus	Excreting
Retention	Ratnasambhava	Feelings	Fire	Eye	Taste	Arms	Going
Recollection	Amitabha	Perceptions	Water	Tongue	Sight	Legs	Taking
Absorption	Vairochana	Forms	Earth	Body	Smell	Genitals	Speaking

Table 9-6: The Thirty-Six Buddhas purified by the Vajra Yoga Path

REVIEW OF KEY POINTS

- The Vajra Yoga Path is a profound teaching that when practiced can produce enlightenment within a single human lifetime. These precious pith instructions are bestowed gradually by the vajra master to students who have demonstrated determination in gathering the prerequisites for practice.

- There are six branches of practice in the Kalachakra Completion Stage: (1) The Yoga of Withdrawal; (2) The Yoga of Stabilisation; (3) The Yoga of the Life-Force; (4) The Yoga of Retention; (5) The Yoga of Recollection and (6) The Yoga of Absorption.

- There are different ways of dividing the six yogas based on different traditions of commentary. Three common divisions are: (1) The Two-Fold Division of Empty-Form and Immutable Bliss; (2) The Three-Fold Division of the Three Purities; and (3) The Four-Fold Division of Approach and Accomplishment.

- The Vajra Yoga Path provides the means to progress along the Five Paths and achieve enlightenment. The first yoga achieves the Path of Accumulation. The following three yogas achieve the Path of Preparation. The fifth yoga achieves the Path of Insight and the sixth yoga achieves the Paths of Habituation and No More Learning.

- During each phase of training, we refine three aspects of Buddha-nature: (1) the appearances of empty-form; (2) the experience of bliss; and (3) the abandonment of duality.

- The Withdrawal Yoga purifies the six constituents of conscious-ness through the practices of night and day time yogas in which ten empty-form signs are generated by bringing the ten winds into the central channel: (1) smoke; (2) mirage; (3) clouds; (4) fire-flies; (5) blazing; (6) moonlight; (7) sunlight; (8) eclipse; (9) lightning and (10) drop.

- The Yoga of Stabilisation purifies the six constituents of space through the practice of five stages of meditation: (1) understand-ing; (2) appreciation; (3) analysis; (4) joy and (5) unwavering bliss. These meditations stabilise our realisation of empty-form and integrate them with awareness.

- The Yoga of the Life-Force purifies the six constituents of wind through the practices of vajra repetition and vase breathing in which the ten winds are refined so they abide within the central channel and converge at the navel chakra.

- The Yoga of Retention purifies the six constituents of fire by holding the winds in the centres of the five chakras: (1) navel; (2) heart; (3) throat; (4) forehead and (5) crown. As the unified winds are held in these points, they absorb into the subtle essences and produce increasingly powerful states of bliss.

- The Yoga of Recollection purifies the six constituents of water by working with the four consorts: (1) a physical consort; (2) a manifested consort; (3) a consort of inner fire; and (4) a great consort of empty-form. On the basis of the first two, we practice inner fire to produce the four joys and refine our subtle essences so we can stabilise our experience of the empty-form consort. This process eventually leads to the experience of immutable bliss.

- The Yoga of Absorption purifies the six constituents of earth by burning up our residual karmic traces with the supreme mind that unifies immutable bliss with empty-form. Over the course of 21,600 moments, we traverse twelve stages which actualise the state of a fully enlightened Buddha.

CHAPTER TEN

The Six Bardos
Bringing Kalachakra into Every Moment

Having received the profound teachings on the complete Kalachakra Path, we are now equipped with a wealth of wisdom and skilful means for clearing the obscurations that cloud our mind and limit our capacity. This extraordinarily comprehensive system provides everything we need to experience greater peace and harmony in our lives, while offering us the means to ultimately reveal the pristine nature of our most sacred truth. Failing to bring these teachings into our lives would be like a foolish man burying a wish-fulfilling jewel beneath his home, fearing someone else might steal it.

To avoid wasting this valuable opportunity, we can refer once again to the verses of Taranatha from the *Divine Ladder*:

During countless aeons, for this one time I have attained this precious human birth, Which is so very hard to achieve and so easy to lose. The time of death is uncertain and the conditions leading to death are beyond my comprehension, This cherished body can die even today!

I shall therefore abandon all worldly concerns that keep me chained to samsara, Including all non-virtues and heavy heinous crimes. Instead I shall use the little time I have left wisely and practise Dharma with urgency, Reflecting on the benefits of liberation.

Of all the realms of experience we could potentially be born into, we have found a precious human rebirth, endowed with a fully functional subtle energetic system of channels, winds and drops. We have the great fortune of living in a world where the authentic teachings that present the methods for working with this subtle body are flourishing and we also have the kind and generous support of compassionate teachers willing to guide us on this path to enlightenment. On the basis of these extraordinary conditions, there is nothing to stop us from embarking on the Kalachakra Path and attaining its immeasurable results.

Unfortunately this precious life is impermanent. The constant threat of death lurks in the background and as we have no idea when this life will end, we cannot afford to succumb to laziness and procrastination. If we do not use our time wisely to practice the Sacred Dharma we are blessed with receiving, when death inevitably comes, we will find ourselves lost uncontrollably in the ocean of our karma.

Recognising this, we will now study the subject of the *Six Bardos* as a means of identifying how we can most effectively practice the Kalachakra teachings in each and every moment of our lives. If we are skilful, we can bring incredible meaning into our activities, while also preparing our mind to approach death without fear or confusion. We will begin with a general overview of the bardos to establish a context for our discussion, followed by an exploration of each individual bardo in detail.

OVERVIEW OF THE SIX BARDOS

The term *bardo* is a Tibetan word often translated as "transitional period". It refers to the way our experiences change over time giving rise to transitional periods in which we shift from one state into another.

These teachings are most commonly associated with the Nyingma tradition but are present in all the major traditions, including the Jonang. As we will explore the bardos from the perspective of the Kalachakra teachings, you may notice some variations in presentation compared to other systems.

There are two major groups of bardos: (1) the Bardos of Life and

(2) the Bardos of Death and Rebirth. Each group contains three bardos giving us a total of six bardos.

The Bardos of Life

These transitional periods span from birth until the onset of the dying process and include:

1. The Bardo of Living
2. The Bardo of Dreaming
3. The Bardo of Meditation

During a single lifetime we transition between these periods on a daily basis. Most people cycle between the bardo of living in the day and the bardo of dreaming at night and if we are fortunate enough to encounter a spiritual path, we may also enter the bardo of meditation through yogic practice. It is within these bardos we need to focus on training our mind so we can develop the control needed in order to take advantage of the bardos of death and rebirth.

The Bardos of Death and Rebirth

These transitional periods begin with the process of dying where the mind separates from the body and continues until the mind either achieves enlightenment or is reborn into another life. They include:

4. The Bardo of Dying
5. The Bardo of Dharmata
6. The Bardo of Becoming

Without training the mind during the bardos of life, our experience of the bardos of death and rebirth will be completely uncontrolled. As our karmic propensities ripen, we are propelled into samsara with no realisation of what is happening to us, but if we can bring awareness into these bardos, it is possible to recognise our Buddha-nature and thereby achieve liberation from suffering.

THE BARDO OF LIVING

The bardo of living provides a valuable opportunity to develop familiarity with the Kalachakra teachings. If we possess the sincere wish to attain enlightenment, during the waking state we need to remind ourselves of this rare chance and endeavour to abandon laziness by entering a spiritual path of learning, reflection and meditation without distraction.

Through the practice of these teachings and by taking the different levels of reality as the path, we understand that there is no place protected from death and we begin to comprehend what we must purify in order to discover the four bodies of a Buddha. We also gain the confidence to relax in the knowledge that we are preparing ourselves for our inevitable death in the best way possible. This is like the swallow who can build its nest with confidence having removed all fear of danger as it has carefully considered the most protective location. If we, however, waste this human body on meaningless pursuits and make no effort to prepare for the next life, when the moment of death dawns we will be ill-equipped to face it and consequently will be filled with regret and panic.

Tantra has the potential to endow us with the means for meeting death with conviction and provides the extraordinary methods for attaining enlightenment in as little as one lifetime. As its practices are made available to us within the bardo of living, this transitional period is considered incredibly important. Using methods of visualisations, mantras and other skilful means, we may wonder how tantra can improve our meditation. Would it not be simpler to just calm the mind and meditate on emptiness? For practice to be successful, both the mind and body must be addressed. Only an integrated and balanced body-mind, free from psycho-physical knots and tension can support the crystal-clear awareness needed in advanced meditation practice.

As we have seen, the practice of Vajrayana consists of the generation stage and the completion stage which together incorporate this necessary balance between mind and body. During the generation stage we transform our perception by visualising ourselves as the Yidam with all the attributes of an enlightened being. In the completion stage we learn to control the subtle energy flow in the body to support the non-dual awareness required for enlightenment. By practising the teachings presented in this book with mindfulness and discipline, we can gradually develop the qualities which come from mastery of these two stages.

Even if we are unable to achieve the high realisations of the Kalachakra completion stage before death arrives, simply striving to practice the Kalachakra Path as much as we can creates the causes to one day achieve the supreme attainment of the Six Vajra Yogas. No matter what stage we currently find ourselves at, every moment we commit to practice is accumulating merit and wisdom. Like money saved in a bank, no virtuous deed that is dedicated towards enlightenment will ever be lost, and therefore every moment we devote to practicing the Dharma is leading us to our ultimate potential.

With the complete teachings of Sutra and Tantra presented within the three books of the *Unveiling Your Sacred Truth* series, you are equipped with the full range of practices that will enable you to bring the Dharma into every situation you encounter. Strive to make full use of your time both on and off the meditation cushion and remember that continuity builds habit. By devoting a portion of each day to developing your mind, each day becomes a stepping stone to progressing along the path. Don't worry if some days are more successful than others and rather than letting setbacks discourage you, cultivate a strong determination to take advantage of each opportunity that life presents.

THE BARDO OF DREAMING

For most people the waking state accounts for approximately two thirds of our lives with the remainder spent sleeping. This means that we spend around thirty years either in the unconscious state of deep-sleep or within the illusory projections of the dream state. This considerable period of time presents us with a unique opportunity to extend our waking state practice.

Each night we experience a dissolution process similar to the process of death. As we fall asleep, our five sensory consciousnesses withdraw and our awareness settles into the unconfigured state of the foundational consciousness. An untrained mind usually traverses this process in a stupor of dullness, blacking out half way through the dissolution. The mind does not stir again until a dream arises and we awaken from the darkness to become aware of a new reality.

This dream reality is generated entirely by the karmic propensities of the mind and as such, is not restricted to the same physical constraints existent within the waking state. It is a far more malleable reality and therefore can manifest in a limitless number of ways. If we can bring awareness into our dreams they can become a powerful support for exploring a much subtler layer of our experience.

The methods we use to do this are collectively known as *dream yoga* and are comparable to turning a light on in a dark room. Most of us enter dreams without comprehension or control, but through the practices of dream yoga we can learn to recognise when we are dreaming, giving us the potential to develop many powerful practices. Just as shining a light in a dark room can reveal countless possibilities, so too can the practice of dream yoga, as engaging in this practice can lead to many extraordinary benefits.

Dream Yoga

Practising dream yoga as a path to enlightenment requires the strong determination to view dreams as an opportunity for practice rather than a time to sleep like an ignorant beast. The practices of dream yoga can be divided into two sets: (1) *daytime practices* which are techniques to strengthen our awareness of the illusory nature of the waking state so we can trigger lucidity in the dream state and (2) *nighttime practices* which we apply when falling asleep in order to work with the illusory nature of our dreams.

The Daytime Practices of the Waking State

The daytime practices of the waking state help us comprehend the illusory nature of conventional reality. We can realise this nature in two ways by either focusing on the falsity of our conventional reality or on the truth of our ultimate reality. In the first case, we reflect on different aspects of our experience to realise the illusory nature of our coarse body, speech and mind:

1. **Seeing appearances as reflections:** Just like the image of our face in the mirror, everything that appears to us is merely a reflection. A reflection can be praised or criticised, but it will never be flattered or offended in the slightest. Similarly we can understand our ordinary waking reality to be the same as a reflection, and in this way the waking state and the dream state are both illusory. Although we believe we are something different from the reflection in the mirror, in truth both are illusions. Our true nature transcends the concepts of "self" and "other", yet we perceive the illusory world of samsara to be real.

2. **Hearing sounds as echoes:** We can also establish the illusory nature of phenomena by practising on a mountain range, in a cave or a large hall where an echo can be produced. We could

345

call out even the harshest self-criticism but it will only be an empty sound we hear, as our words do not truly exist and are merely an echo or illusion of our real voice. This can remind us that everyone's speech is also illusory and similarly, our entire perception appears like an illusion as we have not yet attained the enlightened state.

3. **Seeing thoughts as delusion:** If we look into the sky we see clouds appearing and disappearing without a trace, yet the vast open sky is completely untouched by them. Likewise, the waves of the ocean rise and fall in a never-ending dance, yet the ocean itself remains unmoved. In the same way we can watch our thoughts and perceptions appear and disappear, and yet know there is a far vaster reality in which this performance takes place. The natural world can then become a meditation on our deluded state and how it obscures the true nature of reality.

In the second approach we focus on the practice of pure perception as taught in the generation stage. Here we use the various appearances we encounter as supports to remind us of the enlightened nature of our body, speech and mind:

1. **Seeing all forms as deities:** When looking in the mirror, see yourself as a pure manifestation of Kalachakra. Try to go beyond ordinary illusory appearances by recognising that the purity of the five aggregates is the five male Buddhas and the purity of the five elements is the five female Buddhas. See all gross appearances as the display of the male and female Bodhisattvas, all thoughts as Dakas and Dakinis and all movement or activities, such as eating and drinking, as the enlightened activities of the wrathful protectors. In this way, everything can be a reminder of the "true" reality that is currently hidden from you.

2. **Hearing all sound as mantra:** Likewise, whenever you hear sounds, remind yourself that this illusory world is a manifestation of the innate purity of your Buddha-nature, arising due to the interdependence created by your ignorance. Think of the empty-sounds as mantras—the natural diversity of expressions that we experience as a stream of distinct sounds.

3. **Seeing all thoughts as wisdom:** Be aware of every thought arising and dissolving in your mind as being the brilliant radiance of your Buddha-nature. Recognise that its nature is ultimately empty of any substantial essence and therefore, like space, it is completely free to manifest in whatever way is needed.

By practicing to see the illusory nature of conventional reality we begin to recognise that there is no substantial difference between the appearances of the waking state and the appearances of the dream state. They both assume the feeling of a dream. When this occurs it is valid to generate the thought, "This is a dream", and continuously reminding ourselves of this fact during the day is the simplest way to recognise when we are dreaming.

The Nighttime Practices of the Dream State

The nighttime practices are those we engage in when falling asleep. Through working with our dreams, we bridge the gap between the waking state and the deep-sleep state by developing mastery over the illusory nature of appearances. This training has two phases: (1) recognising the dream state and (2) controlling appearances in that state.

Recognising the Dream State

During this phase we strengthen our awareness of the sleep process so we can develop lucidity in our dreams. This is the awareness that knows when a dream is a dream and if we have practiced diligently during the waking state, this phase can be fairly straightforward. There are however a few points we should consider:

1. **Posture:** When beginning this practice, it is important to align the energy channels by maintaining a good posture, such as the "sleeping lion". For males this involves lying on the right side with the right hand underneath the cheek, legs together with knees slightly bent and the left arm down the left side of the body. For females the posture is reversed with the left hand under the cheek and the right hand resting on the side.

2. **Motivation:** As with any tantric practice, you should begin by taking refuge in the Three Jewels and cultivating the motivation of Bodhicitta, with the wish that your dream yoga practice will bring benefit to all beings. Then develop a strong aspiration to recognise your dream as a dream and hold this aspiration in the mind as you fall asleep.

For those who have a strong daytime practice or a propensity for becoming lucid, these two steps may be enough to achieve your aim. If not, there are several visualisations which can enhance your practice and help induce lucidity:

• For the first method, visualise your Guru at your throat chakra, in the aspect of Kalachakra, the size of the tip of your thumb. At his heart imagine a red four-petalled lotus with the seed syllable OM (ཨོཾ) at its centre, and the syllables AH (ཨཿ), NU (ནུ), TA (ཏ) and RA (ར) positioned on the petals, facing outwards in the four directions. After focusing on the syllable OM, repeat the other syllables silently until you are about to fall asleep. Just before falling into sleep, focus again on the OM and allow yourself to slip into the deep-sleep state. Try to remain single-pointedly with these syllables while holding a strong aspiration to recognise the dream, as well as maintaining the conviction that this is possible with the blessings of the Three Jewels.

- A simpler method is to visualise a small sphere of red light at the throat chakra. Concentrate single-pointedly on the sphere with the determination to recognise your dreams as you fall asleep, allowing your mind to become absorbed in the red light.

- If you continue to have trouble falling asleep, visualise a small black sphere under your feet, as this will draw your awareness downwards, inducing drowsiness.

For some, using visualisations at the time of sleep can lead to insomnia and this is usually a result of holding too tightly to the visualisation. To avoid this, rather than worrying about developing clarity of the specific details, establish a peripheral sense of the forms and loosely rest your awareness in this feeling.

If after trying these variations you still have difficulty recognising or remembering your dreams, emphasise your daytime practices to strengthen your pure perception and awareness of the illusory nature of conventional reality. With determination and mindfulness, strive to carry this recognition into your nighttime practice as well. Continue accumulating merit and strengthening your faith in the Three Jewels, while developing the aspiration that you will be successful in recognising the dream state.

Controlling Appearances in this State

Recognition within our dreams is a powerful ability with the potential for enormous spiritual growth. Because this dream reality is not conditioned by energy, we can perform actions that would normally be impossible, like flying through the sky, instantaneously travelling to faraway places, or multiplying our body and transforming the elements at whim. We can also manifest situations which would usually cause us fear or anxiety in order to realise their illusory quality and free ourselves from underlying grasping. For instance, we could dream that we are dying to help overcome a fear of death, or we could manifest ourselves as a billionaire who becomes destitute to overcome attachment to wealth and aversion to poverty. In this way, our dreams can transform into a laboratory where it is safe to simulate any experience we want.

With mastery of the dream-state we can use the time we spend dreaming as a continuation of our generation stage practices in the waking state. Only now, due to the subtlety of our dream consciousness, when we visualise ourselves as the deity or make vast offerings, everything appears as clearly as it would through our physical eyes. This brings a level of realism to our practice making the virtuous karma we produce considerably more potent.

Sleep Yoga

Before a dream can manifest, our present appearances dissolve back into the foundation consciousness—a process we commonly refer to as "falling asleep". It is generally experienced in a state of thick obscuration with a complete lack of awareness. During a single night, on average we experience five sleep cycles in which our mind transitions from the deep-sleep state into the dream state and back again to deep-sleep. If we can bring awareness to this cycle of dissolution, we can rest our mind in the very subtle consciousness of the deep-sleep state. This method is known as *sleep yoga* and has two approaches: (1) entering into sleep lucidly or (2) dissolving into sleep from a dream.

Entering into Sleep Lucidly

The idea behind this first approach is to allow your body to fall asleep while maintaining awareness throughout the dissolution process. This is very challenging for anyone who has not already achieved a high degree of mental stability as it takes considerable practice to find the right balance between deep relaxation and vivid awareness. If we loosen the mind too much, we slip into dullness and blackout but if we focus our awareness too tightly, we won't be able to fall asleep.

To develop this skill, we can visualise the Guru in the aspect of Vajradhara, manifesting in the centre of the heart chakra. With a mind of devotion, develop the aspiration to merge your mind with the Guru's in the same way as when practicing Guru Yoga. Imagine your body completely melting into light and dissolving into the Guru. Rest your awareness in this feeling, allowing yourself to fall asleep in this state.

When the mind completely dissolves back into the foundation consciousness, it will almost be completely unconfigured, like an embryonic version of the mind. From this state we can choose to continue into deeper states of absorption or we can choose to lucidly transition into a dream state.

Dissolving into Sleep from a Dream

The second approach is a natural extension of our dream yoga practice. Having already established lucidity by recognising the dream as a dream, we can choose to either continue our dream yoga by working with the illusory appearances as they are, or we can choose to shift into sleep yoga by dissolving them back into the substrate from which they arose.

There are a number of methods we can use to trigger the dissolution of a dream from within a dream, the most direct way being to simply close our dream-eyes. Because the dream world is merely a projection of our mind, if we cease to pay attention to it, it will cease to exist.

This process however can be somewhat abrupt and can sometimes cause us to lose our lucidity or to wake up. For this reason, a more gradual method is to practice a form of *Shamatha Without a Sign* (such as the Three Isolations) from within the dream. By establishing the four qualities of single-pointedness, non-conceptuality, non-grasping and effortlessness, the dream world itself will dissolve and the mind will come to rest in the substrate.

The nature of sleep yoga is the dissolution of appearances, whereas the nature of dream yoga is the manifestation of appearances. Together, they can help us develop mastery over the enlightened activity of manifesting emanations for the benefit of sentient beings. Once we gain control over this process, we are no longer in danger of taking an uncontrolled rebirth. Not only will we have the ability to die with complete lucidity, we can also choose where and how we will manifest in the future. In this way, training in the bardo of dreaming is an extraordinarily skilful means for breaking free from cyclic existence.

THE BARDO OF MEDITATION

When our mind abides in profound states of meditative absorption, it has entered the bardo of meditation. In the context of the Kalachakra Path, this bardo is accessed through the meditative practices of the completion stage and through these practices we come to know the ultimate nature of reality.

To experience this bardo, we first need to dissolve the gross mind into the foundation consciousness either through the single-pointed concentration of Shamatha or through the practice of sleep yoga as described above. When the mind rests in its own nature, the analytical absorptions of Vipashyana can be used to cut through the subtle layers of grasping which bind us in our prison of conceptual thought.

Through this type of meditation we can achieve self-liberation of thoughts and perceptions as we realise and then stabilise awareness of our fully-established nature. Initially we have the experience of thoughts being liberated as they arise, like the vanishing of a drawing made on water. With further experience, thoughts liberate themselves like a snake tied in a knot uncoiling itself. Finally, thoughts are naturally liberated like a thief entering an empty house. At this point, we have complete confidence in the pristine nature of the mind.

There are two aspects to practice in the bardo of meditation: (1) cultivating the *mountain-like view* that is the result of directly experiencing the ultimate nature of reality and (2) the *ocean-like practice* that integrates our view with every aspect of our experience. Both can be practiced during meditation sessions or during the periods between them, however we are only considered to be in the bardo of meditation when our mind is actively absorbed in ultimate truth.

Mountain-like View

Realising the generation and completion stages of tantric practice brings absolute awareness to the nature of mind with a complete absence of clinging. This view, the summation of our understanding of the nature of reality, is likened to a mountain; natural, majestic and unshakeable, regardless of the strength of the winds that batter its peak.

This mountain-like view is a direct experience of sublime emptiness, with the comprehension that our inner world has the same limitless nature as infinite space. This view takes no interest in rising phenomena and sees all empty-forms as possessing limitless qualities, all beings are seen as enlightened deities and the world is seen as an enlightened mandala.

Ocean-like Practice

During and after formal meditation sessions the mind is engaged and free from doubt or hesitation. We gain confidence in the self-liberation of phenomena, and the mind is understood to be beyond all notion of dualistic identity and limitation, just as the water beneath the tumultuous ocean surface remains calm and constant.

This practice is without fixation or neurosis and while there is no attachment, every individual action is extremely precise, altering our state of consciousness. We thus experience a transformed state of mind where we no longer cling to external distractions during meditation.

When we realise our primordial nature, we recognise that there is nothing to actually see or gain; there is just the self-liberated awareness of the natural state. We do not need to perceive anything and there is nothing we need to add, we simply realise that this is the ultimate truth and rest within this confidence.

THE BARDO OF DYING

Death from a Buddhist perspective is not an event but a process that leads to the gradual dissociation of the mind from the body, and can take a few moments or several days to complete. When the mind-stream of a person is temporarily associated with the physical body, it is not dependent on it, only conditioned by it. When the mind and body disconnect, enlightenment is close at hand. How close it is will depend on our mastery of spiritual practice when we are alive, especially our ability to recognise the manifestations of Buddha-nature. As a heightened awareness dawns at the moment of death and the mind has an increased ability to transcend ignorance to realise its true nature, great emphasis is placed on the dying state. The practices for this bardo are therefore likened to a king's document which gives us a clear and certain path.

The following section describes the Kalachakra understanding of the six elements and how they relate to the psycho-physical aggregates. We will then outline the process in which these elements of the body and mind dissolve during death, how to avoid an untimely death and the practices for when death cannot be avoided. This includes the unique practice for transferring consciousness at the time of death known as *Phowa*.

The Six Elements of Body and Mind

The Kalachakra uses a system of six elements to describe the basic building blocks of our psycho-physical world. These elements are not individual particles but aspects of phenomena we can experience. Within a single point in space and time, we can find a dominance of one or more of these elements and it is this variation which gives rise to the great diversity of substances we experience. The six elements are as follows:

1. **Earth:** This is the aspect of *solidity* produced by the density of energy particles. When particles are packed tightly together, the substance becomes solid and there is a dominance of the earth element. Examples of this type of substance include flesh and bone.

2. **Water:** This is the aspect of *cohesion* which bonds energy particles together. When the water element is high, particles cluster together even when they are not densely packed. Examples of substances with a high water content are blood, urine and saliva.

3. **Fire:** This is the aspect of *intensity*, created by the accumulation of energy in a single place. The greater the accumulation of energy, the more charge is built up. This is experienced as heat in the body.

4. **Wind:** This is the aspect of *movement* which is felt when energy transforms from one state into another. On a very subtle level this is the vibration of energy within each atom, and on a coarser level, it includes the experiences of breathing and other circulatory processes.

5. **Space:** This is the aspect of *vacuity* in which there is an absence of energy. The space element is particularly dominant in the

orifices of the body as well as in the vacuities between or inside organs.

6. **Consciousness:** This element represents the pervasive presence of the mind within all energy. It is the aspect of *knowing* that allows the mind to influence how energy is shaped.

Type	Element	Quality
Physical	Earth	Solidity
	Water	Cohesion
	Fire	Intensity
	Wind	Movement
	Space	Vacuity
Non-Physical	Consciousness	Knowing

Table 10-1: The Six Elements

During life, the balance between these elements shifts based on changes in our karmic conditions. For instance when we catch a cold, we often experience an excess of fire in the form of fever, or an excess of water in the form of mucous. These experiences are only temporary imbalances and therefore are not considered part of the bardo of dying.

The Dying Process

The actual bardo of dying occurs when the karmic bond holding the aggregates together dissolves to the point where the mind abandons the body. *Death* is then the moment of separation. This process can be divided into two phases of dissolution: (1) the outer dissolution of the coarse body and (2) the inner dissolution of the subtle body.

For each dissolution, the dying person experiences the weakening of one of their elements. This process removes the supports for certain aspects of experience and carries with it specific physical or mental sensations. As the winds related to that element stop circulating in the gross body, they begin to converge in the centre of the heart, triggering the same empty-form signs experienced in the Yoga of Withdrawal.

The Outer Dissolution

As our five physical elements begin to dissolve, we may be aware of our senses gradually ceasing to function. For example, we may hear the sound of voices but cannot decipher any words, or we may see the outline of an object in front of us but are unable to distinguish its details. The first phase of the outer dissolution process is indicated by our inability to fully experience the senses. The next five phases follow the dissolution of each element.

The Dissolution of Earth

At first our body becomes heavy and we lose the strength to move our limbs as they feel as though they are falling, sinking or being crushed by a great weight. We find it difficult to hold anything and we can no longer support our head. These are signs of the earth element withdrawing into the water element as the aggregate of form dissolves. This means the inner wind related to the earth element is becoming less capable of providing a base for consciousness. With the reduction of earth, the water element becomes more obvious, giving rise to visions of *smoke* as an internal sign.

The Dissolution of Water

Progressing through the dying process we may experience discharge from our eyes or become incontinent. We cannot move our tongue, our eyes become dry and our throat and mouth feel sticky. The nostrils close in and we feel very thirsty. As the aggregate of perception dissolves, bodily sensations alternate between pain and pleasure, hot and cold, and the mind becomes frustrated, irritable and nervous. The water element is dissolving into the fire element, taking over its ability to support consciousness. This gives rise to an internal sign of a *mirage*.

357

The Dissolution of Fire

Next, our mouth and nose dry up completely and the warmth of our body begins to leave, starting from the extremities and moving towards the heart. The breath becomes cold and food or liquid can no longer be digested. The aggregate of feeling is dissolving and the mind fluctuates between clarity and confusion, where we cannot recognise our family or who we are. The fire element dissolves into the wind element and is no longer able to function as a base for consciousness. This is accompanied by the inner sign of *clouds*.

The Dissolution of Wind

Later on, breathing becomes increasingly difficult and feels as though air is escaping through our throat. Inhalations become short and exhalations become long. Our eyes roll back into the head and we can no longer move. As the aggregate of conception is dissolving, the mind becomes confused and unaware of the outside world, everything is unclear and the last feeling of contact with the physical environment slips away. The wind element is now dissolving into the space element, and the secondary winds are uniting with the life-supporting wind at the heart. This gives rise to the inner sign of *fire-flies*.

The Dissolution of Space

Subtlety of experience increases further as the space element dissolves into consciousness, and the eye, ear, nose, tongue and body consciousnesses all dissolve into the gross mental consciousness. The inner sign at this stage is a vision of *blazing light*.

After three final long out-breaths, all that remains is a slight warmth at our heart. As all our vital signs have disappeared and none of our sense faculties continue to operate, this is the point when we are considered "clinically dead". If we understand the subtle aspects of this process however, death is not yet complete. Inner dissolution still needs to take place which may continue for approximately twenty minutes. Therefore if possible, it is crucial for the body to be left alone without any noise, as these interruptions can cause aversion to arise in the mind of the dying person, propelling them into a negative rebirth.

The Inner Dissolution

The subtle essences of the white drops are located in the top half of the body while the essences of the red drops are mostly located in the lower half. After the outer dissolution has separated the mind from the gross physical body, the next step is the collapsing of the subtle body. During this process, the inner winds converge back into the heart, carrying with them the energy of the subtle essences distributed throughout the body. This process of gathering the subtle energy into the heart is known as the inner dissolution.

The White Appearance

It begins when the white drops of the father descend down the central channel toward the heart. As an external sign, there is an experience of shimmering whiteness, like *moonlight*. An internal sign is that our awareness becomes extremely clear and the thirty-three states of mind resulting from aversion cease to operate. This phase is known as white appearance.

The Red Increase

The red drops of the mother then begin to rise through the central channel as the winds that held them there cease. The external sign is an experience of warm *sunlight* shining in a pure sky. The internal sign is an experience of bliss as the forty states of mind resulting from attachment cease to function. This phase is known as red increase.

The Black Near Attainment

When the red and white drops meet at the heart, we experience a "blackness", likened to an *eclipse* of the sun, corresponding to the experience of a mind free from thoughts and a feeling of losing consciousness. The seven states of mind resulting from ignorance and delusion are thus brought to an end. Known as black near attainment, this marks the end of one's individual experience of samsara. At this stage the ripening of karma takes over and propels us towards our next rebirth.

The Clear Light of Death

As most people have lost all consciousness by this point, they are unaware of the very subtle dissolutions occurring at the heart as the last subtle winds are gathered and held there. If one were lucid at this stage as a result of previous training in the dissolution process, they would experience the subtle sign of *lightning* followed by the clear light drop, called the *indestructible drop*, which is the complete unification of energy and mind. It is this drop which separates from the body, forming the basis for the next rebirth.

Once this occurs the pure subtle mind of the natural state is experienced like a vast, cloudless autumn sky, empty of form. This is the formless, timeless and unfabricated pristine reality of enlightenment—the clear light of death, also known as the ground luminosity, Dharmakaya or primordial wisdom. In the Tibetan tradition, this is the actual moment of death.

Overcoming an Untimely Death

With knowledge of the death process and an awareness of the various signs that can forewarn us of our death, we have the opportunity to avert an untimely death. This is important as an extended life increases our opportunity to practise the Dharma and transform the dying process.

There are many different signs of approaching death, described extensively in texts such the *Bardo Thodol*, also known as the *Tibetan Book of the Dead*. We can look for these in the physical body, the inner winds and in our dreams.

1. **External Signs:** External or physical signs of death include loss of appetite or loss of clarity to the five senses. Consciousness may become cloudy, thoughts and dreams can lose touch with reality and the colour of our body may change. Other signs include a slow return of normal colour to the skin when a fingernail is pressed down or hair on the back of the head stands up.

2. **Dream Signs:** Dreams can also forewarn of our death, giving us internal signs that we are approaching the end of our life. If they occur late in the evening or around midnight, dreams are generally unreliable, however if they occur between midnight and daybreak, many signs associated with death can be identified. These include riding a white cat, monkey or donkey in an easterly direction, wearing black clothing made of hair, being stuck in a net, having one's ankles chained like a prisoner, dreaming of a tree growing from the top of our head with a bird building a nest in it, or dreaming repeatedly of picking a red flower or staying in a womb. If we only have these dreams once, this is a sign that death can be overcome. Continuous dreams, however, generally mean that death is certain within a year.

Whatever signs of death which may be seen, attempts can be made to overcome them, although the internal signs of death are more difficult to avert than external signs. Of the two types of death, the first occurs with the exhaustion of the karmic lifespan and cannot be overcome. The second is when there is an obstacle to living out our natural lifespan. These obstacles can be overcome either by medical assistance, extensive rituals or the accumulation of merit, depending on the specific conditions present.

The Tibetan Buddhist tradition contains many tantric rituals to overcome an untimely death and as an authentic part of the Buddha's teachings, they often have very tangible results. The following is an example of one such ritual performed by the great master Atisha Dipamkara and is still carried out today by many Tibetan monks. When a person reports seeing certain signs, monks may repeat this ritual for seven days:

Make twenty-one small balls of mud the size of the top of one's thumb, collect twenty-one pieces of kusha grass four fingers in width, make twenty-one images of the dying person from dough, then make twenty-one small balls and small coin-like discs and fill a bowl owned by the person with water. Make as many offerings as you can to the Three Jewels, such as flowers, fruit, incense and perfume, then visualise the twenty-one Taras and all the Buddhas, Bodhisattvas and shravakas, taking refuge and making offerings. Repeat the mantra OM TAG NAG DAG SO HA twenty-one times and blow into the bowl.

Recall the power of the Buddha, Dharma, Sangha, lineage masters, Dakinis and Dharma Protectors, invoking their powers to remove the obstacles to death. Offer them the bowl of water as a substitute for the person's life while reciting the ritual texts and slowly placing the balls, kusha grass, dough images and discs in the bowl of water, requesting Yama the Lord of Death to spare their life.

At the end of the ritual, take all these offerings to the river or ocean and perform a protection ritual to ensure the obstacles which lead to an untimely death never return. Then recite the Ushnishavijaya and Singhamuckha Sutras and the Heart Sutra, followed by dedication and aspiration prayers.

If such a ritual fails to overcome the signs of death, it is likely the person is experiencing a natural karmic death. If this is the case, the practice of phowa will directly help them attain enlightenment or create auspicious conditions for their next rebirth.

Transferring Consciousness at the Moment of Death

Phowa is a powerful technique for directing the consciousness from the body at the time of death, and can also be used to help others direct their consciousness in the period immediately following death. The instructions for the practice of phowa are extremely precise; like a document with clear instructions bearing the king's royal seal.

In general, there are three levels of phowa:

1. **Dharmakaya Phowa:** For advanced practitioners, it is possible to enter the clear light of death lucidly and rest the awareness in the direct experience of the ultimate truth that naturally manifests. In this scenario, such a master abides in this state for as long as is it takes to clear any residual karmic traces. Upon completion, the chains of samsara are completely severed and the enlightened mind can manifest without limits for the benefit of sentient beings.

2. **Sambhogakaya Phowa:** If the practitioner is familiar with the generation and completion stage practices of Kalachakra, these practices can be used at the time of death to generate their mind as the Yidam, bringing it as close as possible to the ultimate truth of Buddha-nature. This effectively induces the death process in a controlled manner, providing the practitioner with the opportunity to recognise their ultimate nature during the subtle transition of the bardo of Dharmata.

3. **Nirmanakaya Phowa:** For everyone else, consciousness can be directed towards the pure land of Shambhala through a visualisation practice. This is done by visualising the mind as the indestructible drop at the heart, the central channel as our path to liberation and Kalachakra as our destination. This practice is designed to ensure specific propensities are ripened at the time of death, allowing for the achievement of a beneficial rebirth.

If we recognise the signs of death or have the feeling that death is imminent, our most important task is to generate detachment from the human realm, letting go of desire for material possessions, social status, relationships and the fulfilment of worldly goals. We should instead reflect on the nature of impermanence by contemplating how all things come and go, just like the seasons, and how all relationships are fleeting. Everyone we have known during this life is like a traveller we briefly met in passing, and to part with them is only natural. Reflecting on how all things in samsara are suffering and worthless by their nature, we give ourselves the chance to break free from cyclic existence. With strong faith in our spiritual teacher and the Three Jewels, we can then train in the phowa practice and gain the ability to transform death into an opportunity for liberation.

The Practice of Phowa According to Kalachakra

While there are many versions of the Phowa practice, the following is suitable for those practicing Kalachakra. During life, try to familiarise yourself with this practice until signs of accomplishment occur. Memorise every aspect so you can perform it without the need for texts or other supports. When the signs of imminent death arise, the practice can be used to transfer your consciousness to the Bodhisattva Pure Realm of Kalachakra—the *Sublime Northern Land of Shambhala*.

Establishing the Visualisation

The first step in the practice is to establish the visualisation by reciting the following text:

The nature of your own physical body transforms instantly into the single deity form of the Body-Vajra Amitabha. Your excellent body radiates white light. With one face and two arms, you are seated in meditative equipoise with legs crossed on a seat of a lotus, with moon, sun, rahu [and kalagni] discs. Your body is naked having abandoned all ornaments and clothing. At its centre is the avadhuti channel, blue and transparent like a glass tube, the size of a bamboo arrow. Its lower end closes below the navel. Its upper end reaches the crown of the head and opens. At the height of the heart centre, the primordial mind abides as a blue drop no larger than a lentil. It naturally glows with a radiance that flickers and throbs.

In the space above your crown, in the centre of many rainbow lights, is a seat made from a lotus, with moon, sun, rahu [and kalagni] discs. On top of this stands your root-lama, inseparable from the Great Sovereign of All Families—the Glorious and Supreme Kalachakra. His body, which is the co-emergence of bliss and emptiness, radiates dark blue light. He has one face with three eyes expressing a mixture of wrath and passion. He has two arms and his hands are holding a vajra and bell while embracing Vishvamata. His red right leg is extended crushing the red Kamadeva, and his white left leg crushes the white Ishvara.

He wears a tiger skin loin cloth, silk garments and is adorned with vajra ornaments. His consort is a goddess of golden colour with one face and two arms. She holds a curved knife and a skull-cup and her body is adorned by the five ornaments while embracing Kalachakra. She is pleased by her clear experience of the union of bliss and emptiness, which radiates five stainless lights in all directions. At the centre of this radiance, on the crown of [Kalachakra's] head, is a crescent moon. Vajrasattva abides there in fully manifest form; the qualities of his three secrets are limitless.

This body, endowed with all supreme aspects is the Sambhogakaya, the Lord of the Mandala, the All-Pervasive Sovereign, the Lama of Suchness, the Supreme Yidam and the Solitary Form that is the Source of the Three Refuges.

Spend as much time as you need to develop a clear impression of the visualisation elements. In particular, make sure you have a strong feeling of Guru Kalachakra's presence above your head and of your mind as the indestructible drop at your heart.

Developing Mindfulness of the Enlightened Mandala

Before attempting to transfer your consciousness, it is important to establish a strong feeling of devotion towards Guru Kalachakra by reciting prayers to strengthen your mindfulness of the Enlightened Mandala. Bringing these thoughts to mind at the time of death ripens the virtuous karmic propensities that have the capacity to propel us towards Shambhala.

As you recite each of the following verses, imagine the energy distributed throughout your body as the enlightened deities of the mandala. With each verse, the energy melts into light and dissolves into the indestructible drop at your heart.

Mindfulness of the Essential Mandala

NAMO KALACHAKRAYA
Homage to Kalachakra!

Endowed with all Supreme Aspects, Immutable Great Bliss;
Body that Enjoys All Things, Primordial Wisdom of Union;
Glorious Original Buddha, Kalachakra;
Sovereign of All Families, Fierce Vajrasattva:

I pray from my heart with faith and devotion!
May the appearance of this drop of basic space and clear awareness
Pass up the central channel and leave through the crown of my head.
May I enter the heart of Kalachakra!

Dancing in the Primordial Wisdom of Great Emptiness, Perfection
of Wisdom; Body of the Beautiful Vajra Goddess with All Aspects;
The Self that Produces the Display of the Ten Shaktis;
Primordial Buddha, the Deity that Embodies All Families:

I pray from my heart with faith and devotion!
May the appearance of this drop of basic space and clear awareness
Pass up the central channel and leave through the crown of my head.
May I enter the heart of Kalachakra!

Mindfulness of the Great Bliss Mandala

The Six Buddhas, the Omniscient Ones Gone to Bliss;
The Six Female Buddhas, the Goddesses Who are the Union of Bliss
and Emptiness; The Foundation for the Manifestation of Infinite
Miraculous Emanations; The Creator of All, Glorious Lord of the
Mandala:

I pray from my heart with faith and devotion!
May the appearance of this drop of basic space and clear awareness
Pass up the central channel and leave through the crown of my head.
May I enter the heart of Kalachakra!

Mindfulness of the Mind Mandala

From the play of the Glorious Vajra-Mind
Comes the wondrous manifestations of the Male and Female Bodhisattvas;
Pure forms pleasing all of the Victorious Ones;
Perfect peace of the Dakas and Dakinis, the True Self.

I pray from my heart with faith and devotion!
May the appearance of this drop of basic space and clear awareness
Pass up the central channel and leave through the crown of my head.
May I enter the heart of Kalachakra!

Supreme Mind of Peace arising as the Wrathful Primordial Wisdom;
That Terrifying and Wrathful One is the Mother of All Families.
Her fearful manifestations destroy the demons of the three realms.
Maker of All Pure Manifestations:

I pray from my heart with faith and devotion!
May the appearance of this drop of basic space and clear awareness
Pass up the central channel and leave through the crown of my head.
May I enter the heart of Kalachakra!

Mindfulness of the Speech Mandala

The Yoginis are the ornaments of Primordial Wisdom's glorious
manifestation; The secret field of hundreds of thousands of innate
assemblies Always performing pure activities throughout the three
realms; The Principal Sovereigns of more than Seventy Goddesses:

I pray from my heart with faith and devotion!
May the appearance of this drop of basic space and clear awareness
Pass up the central channel and leave through the crown of my head.
May I enter the heart of Kalachakra!

Mindfulness of the Body Mandala

The Great Deity, the Hero, the Ruler of Existence,
Together with a Retinue of Three Hundred and Sixty Goddesses,
The activities of the Twelve Principal Ones is unmatched;
Each of them is a miraculous manifestation of Vajrasattva.

I pray from my heart with faith and devotion!
May the appearance of this drop of basic space and clear awareness
Pass up the central channel and leave through the crown of my head.
May I enter the heart of Kalachakra!

The wondrous radiance of merit and wisdom, as vast as space;
The unceasing wish-fulfilling activities of the Ten Naga Kings;
This mode of skilful means and wisdom
Is the magical display of the manifestations in the sphere of reality.

I pray from my heart with faith and devotion!
May the appearance of this drop of basic space and clear awareness
Pass up the central channel and leave through the crown of my head.
May I enter the heart of Kalachakra!

Mindfulness of the Universe Mandala

When the appearance of the wisdom of great bliss increases,
The pacified mind appears as incredibly wrathful.
The Ten Very Wrathful Goddesses are in a frenzied dance of method
and wisdom; Their great qualities appearing in every direction.

I pray from my heart with faith and devotion!
May the appearance of this drop of basic space and clear awareness
Pass up the central channel and leave through the crown of my head.
May I enter the heart of Kalachakra!

Furthermore, the many manifestations of this magical display
Such as the assemblies of Desire and Detachment Goddesses,
And the thirty five million Gods and Demons,
Are all protectors manifesting freely as the animate and inanimate
world.

I pray from my heart with faith and devotion!
May the appearance of this drop of basic space and clear awareness
Pass up the central channel and leave through the crown of my head.
May I enter the heart of Kalachakra!

Mindfulness of the Union of Immutable Bliss and Empty-Form

The Great Immutable Bliss of Kalachakra;
The Empty-Form endowed with All Supreme Aspects of Luminosity;
The Ornament of the Display of the Innate Sphere of Reality, Samsara
and Nirvana; The Profound Realisation of the Expansive Exalted
Mind, the Object of Great Transference;

I pray from my heart with faith and devotion!
May the appearance of this drop of basic space and clear awareness
Pass up the central channel and leave through the crown of my head.
May I enter the heart of Kalachakra!

The Innate Kalachakra of the Primordially Abiding Dharmakaya;
The Self-Nature of Unchanging Luminosity, the Great Transference;
The Natural, Primordially Liberated, Self-Illuminating Expanse;
Consciousness and Exalted Mind, dissolve indivisibly in the
Great Union.

The Actual Transference of Consciousness

For the actual transference, allow your awareness to absorb completely into the indestructible drop, as though you were in the centre of your heart, with the central channel above you like a long tunnel. With the sound PHAT, the drop of consciousness shoots upwards to the opening of the crown chakra. With a second PHAT, it continues ascending to the heart of Kalachakra, and with a third PHAT, your mind melts into the guru's mind so that they become inseparable.

You should repeat the above sequence three times, for a total of nine recitations of PHAT. Tantric masters such as Naropa claim that if we are proficient at controlling the inner winds, it is not necessary to recite PHAT, but if we do not have such control, these instructions should be followed precisely.

With the last PHAT, the consciousness completely merges with Guru Kalachakra's heart. Rest your awareness for a few moments in this state and then bring your consciousness back to the body again by visualising the drop at the centre of your heart. Finally, imagine that Kalachakra melts into light and dissolves into your body. Signs of accomplishment of the phowa practice include a small protrusion on the crown of the head, hairs may also fall out from the crown or a clear liquid may be found at the crown.

Practicing too rigorously may cause breathlessness or sudden head-aches. If these occur, visualise your crown chakra completely closed. Follow this with a visualisation of a heavy golden vajra entering your chakras and exiting through your lower body, meeting a large golden Dharma wheel under the ground. As the golden vajra sits in the centre of the Dharma wheel, remain there single-pointedly. If you focus on this image for a long time or repeat the visualisation, obstacles to your practice will be overcome.

When performing this phowa practice at the moment of death, generate a strong and powerful inner wind projecting your consciousness into the guru's heart with great force so that it will not return and instead of the guru melting into you, you should melt completely into the guru's heart. When facing death, remain with your guru in a non-conceptual state of mind, letting go of your memories of pain and loss, as well as attachment to your former life, such as achieve-ments, status and bonds to relatives and loved ones. Accomplished Kalachakra practitioners will have countless visions of empty-forms, although even without such visions, you can still remain inseparable from your guru's non-conceptual mind. All the past Kalachakra lineage masters practiced in this way, attaining the state of Buddhahood.

In essence, the profound practice of Phowa can have the incred-ible result of allowing us to consciously direct ourselves into the state of clear light, but it requires preparation whilst we are alive. If we practice well, death can be transformed into a time of immense joy, as we can potentially merge our consciousness with the enlightened state or attain rebirth in a pure realm. It is best for practitioners to conduct the Phowa practice for themselves, although it can certainly help to have highly realised beings perform the practice on our behalf.

THE BARDO OF DHARMATA

When the five elements and inner winds dissolve at the moment of death, the primordial experience of the Dharmakaya state naturally occurs for every sentient being and this is true for practitioners and non-practitioners alike. As ordinary beings have not become familiar with this state as their primordial reality through spiritual practice, they do not recognise it in death. Most of us are therefore unaware that death allows us to completely realise the enlightened mind, presenting us with the extraordinary opportunity for liberation.

Exceptional practitioners who have perfectly prepared for death will recognise the Dharmakaya state for what it is and so do not have to experience the bardo of becoming. The Dharmakaya is the source of enlightened activity and is the enlightened aspect of Dharmadhatu, the all-pervading space or ground for all beings, and the source of all phenomena. The three kayas of enlightenment manifest from this reality as well as all conventional phenomena.

Recognition of the Dharmakaya state results in instant enlightenment. The clear light state of child luminosity, established through practice, mixes with the mother luminosity of the Dharmakaya state. This union is likened to a child recognising its mother, remaining together in comfort, joy and security; a state leading directly to Buddhahood which is known as the *Dharmakaya Realm of Shambhala*.

If we do not achieve this realisation, many manifestations of the Dharmadhatu will dawn upon us as luminous appearances or Sambhogakaya forms and this display is the bardo of Dharmata.

Recognising this as the empty-form manifestation of our Buddha-nature will result in the *Sambhogakaya Realm of Shambhala*.

The first manifestations of the bardo of Dharmata generally occur with the arising of the *Vision of Five Lights*, before the bardo of becoming. We say that our true nature "appears" to us in the form of various brilliant coloured lights. Depending on our degree of ignorance, these lights can blind us with their luminosity and make us flee to the shadows of our ego, or they can be seen and recognised for what they actually are, a display of our mind's true nature.

The different colours perceived in this primordial state are the natural expression of the fundamental qualities of our mind. Each dazzling light is a link communicating between body and mind, and although one's being is absorbed in luminosity, there is still an awareness present possessing a sharp and precise quality.

The element of consciousness is perceived as blue light, space as green, wind as dark-blue, fire as red, water as white and earth as yellow. These colours express the elemental qualities of the mind, as described in the bardo of dying, only this time they arise in reverse order.

What we originally see as different coloured rays of light evolve into luminous spheres of various sizes. Within these spheres we experience hosts of peaceful and wrathful deities, perceived as enormous spherical concentrations of light in which the deities emanate a brilliant radiance.

From the ultimate level, the mind that perceives a deity and the deity itself are inseparable, yet as long as we are not enlightened, we have the perception of a separate "I" which has the experience, and takes that which is experienced as "other". This egocentric view results in a tendency for the mind to feel threatened by the radiant pure forms of the deities, as the experience can be overpowering, like looking directly into the sun. As a result, we are more likely to be attracted to six dimmer lights connected to the six realms of samsara, drawing us towards rebirth in one of those realms.

If however we have familiarised ourselves with the extensive deities of the Kalachakra Mandala, we can bring greater awareness to these appearances of light. Rather than being frightened by them, we see them as empty-form manifestations of the enlightened mind. Having this recognition means we can use this display as an opportunity to realise our ultimate nature and therefore stop the process of rebirth. Instead of continuing within the bardo of becoming, we can abide in the very subtle Sambhogakaya manifestations until such point as they dissolve back into the sublime emptiness of Buddha-nature.

Even without attaining realisation of our ultimate truth in this state, we may still have the opportunity to be reborn into a Buddha realm. If our mind does not grasp onto the appearances, it may abide in this extremely subtle realm of existence. This can happen due to strong faith, unbroken samaya, perfect pith instructions and a strong habituation to spiritual practice. This is the principle behind the pure land practice of Amitabha. Such practitioners may also have the ability to recognise the signs of a favourable birth and can choose to be born in an impure land if they desire.

The experience of confronting the mandalas of deities takes place only briefly and if the opportunity for liberation is not recognised, the mind swiftly enters into the bardo of becoming. Here we reawaken to a situation similar to our experience in a lucid dream state, and we are gradually driven towards our next rebirth in one of the six samsaric realms.

THE BARDO OF BECOMING

The bardo of becoming, often referred to as simply "the bardo", describes the transitional period between death and the following rebirth. It begins with the reawakening of our habitual tendencies after death and continues until we either enter the womb of our mother in our next rebirth, or when we enter an egg or other environment before being born. The teachings outline several methods for attaining liberation during this transitional period and by familiarising ourselves with these we can gain certainty of the direction of our rebirth; just like still water being directed through a narrow channel.

The Experience of a Bardo Being

When we fail to recognise either the clear light state at the moment of death or the luminous appearances of the bardo of Dharmata, a reverse process of dissolution takes place. The karmic winds reappear, along with the thought states connected with ignorance, desire and aversion. As the memory of our past karmic body is still fresh in our mind, we assume a mental body and the seeds of our habitual tendencies are activated and reawakened. This mental body possesses the four aggregates of feeling, perception, formation and consciousness. Although there is no physical form aggregate, most beings continue to perceive their previous body, which is merely a mental projection. Before being reborn we experience many signs of rebirth and see our new parents in sexual union, causing desire to arise. Attraction to the father means rebirth as a girl, whereas attraction to the mother signifies rebirth as a boy.

In this bardo our mind is nine times more subtle than the normal human mind and therefore good practitioners with strong aspirations attained through the power of their previous practice will have the ability to chose their parents. Particularly good practitioners visualise their father as Kalachakra, their mother as Vishvamata and themselves as Kalachakra Yab-Yum. Conception follows and this type of being is regarded as a *tulku*; a recognised reincarnation of a lama or yogini. This term is often thought to mean "manifestation of Buddha", in accord with the Chinese translation for lama as "living Buddha", but we cannot judge if a being is a manifestation of a Buddha, as highly realised beings sometimes manifest in very humble forms. A tulku, however, is a being who has the experience of controlling their rebirth or circumstances of conception. Lamas generally choose to be reborn in this way, although this is different from a Dharmakaya manifestation such as Buddha Shakyamuni, known as a Supreme Emanation Body.

Good Vajrayana practitioners with control of their inner winds and subtle essences can mix the two together. This means they can direct the inner wind into the central channel and control the subtle essences, unifying consciousness and the inner wind. When they die they have the ability to breathe in with their last inhalation, without exhaling. Most people have no control of the subtle inner winds and therefore exhale with their final breath and so are driven uncontrollably by the winds of karma as soon as they die.

If we have done little spiritual practice during life or have failed to live virtuously, the bardo of becoming can be a terrifying experience. If ignorance and lack of faith are our predominant negative tendencies, we create the karma to see unpleasant and disturbing black visions and sometimes the only thing we see is a menacing black colour. If desire is our chief downfall, we may witness disturbing red visions, while anger and hatred cause us to see terrifying grey visions. These are known as the three frightening appearances.

As the winds of the elements return, we often experience five terrifying sounds. Firstly we may hear a very strong, loud and frightening wind, as if a mountain was collapsing. Then we may experience the sound of the ocean like a giant tsunami, followed by the sound of fire, where it seems as though the entire universe is burning. Then the sound of a wind like many hurricanes confronts us, and finally the sound of a thousand thunderclaps.

Those who are inadequately prepared for death and are lacking wisdom, suffer greatly when confronted by these terrifying sounds, and yet they are only seeing and hearing the obscurations to their intrinsic nature; the effects of their negative karma. Good practitioners on the other hand realise that everything occurring in the bardo state is a manifestation of their own intrinsic nature. Everything arises due to their previous karma and so there is no need to cling to the experience, whether frightening or pleasant. Furthermore, by remembering our spiritual practice, we can access an opportunity for liberation or at least ensure an auspicious rebirth.

There are six fixed or certain signs that occur for all beings in the bardo. They can pass through anything solid such as walls or rocks and therefore are able to go anywhere. They can speak and see their family and friends, although no-one can hear them. They cannot see the moon, sun or stars in the sky, they leave no footprint nor have a shadow. Finally, they possess limited clairvoyance, such as direct knowledge of what their family is thinking about them and their possessions. This can lead to an angry or resentful state of mind, thus creating more negative karma.

In addition, there are six uncertain signs which occur. Firstly, beings in the bardo are uncertain about their location and environment. Human beings and animals reside in a particular location at a particular time but bardo beings do not. Secondly, living beings have knowledge of what to eat and what not to eat, however there are no certain foods for bardo beings so they mostly rely on odours for sustenance, such as incense or burnt offerings. Thirdly, living beings know what to wear as clothing whereas bardo beings do not have this certainty and there-fore wear anything for clothes, such as leaves.

Virtuous actions during life give rise to pleasant appearances while non-virtuous actions give rise to frightening or unpleasant appear-ances. Eventually a bardo being's craving for the support of a physical body drives them towards rebirth in one of the six realms. They are attracted to the light corresponding to their most predominant afflictive emotion and they experience many signs forewarning of their rebirth.

Following Tibetan tradition, the family of a deceased person may perform many rituals and accumulate merit in order to benefit their loved one during their journey through the bardo, so that they may gain an auspicious rebirth. Traditionally this takes forty-nine days, as beings typically remain in the bardo for no more than seven weeks before the consciousness takes physical form once again, although this transition period has no definite or fixed duration. The bardo of becoming ends when the consciousness enters one of the four types of births—in a womb, in an egg, in moisture or instantaneous. When physical birth takes place the bardo of living begins.

Taking Rebirth in Shambhala

Assuming we have been unable to take advantage of the various opportunities presented to us during our death, the final thing we can do is try to direct our mind towards a conducive rebirth where we can continue our practice of the path and achieve enlightenment at a later time.

In the Kalachakra tradition, the optimal conditions for spiritual practice are found in the *Sublime Nirmanakaya Realm of Shambhala*. This subtle human realm has been emanated by tenth level Bodhisattvas as a place for sentient beings to achieve enlightenment through the practices of the Vajrayana. Once born in this realm, you are guaranteed to achieve enlightenment within a single human lifetime. This is like a flash of lightning when compared to the aeons spent achieving the same aim within a pure realm such as Sukhavati.

As Shambhala is a karmic realm, one of the causes for being born there is the creation of strong karmic connections through the practice of the Kalachakra Path and from familiarising ourselves with the features of this realm. We can do this by reciting the following prayer at the end of the day. Then as you fall asleep, develop the strong aspiration to be reborn in this sublime realm.

OM AH HUNG HO

To the north of the centre on the southern continent is the pure and hidden realm of Shambhala—subtle and secret. In the shape of an eight-petalled lotus, surrounded in all directions by a boundary of snow mountains, everywhere there are rivers, lakes, forests and flowers, their exquisite beauty rivalling the glory of the god realms.

In each of the petals there is twelve kingdoms. In each kingdom there is ten million cities, making nine hundred and sixty million in all. Ninety-six emanated governors watch over these kingdoms. This noble land—this excellent and sublime realm of mantra—is always protected by the enlightened minds of the Kalki Kings.

At its centre is Mount Kailasha, on which sits the capital of Shambhala—Kalapa. Between lotus-filled lakes, within the marvellous pleasure groves, lies the wondrous mandala of Kalachakra.

May I be blessed to be born in this perfect and sublime realm,
Free from enemies and contagious diseases;
Free from disputes, sorrow, suffering and terror;
Free from discrimination between high and low, rich and poor:

Where everyone practices the authentic teachings,
Especially the Vajrayana path of Kalachakra—the King of Tantra.
Dispelling all outer, inner and secret obstacles,
This practice naturally flows from the sacred Dharma.
May I perfectly experience this pure realm and
May I actualise the result of this path of the two stages.

Having traversed the five paths and the ten levels within a single lifetime, Attaining perfect Buddhahood by accomplishing the four kayas and the four wisdoms, May I be able to emanate immeasurable forms for the benefit and happiness of all beings without exception.

Nature of phenomena, the primordial purity of reality itself;
Conventional phenomena, unfailing interdependence;
The superior intention, completely pure accumulation of merit;
May I quickly accomplish everything in accordance with these aspirations.

* * *

The following table summarises the states of mind that are most active during each bardo as well as the main practices which are recommended for taking advantage of these periods.

Group	Bardo	State	Practices
Life	Living	Waking	Three Vows, Guru Yoga, Deity Yoga
	Dreaming	Dream	Deity Yoga, Dream Yoga
		Deep-sleep	Sleep Yoga
	Meditation	Blissful Absorption	Three Isolations, Six Vajra Yogas
Death	Dying	Deep-sleep	Phowa, Yoga of Withdrawal
	Dharmata	Blissful Absorption	Yoga of Stabilisation
	Becoming	Deep-sleep	Sleep Yoga
		Dream	Dream Yoga, Deity Yoga, Shambhala

Table 10-2: Overview of the Six Bardos

REVIEW OF KEY POINTS

- Bardo is a term meaning "transitional period". It is used to refer to the periods of transition from one state to the next. In general, there are six bardos divided into two groups of three: (1) the Bardos of Life and (2) the Bardos of Death and Rebirth.

- The six bardos are: (1) the Bardo of Living; (2) the Bardo of Dreaming; (3) the Bardo of Meditation; (4) the Bardo of Dying; (5) the Bardo of Dharmata and (6) the Bardo of Becoming.

- The bardo of living occurs during the waking state of our present life. It is primarily useful for practicing a spiritual path that helps us purify obscurations and cultivate virtues. In the Kalachakra Path this means practicing the stages of generation and completion.

- The bardo of dreams occurs when we fall asleep until the moment we wake up. It consists of withdrawing into the deep-sleep state and arising in the dream state. The main practices used to familiarise ourselves with these states are known as dream yoga and sleep yoga.

- Dream yoga consists of daytime practices to heighten our awareness of the illusory nature of conventional reality and nighttime practices which assist us to become lucid in dreams, so they can then be used on the path.

- Sleep yoga is mainly concerned with cultivating awareness of the dissolution process so we can rest the mind in the deep-sleep state of the foundation consciousness. It is essentially a practice of Shamatha Without a Sign.

- The bardo of meditation occurs when the mind enters the blissful absorption of deep meditative concentration. There are two aspects to this practice: (1) cultivating the mountain-like view that is the result of directly experiencing the ultimate nature of reality and (2) the ocean-like practice that integrates our view with every aspect of our experience. On the Kalachakra Path this is done through the practice of the Six Vajra Yogas.

- The bardo of dying occurs when the final dissolution of body and mind begins, until the mind completely separates from the body. It involves the outer dissolution of the coarse body and the inner dissolution of the subtle body.

- If we recognise the signs of approaching death, it is possible to take action to avoid the untimely loss of life. When the signs are caused by obstacles to life we can use medical treatment or rituals to remove the obstacle. However, if the signs arise due to the exhaustion of our karmic lifespan, there is nothing we can do.

- The practice of Phowa is used to direct the consciousness at the time of death in order to create the conditions for an auspicious rebirth. There are three types of Phowa used by different levels of practitioners: (1) Dharmakaya Phowa in which the practitioner rests their awareness in suchness; (2) Sambhogakaya Phowa in which the practitioner generates themselves as Kalachakra; and (3) Nirmanakaya Phowa in which the practitioner visualises merging their consciousness with their Guru.

- The bardo of Dharmata occurs from the moment of death through to the re-activation of the gross conceptual mind. During this period, the mind experiences a range of dazzling lights. If we can recognise them as empty-form manifestations of our Buddha-nature, we can rest the mind in this very subtle state and subsequently achieve liberation.

- The bardo of becoming occurs when the mind takes the subtle form of a bardo being due to the strength of their karmic propensities. Such a being manifests a series of dreamlike experiences until eventually being drawn into a womb and taking another rebirth.

- In case you are unable to achieve liberation during the bardos of death and rebirth, you should spend time during this life cultivating familiarity with the Sublime Realm of Shambhala so that when you experience the bardo of becoming, you can direct yourself to this most auspicious Vajrayana pure land.

Conclusion

It is my sincere hope that you will take the precious teachings presented in the *Unveiling Your Sacred Truth* series and put them into practice, so that you and all those you meet may encounter greater peace and harmony in your lives. As a means of helping you remember these teachings, I would like to offer you a dedication prayer that summarises the essential meaning of the Kalachakra Path:

གཞོན་པའི་ལང་ཚོ་སྤྱོད་འདོད་རྣམ་གཡེང་དང་། །གཉིད་ཀྱི་ལོངས་སྤྱོད་མི་ཚེའི་རྒྱས་སྤྲོས་སོགས། །
དགེན་པའི་མི་ལོ་སུམ་བཅུའི་ལེགས་འབྲས་འདིས། །བསྐྱན་འགྲོའི་རྒྱུད་སེལ་ཞི་བདེའི་དཔལ་སྤྱིན་ཤོག །

May this excellent result of foregoing the pleasures and distractions of youth,
The richness of sleep, and the luxuries of living
Heal the sorrows of all beings and strengthen
The glorious Dharma of genuine peace and harmony.

ཕྱི་རྩོལ་ཕྱུལ་གྱི་རྣམ་གཞག་མཐའ་ཡས་ཀྱང་། །ཕྱུལ་ཅན་ཀུན་བྱེད་རྒྱལ་མོའི་ཚོ་འཕྲུལ་ཙམ། །
བརྒྱུ་སྤྲོང་སེམས་ཀྱི་ཕྱི་ནང་གསང་བའི་དོན། །ཤེས་ཤིང་གོམས་ན་སྒོམ་བྱུང་ཡེ་ཤེས་སྟེད། །

However boundless the external projections may be,
They are all created by the queen—your mind.
If you come to know and familiarise yourself with its many layers,
The wisdom of meditation will be revealed.

སྒོམ་བྱུང་རིགས་པས་ཀུན་ཉོན་འཁོར་བ་ཡི། །མཆང་ཆེན་བཙལ་ན་འཇིག་རྟེན་ཆོས་བརྒྱད་ལ། །
ཆགས་སྤང་སྒོལ་བས་ཡང་དག་ལམ་དུ་སྤྲོ། །དོས་དང་བརྒྱུད་ནས་རྣམ་དག་འགྲོག་པ་སྟེ། །

From authentic meditation comes awareness
Of the faults of Samsara and its origination.
By freeing yourself from the eight worldly dharmas,
The authentic path of Nirvana is reached.

ཕྱོགས་མེད་དག་ཆོས་ཟབ་མོའི་ལམ་སྒོལ་ཀུན། །རིས་མེད་དུ་ཡངས་རྣོ་ཡིས་བསྒྲུབ་པ་ཡིས། །
རང་ལ་མཆོག་ཏུ་འཆམ་པའི་ཡང་དག་ལམ། །ཉི་དགར་རྟེན་པ་དཏོས་པོའི་གཤིས་སུ་རིས། །

With a mind that is open to spiritual diversity
And free from the bias of culture and custom,
The purest and most suitable Dharma
Will naturally be found.

དེ་སླུར་རིས་ཤེས་ཟབ་མོས་དྲངས་བ་ཡིས། །ཡང་དག་སྐྱབས་འགྲོ་རྒྱལ་སྲས་སེམས་དཔའི་ལམ། །
གོ་ཏོགས་ཟབ་མོས་གསལ་སྤྲད་དང་འབྲེལ་ན། །རྒྱ་ཆེན་ཚོགས་གཉིས་འཛིན་པའི་རྩ་བ་བརྟན། །

This profound realisation brings true refuge
And awakens the path of Bodhicitta;
Joined with activities of purification and merit,
The root of the two accumulations is stabilised.

རྩ་ཡན་ལག་ཉིང་ལག་ལ་སོགས་པས། །སོ་ཐར་ཚུལ་ཁྲིམས་གཙང་མས་དང་ཚུལ་བཙུན། །
འདའ་མཆམས་བཀག་སྤྱང་སོར་རྒྱུ་ཐབས་སགས་ཀྱིས། །བྱང་རྒྱུབ་སེམས་དཔའི་བསྒྲུབ་པས་རང་རྒྱུད་འདུལ། །

Through discrimination of what is primary and secondary,
The pure conduct of Personal Liberation will remain.
Through the clarity of methods and purification,
The Bodhisattva pledges are restored and the mind is tamed.

རྣམ་དག་ལེགས་ལམ་སྟོན་པའི་བཤེས་གཉེན་ཀུན། །ཚུལ་བཞིན་བསྟེན་པ་བླ་མའི་རྒྱལ་འབྱོར་ཀྱིས། །
ཟབ་ལམ་བྱེག་པའི་སྒོ་འབྱེད་བྱིན་རྒྱབས་འཇུག །ཟབ་དོན་རིགས་ཀྱི་ས་བོན་སྙིང་དུ་སྦྱང། །

Understanding it is the teacher who shows
The true path of virtue and opens the door
To the blessings of the profound path,
The sacred meanings are imprinted on the heart.

རྡོ་རྗེ་སློབ་དཔོན་སངས་རྒྱས་ཀུན་འདུས་སུ། །ཤེས་ནས་བྱིན་རླབས་དབང་གི་རིམ་པ་ཡིས། །
ཕྲ་གསང་རྩ་རླུང་ཐིག་ལེའི་མདུད་རྒྱ་རྣམས། ། གྲོལ་ཏེ་དག་སྣང་ཐབས་མཐའི་ས་བོན་སྨིན། །

When realised as the embodiment of all enlightenment,
The Vajra Master bestows the empowerments
To release the subtle channels, winds and essences;
Ripening all propensities of pure appearance.

འདི་སྣང་སྒྱུ་མར་ཤེས་པའི་སྟོང་སྤྱོང་དང༌། །དག་སྣང་ལྷ་སྒྱུར་ཕྱར་བའི་རྣལ་འབྱོར་གྱིས། །
སྐྱེ་ཤི་བར་དོ་རིམ་གྱིས་སྦྱང་བའི་དོན། །གནས་སྐབས་གསུམ་གྱི་སྣང་བ་དག་པར་འགོ །

Understanding all appearance as illusory and dissolving into emptiness,
Pure perception reveals appearances as the deities of enlightenment.
Purifying birth, death and bardo,
The three stages are conquered.

ཐུན་མོང་སྟོན་འགྲོ་ཐུན་མིན་ཉེར་སྤྱོག་གིས། །ཐུན་མོང་ཞི་གནས་ཐུན་མིན་ལྷག་མཐོང་འཛེན། །
ཟབ་མོའི་ལམ་ལ་དབེན་པ་གསུམ་སྤུན་དང༌། །སྤོང་མེད་བཞི་ལྷུན་རྣལ་འབྱོར་རྣམས་བཞི་རྟོགས། །

With the common and uncommon preliminaries,
The states of calm abiding and special insight are brought together.
Through the profound path of the Four Disregards and the Three Isolations,
You accomplish the Four Absorptions.

རྟགས་བཅུ་འབྱམས་པས་ཐ་མར་སྣང་བ་འགག །སྟོང་གཟུགས་རྣམས་སྣང་བས་རྟོགས་རྣལ་ཡེ་ཤེས་འཛིན། །
ཡུལ་དང་ཡུལ་ཅན་ཆད་བཞི་སྟོང་གཟུགས་ཀྱིས། །ཚོགས་དྲུག་བྱིངས་སུ་དྲངས་བ་དག་པའི་ཉམས། །

When the ten signs arise, the impure appearances dissolve;
Empty-form with non-conceptual wisdom.
The six collections of consciousness are replaced
By the vastness of pure appearance.

སྟོང་གཟུགས་སྲོག་ཏུ་འཛིན་པའི་འབར་སྡུང་གིས། །ཡེ་བབས་མེ་ས་བརྟེན་གཏུམ་མོས་ཞི་བདེ་འཇེན། །
དགའ་བཞིའི་སྟོང་བ་གོམས་པས་ཕྱག་ཆེན་འབྱུང་། །ཕྱག་རྒྱ་ཆེན་མོས་བདེ་ཆེན་ཡེ་ཤེས་འཇེན། །

Empty-form merges with inner wind at the navel,
The Inner Fire blazes, melting the drops,
Producing the Four Joys and
Resulting in the union of great bliss and primordial wisdom.

རྣམ་ཀུན་མཆོག་ལྡན་སྟོང་གཟུགས་ཕྱག་རྒྱ་ཆེ། །མཆོག་ཏུ་མི་འགྱུར་བྱང་འཇག་བདེ་ཆེན་པོ། །
ཁ་སྦྱོར་བདུན་ལྡན་ཡེ་ཤེས་རྡོ་རྗེའི་སྐུ། །འདི་ཕྱི་བར་དོ་གསུམ་དུ་མངོན་འགྱུར་ཤོག །

May I accomplish the union of
The unsurpassable Great Consort of Empty-Form
And the Sublime Body of Immutable Bliss—
Vajradhara with seven enlightened qualities.

དགེ་བ་འདི་ཡིས་སྐྱོ་བུར་རྗེ་མའི་ཚོགས། །སྒྲོག་དང་རྦུར་སེལ་རྩ་རྡང་སྟུན་ཙིག་ཏུ། །
འཚོམས་པར་ནུས་པའི་ཐབས་ཟབ་ལ་བརྟེན་ནས། །གཞན་མཆོག་བདེ་གཤེགས་སྙིང་པོ་སྐྱུར་སྟོབ་ཤོག །

By these virtues, may the collection of temporary stains,
And the gross winds and channels be destroyed,
So that through this profound method
The sacred truth of our Buddha-nature may be revealed.

འདིར་འབད་དགེ་བ་རྣམ་པར་དཀར་བས་མ་ཐུས། །བདག་ཕྱས་བོར་ཆེ་དཔལ་ལྡན་ཤམྦྷལར། །
རིགས་ལྡན་རྒྱལ་པོའི་འཁོར་དུ་ལེགས་སྐྱེས་ནས། །དུས་འཁོར་བསྟན་ལ་ཕྱུ་བ་བྱེད་པར་ཤོག །

Through the power of this effort, when I die
May I reach the Sublime Realm of Shambhala.
May I attain a fortunate rebirth within the retinue of the Kalki
And serve the Kalachakra Tantra for the benefit of all beings.

མདོར་ན་ད་ལྟའི་རིང་ནས་བཟུང་སྟེ། །ནད་མཚོན་དམག་འཁྲུག་དབུལ་ཕོངས་ལ་སོགས་པ། །
ས་ཆེན་འདི་ཡི་རྒུད་པ་ཀུན་སེལ་བའི། །རིགས་ལྡན་སེམས་དཔའི་སྲས་སུ་བདག་གྱུར་ཅིག །

From this day forward,
May I heal all sickness, poverty, war and conflict.
May I be a champion of the Kalkis.

སྐྱེ་བ་འདི་ནས་ཚེ་རབས་ཀུན་ཏུ་ཡང་། །ཤམྦྷ་ལ་དུ་རིགས་ལྡན་རྒྱལ་བའི་སྐུར། །
བཞེངས་སྟེ་ཕྱོགས་མེད་འགྲོ་བའི་རྒུད་པ་སེལ། །འཛམ་གླིང་ཀུན་ཕན་ཞི་བདེའི་དཔལ་སྐྱིན་ཤོག །

In all my future lives, may I be born a Dharma King of Shambhala
And eliminate the sorrow of all beings throughout space.
May genuine peace and harmony prevail.

མི་ལུས་རིན་ཆེན་སྨྱིན་པའི་ཕ་མ་དང་། །མཁན་སློབ་བཤེས་གཉེན་རྩ་བའི་བླ་མ་མཆོག །
ལེགས་འབད་འདི་ལ་རས་འདེགས་སྟོགས་སུ་གྱུར། །སྐྱེ་ཀུན་ཟབ་མོའི་ཆོས་ལ་མཉམ་སྤྱོད་ཤོག །

To all of my precious parents and teachers—
especially my sublime Root Lama—
As well as those who have assisted and contributed in the process of this work,
May we all enjoy this profound Dharma together for all our future lives.

ཁྱད་པར་རྗེན་ཅན་ཨ་མས་ལོ་མིང་རིང་། །མངལ་ཁྲོད་བསྐྱེད་བསྲིང་རི་ལྷུང་མང་བོའི་བར། །
དཀའ་སྤྱད་ལ་དུབ་འཛིན་སྐྱོང་ཁྲོད་བསད་ཏེ། །ལུ་ལ་མ་ཐུན་རྒྱུ་སྐྱར་བའི་དོན་དུ་བསྔོ། །

In particular, I wish to dedicate this virtue to my dearest mother
Who carried me in her womb and for many years
Supported me while experiencing much sorrow and hardship.

ཆོས་དབྱིངས་བདེ་གཤེགས་སྙིང་པོའི་བདེན་པ་དང་། །ཆོས་ཅན་རྟེན་འབྲེལ་བསླུ་བ་མེད་པ་དང་། །
རྣམ་དག་བསམ་པ་སྤྲས་བཅས་རྒྱལ་བ་ཡི། །སྨོན་ལམ་ཇེ་བཞིན་ལྷུར་དུ་སྤྲིན་གྱུར་ཅིག །།

By the ultimate truth of Buddha-nature,
And the relative truth of interdependence,
May my pure intention unite with the aspirations of the mighty ones
And may I accomplish all my goals.

Appendices

The Tantric Vows and Commitments

THE TANTRIC COMMITMENTS OF KALACHAKRA

The Kalachakra training in ethical discipline consists of three sets of pledges: (1) The Common Pledges of the Five Buddha Families; (2) The Uncommon Pledges of Kalachakra; and (3) The Twenty-Five Conducts of Kalachakra.

The Common Pledges of the Five Buddha Families

As part of our commitment to the Five Buddha Families, we promise to uphold the following pledges:

The Pledges of the Buddha Family

1. Take refuge in the Buddha.
2. Take refuge in the Dharma.
3. Take refuge in the Sangha.
4. Abandon non-virtue.
5. Cultivate virtue.
6. Benefit others.

The Pledges of the Vajra Family

1. Maintain mindfulness of the vajra.
2. Maintain mindfulness of the bell.

3. Visualise oneself in the aspect of the Yidam.

4. Practice devotion towards the Vajra Master.

The Pledges of the Jewel Family

1. Give material wealth.

2. Give fearlessness.

3. Give Dharma.

4. Give loving-kindness.

The Pledges of the Lotus Family

1. Uphold the teachings of the Sutrayana.

2. Uphold the teachings of the Lower Tantras.

3. Uphold the teachings of Highest Yoga Tantra.

The Pledges of the Action Family

1. Maintain the discipline of the three vows.

2. Make extensive offerings.

The Uncommon Pledges of Kalachakra

As part of our commitment to the path of Kalachakra, we promise to uphold the provisional and definitive pledges of the Six Buddha Families:

Six Provisional Pledges

1. **Akshobhya**—Unify the body, speech and mind through the practice of Deity Yoga.

2. **Ratnasambhava**—Make extensive offerings through the practice of Tsok Feasts.

3. **Vairochana**—Maintain mindfulness of the purity of phenomena by working with the ten impure substances.

4. **Amoghasiddhi**—Reduce grasping onto ordinary bliss by offering all blissful experiences to the enlightened mandala.

5. **Amitabha**—Recognise the purity of bliss by working with a visualised consort.

6. **Vajrasattva**—Cultivate the aspiration to abide in the union of immutable bliss and empty-form by maintaining mindfulness of the sacred aspect of sexuality.

Six Definitive Pledges

1. **Akshobhya**—Unify the body, speech and mind through the practice of the Six Vajra Yogas.

2. **Ratnasambhava**—Experience all perceptions as empty-forms by bringing the ten winds into the central channel.

3. **Vairochana**—Gather all subtle essences into the central channel.

4. **Amoghasiddhi**—Release grasping onto bliss by working with the practice of Inner Fire.

5. **Amitabha**—Gather all subtle essences at the lower tip of the central channel by working with a consort.

6. **Vajrasattva**—Abide in the union of immutable bliss and empty-form.

The Twenty-Five Conducts of Kalachakra

In order to ensure that our actions of body and speech are in accord with the Kalachakra teachings, we should abandon the following actions:

The Five Major Negative Karmas to Abandon

1. Taking life.

2. Speaking lies.

3. Taking what is not given.

4. Inappropriate sexual conduct.

5. Taking intoxicants

The Five Minor Negative Karmas to Avoid

6. Gambling.

7. Eating unseemly meat.

8. Reading ignoble words.

9. Making offerings to spirits.

10. Following extremist practices.

The Five Forbidden Killings

11. Killing animals.

12. Killing children.

13. Killing women.

14. Killing men.

15. Destroying representations of enlightened body, speech and mind.

The Five Attitudes of Disrespect

16. Hating friends who benefit Dharma or the world in general.

17. Hating leaders or elders worthy of respect.

18. Hating spiritual teachers or Buddhas.

19. Hating members of the Sangha, in particular Arya beings.

20. Hating those who trust us.

The Five Attachments

21. Attachment to sights.

22. Attachment to sounds.

23. Attachment to smell.

24. Attachment to tastes.

25. Attachment to sensations.

THE TANTRIC VOWS ACCORDING TO KALACHAKRA

The tantric vows that are specifically mentioned in the Kalachakra Tantra are: (1) the Fourteen Root Vows and (2) the Eight Branch Vows.

The Fourteen Root Vows

1. The following actions should be abandoned completely:

2. Disturbing the mind of one's vajra master.

3. Transgressing the words of one's vajra master.

4. Showing contempt towards one's vajra family.

5. Abandoning the mind of love.

6. Damaging one's Bodhicitta.

7. Criticising philosophical tenets.

8. Proclaiming secrets to those who are unripe.

9. Despising one's aggregates.

10. Making others uncertain about the Sacred Dharma.

11. Holding deceitful love.

12. Developing self-fabricated concepts about the ultimate nature of reality.

13. Speaking about the faults of those who are pure.

14. Abandoning the sacred substances.

15. Disparaging women.

The Eight Branch Vows

The following actions should be avoided as much as possible:

1. Relying on an unqualified consort.

2. Entering into union without maintaining an awareness of emptiness.

3. Demonstrating tantric implements and practices to those who are unsuitable.

4. Creating conflict during an offering feast or ceremony.

5. Leading astray those with genuine faith.

6. Spending long periods of time with those who do not believe in the vajra path.

7. Boasting about your spiritual accomplishments.

8. Teaching the Dharma to those who have no faith in the teachings.

Outline of Book Three

PART TWO: GENERATING THE ENLIGHTENED MANDALA

PART THREE: ACTUALISING THE STATE OF KALACHAKRA

7. Pointing Out the Nature of the Mind

About the Author

Khentrul Rinpoché Jamphel Lodrö is the founder and spiritual director of Dzokden. Rinpoche is the author of many books including Unveiling Your Sacred Truth, The Great Middle Way: Clarifying the Jonang View of Other-Emptiness, A Happier Life, and The Hidden Treasure of the Profound Path.

Rinpoche spent the first 20 years of his life herding yak and chanting mantras on the plateaus of Tibet. Inspired by the bodhisattvas, he left his family to study in a variety of monasteries under the guidance of over twenty-five masters in all the Tibetan Buddhist traditions. Due to his non-sectarian approach, he earned himself the title of Rimé (unbiased) Master and was identified as the reincarnation of the famous Kalachakra Master Ngawang Chözin Gyatso. While at the core of his teachings is the recognition that there is great value in the diversity of all spiritual traditions found in this world; he focuses on the Jonang-Shambhala tradition. Kalachakra (wheel of time) teachings handed down from the Kalki Kings of Shambhala, contain profound methods to harmonize our external environment with the inner world of body and mind. This tantra is connected directly to the Karma of our earth to bring about the Golden age of Peace and Harmony (Dzokden). Khentrul Rinpoche has made it his life mission to spread these precious teachings in as many languages as possible globally so that we can truly transform our world, one person at a time from their inside out.

RINPOCHE'S VISION

Dzokden was founded with the express purpose of supporting Khentrul Rinpoche in realizing his vision to bring about the Golden Age of peace and harmony in this world. As our community continues to grow and develop, more and more people are getting involved with this extraordinary effort.

To provide a sense of the scope of Rinpoche's vision, we can speak of eight goals that reflect Rinpoche's short and long term priorities:

Immediate Goals

Ultimately speaking, lasting genuine happiness is only possible through profound personal transformation. Now more than ever, we need methods to develop our wisdom and actualise our greatest potential. It is for this reason that Rinpoche places such a heavy priority on the preservation of the Jonang Kalachakra Lineage. There are four ways in which Rinpoche proposes to do this:

1. **Create opportunities to connect with an authentic and complete Kalachakra lineage in close collaboration with dedicated meditators in remote Tibet.** Our goal is to create all of the supports for practicing Kalachakra in accordance with the authentic lineage masters who have upheld this tradition for thousands of years. We do this by commissioning statues and paintings, writing books and giving teachings around the world. We place particular emphasis on ensuring the authenticity of our materials, drawing on the profound experience of highly realised meditators who are dedicating their lives to these practices.

2. **Establish international retreat centres for the study and practice of Kalachakra.** In order to integrate the teachings into our mind, it is crucial to have the opportunity to engage in periods of intensive practice. Therefore, we are working to create the necessary infrastructure to support and nurture the members of our community to engage in both short and

long-term retreats. This includes the purchase of land and the construction of everything needed to conduct group and solitary retreats. Our long-term aim is to develop a network of such centres around the world, forming a global community that supports a wide variety of practitioners.

3. **Translate and publish the unique and rare texts of Kalachakra masters.** The Kalachakra System has been the subject of countless texts over the course of Tibet's long history. So far, only a small fraction of these texts has been translated and made accessible in the West. While the theoretical texts are important, we aim to focus particularly on the pith instructions which will guide dedicated practitioners to a deeper experience of these profound teachings.

4. **Develop the tools and programs for a structured learning experience.** With pockets of students distributed throughout the world, we believe it is important to make the most of modern technologies to facilitate the process of learning for our students. Our aim is to develop a robust online educational platform that allows our international community to access quality study programs that are intuitive, structured and engaging.

Long-Term Goals

Whilst we each work towards achieving ultimate peace and harmony in our own mind, we must not lose sight of the fact that we exist within the context of a world filled with a great diversity of individuals. These individuals give rise to a wide variety of beliefs and practices that in turn shape how we relate and interact with each other. In this interdependent reality, it is vital to find viable strategies for promoting greater tolerance and respect. To this end, Rinpoche proposes four specific areas of activity:

1. **Promote the development of a Rimé Philosophy through dialogue with other traditions.** With the desire to be constructive members of a pluralistic society, we need to learn ways of reconciling our differences. We therefore aim to help people develop the positive qualities that promote an attitude of mutual respect, openness to new ideas and an inquisitive desire to overcome our ignorance.

2. **Develop highly realised role models by offering financial support to dedicated practitioners.** To ensure the authenticity of our spiritual traditions, it is imperative that there are people who actualise the highest of realisations. Therefore, we aim to create a financial scholarship program which facilitates genuine practitioners who wish to dedicate their lives to spiritual development, regardless of their system of practice. By helping people actualise the teachings, they become positive role models for those around them, inspiring and guiding the generations to come.

3. **Actualise the great potential of female practitioners by developing specialised training programs.** The Tibetan culture has a long history of cultivating highly realised masters through the intensive training of those who are recognised to have great potential. Unfortunately, all too often the search for potential has focused only on male candidates. Rinpoche believes that it is increasingly important to have strong, highly realised, female role models who can help bring greater balance into our world. For this reason we are working to develop a unique training program to provide women with the opportunity to actualise their spiritual potential. It is our aim to design a specialised curriculum as well as the financial infrastructure to fully support all aspects of their education.

4. **Promote greater flexibility of mind and a broader understanding of reality through modern educational programs.** In a world that is rapidly evolving, we need to rethink the types of skills we are teaching our children. The rigid structures of the past are often ill equipped to prepare students for the challenges they will face during their lives. Therefore, we aim to develop a variety of educational programs that can help children to become more flexible and more capable of adapting to their environment. An important part of these programs is the development of greater awareness of the role that our mind plays in our day-to-day experiences. We also aim to bring reforms into the monastic education system to help make them more relevant for this modern world.

HOW CAN YOU HELP?

The above will not be possible without your support and participation. A vision of this magnitude requires a great deal of merit and generosity from many benefactors over many years. If you would like to offer your support, please do not hesitate to contact us.

Dzokden

3436 Divisadero Street

San Francisco, California 94123

United States of America

www.dzokden.org

www.ingramcontent.com/pod-product-compliance
Lightning Source LLC
Chambersburg PA
CBHW081652120626
46550CB00010B/2864